Personnel Economics in Imperfect Labour Markets

Personnel Economics in Imperfect Labour Markets

Pietro Garibaldi

OXFORD
UNIVERSITY PRESS

OXFORD
UNIVERSITY PRESS

Great Clarendon Street, Oxford OX2 6DP

Oxford University Press is a department of the University of Oxford.
It furthers the University's objective of excellence in research, scholarship,
and education by publishing worldwide in

Oxford New York

Auckland Cape Town Dar es Salaam Hong Kong Karachi
Kuala Lumpur Madrid Melbourne Mexico City Nairobi
New Delhi Shanghai Taipei Toronto

With offices in

Argentina Austria Brazil Chile Czech Republic France Greece
Guatemala Hungary Italy Japan Poland Portugal Singapore
South Korea Switzerland Thailand Turkey Ukraine Vietnam

Oxford is a registered trade mark of Oxford University Press
in the UK and in certain other countries

Published in the United States
by Oxford University Press Inc., New York

British Library Cataloguing in Publication Data

Data available

Library of Congress Cataloging in Publication Data

Data available

Typeset by Newgen Imaging Systems (P) Ltd., Chennai, India
Printed in Great Britain
on acid-free paper by
Biddles Ltd., King's Lynn, Norfolk

ISBN 0–19–928066–5   978–0–19–928066–7
ISBN 0–19–928067–3   978–0–19–928067–4

10 9 8 7 6 5 4 3 2 1

to Giulia Tommaso and Alessandra

THE AIM OF THE BOOK

Personnel economics, the use of economics for studying human resource issues, is becoming a standard course in business and economics departments around the world. Indeed, after being successfully introduced in North American business schools by the pioneer books of Lazear (1995, 1998), the teaching of personnel economics is now growing in Europe and in the rest of the world. Yet, most of the traditional analysis of personnel economics assumes perfectly competitive labour markets, a situation in which wages are fully flexible and dismissals can take place at no cost. Such a setting is hardly appropriate for most European markets, where wage rigidity and wage compression are widespread phenomena, and where employment protection legislation is very stringent. Personnel Economics in imperfect labour markets aims at describing key personnel issues when firms and human resource managers act in highly regulated labour markets. Few standard questions are easily identified. Should hiring take place under temporary or permanent contracts? How can we provide compensation related incentives when minimum wages are binding? How do we solve the employment/hours trade-off? What is the optimal workers' separation policy when employment protection legislation is very stringent? Should general training be sponsored by the firm when wage compression is widespread? While the underlying methods are the standard in the field (i.e. the use of microeconomics for studying and solving human resource problems) some of the questions and most of the answers provided by the book are fairly original, and have so far been left to technical and specialized academic journals, not readily available to most students and to a broad public.

POSITION OF THE BOOK IN THE LITERATURE

Most labour economics textbooks devote one chapter to personnel economics. Borjas (2004), Ehrenberg and Smith (2003), McConnell *et al.*(1999), Elliot (1999) are just a few examples. In these chapters, the basic issues in personnel economics are just briefly touched upon, and there is no attempt to see how the standard issues change when labour markets are not competitive. Yet, there are two books entirely devoted to personnel economics, and they have both been written by Lazear. The 1995 MIT book (*Personnel Economics*) is a good reference for introducing the educated scholar to the field. It is quite broad and it is not too technical. Conversely, the 1998 Wiley book (*Personnel Economics for Managers*) is thought out and written to be accessible by students of North American business schools. While these books represent the obvious comparison for personnel economics in imperfect labour markets, many chapters and issues covered in the new book are totally absent in the two Lazear textbooks. The reason for such a difference is that the new chapters refer to issues which are mostly relevant for regulated labour markets, a standard situation outside North America.

AUDIENCE

Students are the primary audience for the book. Specifically, the book is written with three types of student in mind. First, all the material covered in the book can be easily taught at the undergraduate level in programmes that specialize in economics and business. Second, the book can be used in business schools where human resource-oriented courses are taught by economists. Third, labour economics courses taught in Europe will find many chapters in the book a very useful reference, and can use it as a key reference in an otherwise standard labour economics course. In addition, scholars in the field are likely to find the book a useful reference text, and may wish to have it in their personal library.

PREREQUISITES AND TECHNICAL LEVEL

In light of the audience in mind, the technical level required by the book is supposed to be very modest. Ideally, readers should have taken an introductory course in microeconomics, a semester of calculus, and an introductory course in statistics. In practice, it will be possible to read the book even when these prerequisites are partially or totally unfulfilled. The viability of the latter option will rest on the various numerical examples presented in the book. In such simple examples, all the main arguments are presented and the main results outlined, even though they lack the rigour and the generality that the use of algebra allows.

CASE STUDIES

An important feature of the book is the analysis of a few key case studies in personnel economics. Such case studies rely on personnel data and analyse key issues with an econometric perspective. They are a distinctive feature of the book, and they should be analysed by all audiences, even though some basic econometrics may be required. A first case study analyses the change in overtime regulation in France in 1982. A second study refers to the introduction of a performance pay plan in a window glass installer in the United States. A third study analyses the role of the temporary help industry in the provision of training. A fourth study analyses relative performance pay in the context of broiler production in the United States. A final study looks at the benefits of team production in terms of firm productivity.

COURSE ORGANIZATION

There are fourteen chapters in the book. Each chapter is written with a lecture topic in mind. Most of the chapters can be easily taught in a two-hour meeting, even though some chapters require marginally more time. The (marginally) more technical material is left to the appendices, so that the interested reader can find more details if needed. A thirty-hour course, with fifteen meetings, can easily cover most chapters of the book and leave some hours for setting and solving problems.

ACKNOWLEDGEMENTS

The idea of this book started in the late 1990s at one of the first editions of the European Summer Symposium in Labour Economics, a yearly CEPR conference held in Amersee, Germany. Ed Lazear was one of the keynote speakers and gave a lecture on the future and the challenges of personnel economics, as both a research field and a teaching course. I was fascinated by the lecture, and immediately realized that teaching 'labour economics inside the firm' or 'personnel economics' was an obvious opportunity for Bocconi, the university that hired me back in 1999. Tito Boeri took me seriously, and immediately gave me the opportunity to teach personnel economics in Bocconi University. Personnel economics is now a mandatory course in the Economics and Management degree inside Bocconi. Another course has been recently introduced at a graduate level. Without Tito, this project would have never seen the light. I am highly indebted to him.

Teaching personnel economics to future European managers was immediately fascinating. In the first years I realized that a proper European course had to seriously consider the institutional dimensions of the labour market. In those years most of my research output was linked to the interplay between labour demand and labour market institutions, notably employment protection legislation. I realized that a proper European version of personnel economics had to take this institutional dimension into consideration. I discussed the issue with Ed Lazear again in 2002 in Amersee. He encouraged me to go forward with the project, and I am certainly indebted to him.

I am also indebted to my various research co-authors, since many ideas brought forward in the various chapters have benefited from their insights, notably Gianluca Violante, Giuseppe Bertola, Lia Pacelli, and Etienne Wasmer. Michele Pellizzari, Marco Leonardi and Lorenzo Cappellari taught preliminary chapters, and offered important comments.

The role of students has obviously been crucial. Various versions of this course were taught in Bocconi University, at the University of Turin, at the State University of Milan, and at Brussels University. All these students saw various drafts of the chapters, and accepted the inevitable mistakes that earlier drafts incorporate. Paola Monti stands out among these students.

☐ CONTENTS

☐ LIST OF FIGURES

☐ LIST OF TABLES

1 Personnel Economics and Non-Competitive Labour Markets

1.1 Introduction

Personnel economics analyses personnel issues inside the firm. Yet, each firm operates inside a labour market, and the functioning of such a market has important consequences for personnel economics. The view of personnel economics analysed in this book is based on two key properties of the labour markets:

- labour markets are imperfect and jobs are associated to rents;
- labour market institutions interact with personnel policies. Notably,

    - wages are partly set outside the firm–worker pair (minimum wages and collective agreements are widespread)
    - job termination policies are affected by a sizeable and binding employment protection legislation.

In an imperfect labour market the traditional competitive view of the labour market does not hold. In a competitive labour market, the wage is fully set by market forces and firm–worker pairs have no control over its value. In addition, in a perfect labour market the workers are just indifferent between working for the firm or working for somebody else. The resulting equilibrium wage is fully flexible, and whenever business conditions change, wages can be adjusted in response.

Things are different when the labour markets are imperfect. When the labour markets are imperfect, a job is associated with a market rent. This means that a job brings some *pure surplus* to both the firm and the worker. In other words, the firm and the worker are better off when they are together than when they are separated, and if a given job were to be suddenly severed, both parties would lose. The surplus can be thought of as some extra value that the parties enjoy when they are together. Such extra value has to be split between the firm and the employees. This brings the issue of wage determination, which is one of the key topics in personnel policies. In the book we explore three basic possibilities for wage determination: wage setting by the firm, wage bargaining by the firm and the worker, and wage determination made outside the firm and the worker, i.e. by collective agreements. The book uses these three possibilities interchangeably.

In an imperfect labour market wages are also rigid and do not fully respond to business fluctuations. This implies that firms have to use different instruments (other than wages) to respond to changes in business fluctuations. And when prices cannot easily move firms have to rely on quantities. The problem is that in an imperfect labour market, interrupting an employment relationship is far from straightforward. This is the case because there is pervasive and abiding employment protection legislation.

The next section establishes the concepts introduced in this chapter in a more formal setting, while sections 1.2 and 1.3 briefly discuss the nature of labour market institutions introduced in these paragraphs.

1.2 **The Job in an Imperfect Labour Market**

The Job is defined as a firm–worker match engaged in a production setting. We imagine that a firm and a worker have been brought together in the past. The focus here is on a single job rather than firms.

The Value of Production is y. y indicates the value of the labour product obtained when the firm and the worker engage in production. Let's say that y is measured in euros. One can think of y as the revenues from the job, so that y is the product of a quantity of output produced times the price of output. y corresponds also to the value of the marginal labour product to the worker.

The worker's outside option is v. v can be thought of as the wage that the worker would get if he or she had to leave the current job and find a position elsewhere. It can also represent the alternative value of leisure. It is not essential to emphasize which of the two interpretations is used, but in any case we measure its value in euros.

The wage that the worker receives for the current assignment is w.

The firm's marginal profit from the job is the difference between the revenue from the job and its cost. The focus here is just on the labour cost associated with this job, and we assume that there are no other specific costs. We can call the profits from the job the firm surplus from being with the worker and we shall indicate it by S_π

$$S_\pi = y - w$$

The wage w is measured in the same unit of y.

The worker surplus from being in the current job can be similarly defined as the difference between the wage obtained in the current relationship and the outside option. In formula this reads

$$S_w = w - v$$

Each part is interested in its own surplus. Yet, since we are measuring each surplus in euros, we can simply sum up the two marginal surpluses so as to obtain an expression for the total surplus S. In formula, the total surplus from the job is defined as

$$S = S_\pi + S_w$$
$$S = y - v$$

or as the different between the marginal revenue product y and the outside option v. In the definition of the surplus, the wage does not enter. This should not be surprising, since the wage enters positively in the worker's surplus and negatively in the firm's profit. One extra unit of wage reduces firm profits by 1 euro and increases the worker's surplus by the same euro. This suggests that the wage is a way to transfer utility from one party to the other. Since it acts as a pure transfer, it does not enter into determination of the total surplus, which is an expression for the pure value associated with a given position.

1.2.1 PERFECT LABOUR MARKET

In a perfect labour market there is no surplus from the job. This implies that when the labour market is competitive and market forces operate without any obstacle, the total surplus from the job is zero and

$$S = 0$$
$$y = v$$

The worker is paid exactly the value of the marginal product

$$w = y$$

The worker is indifferent between working at the firm and its best alternative

$$w = v$$

Let's discuss the consequences of these results. The firm–worker pair generates a value of the labour product that is equal to y. In a competitive market such value y is identical to the wage, so that we can say that the worker is the full residual claimant of the marginal product generated by the job. But the worker does not enjoy any pure surplus, since the wage turns out to be also equal to its alternative use of time, which we formally indicate with v. Further, the firm also makes zero profits, since the marginal revenue product is equal to the wage.

1.2.2 IMPERFECT LABOUR MARKET WITH WAGE SET BY THE FIRMS

In an imperfect labour market there is surplus from the job

$$S > 0$$
$$S = y - v$$
$$y > v$$

An alternative way to express the same concept is to say that in an imperfect labour there are rents. The working of competition is not sufficient to eliminate these pure surpluses, and firm–worker pairs enjoy such rents.

If the labour market is imperfect and the *firm can freely set the wage*, it will set the wage so as to maximize profits. The firm has an interest in setting a wage that is as low as possible, but it has to take into account the worker's outside option. In other words, the worker has a participation constraint which can be written as

$$w \geq v$$

which is a condition that implies that the worker will accept working for the firm as long as the wage is larger than his or her outside option. In formula, the firm problem is the following

$$Max_w \, S_\pi = y - w$$
$$s.t. \, w \geq v$$

This implies that the wage chosen in this case will be

$$w = v$$

and the firm will make positive profits equal to

$$S_\pi = y - v$$

1.2.3 IMPERFECT LABOUR MARKET WITH SURPLUS SPLITTING

As we mentioned above, in an imperfect labour market there is surplus from the job

$$S > 0$$
$$y > v$$

We now assume that the surplus is split between the firm and the worker, and the worker gets a fraction β of the total surplus

$$w_\beta = v + \beta S$$
$$w_\beta = v + \beta(y - v)$$
$$w_\beta = (1 - \beta)v + \beta y$$

Wages are obtained as the weighted average between the worker's outside option and the marginal productivity on the job. The weight corresponds to the worker's bargaining share β.

The firm makes profits

$$S_\pi = y - w_\beta$$
$$S_\pi = y - \left[v + \beta(y - v)\right]$$
$$S_\pi = (1 - \beta)(y - v)$$

and the worker enjoys a surplus vis-à-vis his or her outside option, since $S_w = \beta(y - v)$.

1.2.4 IMPERFECT LABOUR MARKET WITH EXOGENOUS WAGE

In an imperfect labour market there is surplus from the job

$$S > 0$$
$$y > v$$

Assume that the wage is set outside the firm worker pair and equal to $\bar{w}$. The worker will accept the job if

$$S_w = \bar{w} - v \geq 0$$

The firm will operate if the profits are non-negative

$$S_\pi = y - \bar{w} \geq 0$$

1.3 **Minimum Wage Constraints and Union Density**

The minimum wage is a labour market institution that sets a lower bound to the wage paid to individual workers. While the conceptual definition is very simple, and most countries in the world have some form of minimum wage, the scale, eligibility, and operation details vary from country to country, so that it is very difficult to provide a unique and comparable cross-country definition of the minimum wage.

Some countries opt for a single national minimum rate, which can be set on an hourly, daily, weekly, or monthly basis. Beyond the single national wage there is often a reduced or sub-minimum rate for some groups of workers, and notably the young. Often, sub-minimum rates do not exist *de jure*, but they do exist *de facto*, since special employment programmes allow employers to pay lower wages to youth workers or lower their social security charges.

In some countries, there exist minimum wage premia related to various workers' characteristics. For example, the minimum wage may rise with workers' experience, workers' qualification, and family status. The minimum wage may or may not be indexed to price inflation, even though such indexation schemes exist now in a very few OECD countries.

The setting of the minimum wage also changes according to two main criteria. In some countries, the minimum wage is unilaterally set by the government while in other countries it is part of a negotiation with workers and firm representatives.

Despite the various differences that we pointed out, one can still try to compare minimum wages across countries by measuring their value relative to some measure of average wage. Such a ratio (often referred to as the Kaitz index) depends on how both the numerator (the minimum wage) and the denominator (the average wage) are measured. In principle, using median rather than average wage provides a better measure of the denominator, since it also takes into consideration the dispersion of earnings. Special attention should also be paid to using the appropriate earning measure, which should exclude any overtime and bonus payment. The OECD (1998) has compiled indices of minimum wages for most OECD countries. High minimum wages are considered those for which the Kaitz index is more than 60 per cent as in France and Belgium, while it is considered low in countries in which the index is around 30 per cent (Spain, Czech Republic).

In an imperfect labour market, trade unions play an important role in wage determination. There are various ways to assess the importance of trade unions in the labour market. The first way is to look at union density, i.e. the fraction of workers registered to a trade union. Table 1.1 suggests that union density in Europe is much larger than in the USA: 44 per cent of European workers are registered to a trade union while in the United States the same figure is 14 per cent.

In some continental European countries trade union density is not very high and, perhaps surprisingly, it appears larger in the United States than in France. How is this possible when most people would think of France as the realm of the general strike? In order to correctly estimate the importance of trade unions it is necessary to consider the degree of trade union coverage, i.e. the percentage of workers whose salary has been negotiated by a trade union. While

Table 1.1. Union density and wage-setting institutions in different countries

	Density[a]	Coverage[b]	Centralization[c]
France	9.1	95.0	2.0
Germany	29.0	92.0	2.0
Spain	21.1	78.0	2.0
Italy	23.7	82.0	2.0
United States	14.3	18.0	1.0
Japan	24.0	21.0	1.0
European Union	43.1	82.3	1.9

[a] Percentage of workers belonging to a trade union.
[b] Percentage of workers whose wage is negotiated by a union.
[c] Degree of centralization in bargaining. 1 at firm level, 3 central.

Source: OECD 1999.

in the United States the difference between the trade union density and the degree of coverage is not very important, for countries like France, Germany, and Italy, the degree of trade union coverage is around 90 per cent. This means that in Europe nine workers out of ten have their wage negotiated by trade unions, even though only four out of ten are union members. Table 1.1 also collects information on the degree of centralization of collective bargaining, i.e. the level at which contracts are negotiated. While in the United States the negotiation is mostly at the level of the firm, in Europe it takes place mostly at the sectoral level. From the labour market point of view, strong trade unions can have adverse effects on the costs of labour, and can ultimately reduce employment. However, trade unions may also play a key role in society and boost workers to improve workers' morale and productivity.

1.4 **Employment Protection Legislation**

Employment Protection Legislation (EPL) is one of the most important institutions of the labour market. It refers to the set of norms and procedures to be followed in cases of dismissal of redundant workers. In almost every country, EPL forces employers to transfer to the worker a monetary compensation in the case of early termination of a permanent employment contract. Moreover, complex procedures have to be followed in the case of both individual and collective lay-offs. Finally, in some countries, the final decision on the legitimacy of a lay-off depends on a court ruling. From the viewpoint of economic analysis, it is very important to note that the firing decision is not only up to the worker and/or the employer, but can involve the participation of a court, which can be asked to assess the legal validity of the lay-off.

The most traditional dimensions of EPL are the severance payments and advance notice. Severance payments refer to a monetary transfer from the firm to the worker to be paid in the case of firm-initiated separation. Advance notice refers to a specific period of time to be given to the worker before a firing can actually be implemented. Note that the severance payment and advance notice that are part of EPL refer to the minimum statutory payments and mandatory rules that apply to all employment relationships, regardless of what is established by labour contracts. Beyond mandatory payments, collective agreements may well specify larger severance payments for firm-initiated separations. Such party clauses, albeit important, are not considered in this report.

Another important dimension of EPL consists of the administrative procedures that have to be followed before the lay-off can actually take place. In most countries, the employer is often required to discuss the lay-off decisions with the workers' representatives. Further, the legislative provisions often differ depending on business characteristics such as firm (or plant) size and industry of activity. As this simple introduction shows, it is obvious that the EPL is a multidimensional phenomenon.

In most countries the legislation distinguishes between individual and collective dismissals. Individual dismissals should be further distinguished between economic dismissals and disciplinary dismissals, with most EPL clauses applying only to the former case. Disciplinary dismissals (i.e. worker's fault dismissals), do not typically involve monetary transfers. The procedure for collective dismissal applies to large-scale firm restructuring, and requires the dismissal of at least a specific proportion of the workforce. When a collective dismissal is authorized by the relevant authority (often a court) the firm can then implement a large dismissal without a large transfer. Yet, such procedure requires a much tighter administrative burden, in the form of prolonged consultation with the workers' representatives.

From the viewpoint of economic analysis, the multidimensionality of the EPL can be reduced to two components. The first component is simply a monetary transfer from the employer to the worker, similar in nature to the wage. The second, instead, is more similar to a tax, because it corresponds to a payment to a third party, external to the worker–employer relationship. Conceptually, the severance payment and the notice period correspond to the transfer, while the trial costs (the fees for the lawyers, etc.) and all the other procedural costs correspond to the tax (in Italy, the transfer part corresponds to approximately 80 per cent of the total cost of the lay-off).

Unavoidably, the complexity of the firing regulations is costly for the employer. It is quite difficult to quantify the total cost of a lay-off, mainly because its exact amount depends also on the probability of the worker filing the case to a court, and on the probability of the court invalidating the firm's firing. In the Italian case, in particular, if the firing decision is overruled by the judge, the firm can be forced to take the employee back on the payroll. Despite the difficulty of carrying out precise calculations of the average cost of a lay-off, a number of studies have tried to assign a reasonable value to such a cost. Garibaldi and Violante (2006) estimate that an Italian employer with more than fifteen employees who fires a worker and whose decision is overruled by a court a year after the lay-off with 80 per cent probability will have to bear a cost of fifteen months' wages, i.e. a year and three months of wages.

From a cross-country perspective, it would be interesting to measure the average cost of a lay-off in the various countries. Unfortunately, homogeneous measures of such cost relative to the average wage do not exist for all countries. In order to carry out international comparisons of the employment protection regimes, economists use the so-called method of the 'hierarchies of the hierarchies'. This method consists in assigning a number (say from 1 to 6) to every country for any single feature of the protection regimes. Higher numbers denote more rigid regimes. Taking the average of the several components, a single synthetic measure of the rigidity of the EPL is obtained.

The synthetic indicators, originally compiled by the OECD, are now available for transition economies as well as for Latin American countries. In order to obtain the overall indicator of the rigidity of a country, it is necessary to consider simultaneously (a) the rigidity of the individual firing regulation of workers under permanent contract, (b) that of workers under temporary contracts, and (c) the rigidity of collective dismissals. The average of these three measures gives the overall indicator. Obviously, each of the three measures is obtained, in turn, through an average of some other sub-measures. As an example, consider the indicator for individual firings of workers under permanent contracts. Such a number is obtained as an average of 4 sub-indicators: (1) the administrative procedures, (2) the length of the notice period, (3) the amount of the severance payment (4) the severity of the enforcement (the more or less important role of judges on firing disputes). Clearly, in order to construct the synthetic indicators, it is necessary to consider a great number of dimensions.

Table 1.2 displays the relative position of the six countries. The United States turns out to be the most flexible country, while EPL is much tighter in countries such as Italy, Spain, and Germany. The table also shows the EPL rigidity indicators in the 1980s, thus allowing us to observe the evolution over time of the firing regulations. As far as the 'regular' contracts are concerned, the table clearly shows that the European countries have made very little change to the firing regulations. As a matter of fact, the level of protection is practically unchanged. Conversely, the regulation of temporary contracts has been eased in most European countries.

These indicators are undoubtedly useful for the economic analysis, as they are often used to empirically test the predictions of the economic models. However, it is worth recalling the reasons why such indicators are not perfect. First, it is very difficult to get time series of these indices (the latest OECD

Table 1.2. Strictness of employment protection legislation in different countries

	Regular employment		Temporary employment		Overall index	
	1980s	1990s	1980s	1990s	1980s	1990s
France	2.3	2.3	3.1	3.6	2.7	3
Germany	2.7	2.8	3.8	2.3	3.2	2.5
Spain	3.9	2.6	3.5	3.5	3.7	3.1
Italy	2.8	2.8	5.4	3.8	4.1	3.3
Japan	2.7	2.7	...	2.1	...	2.4
United States	0.2	0.2	0.3	0.3	0.2	0.2
European Union	2.5	2.3	2.9	2.2	2.7	2.3

Note: Degree of centralization in bargaining. 1 at firm level, 3 central.

Source: OECD 1999.

numbers refer to three points in time). Second, the method of the 'hierarchies of hierarchies' assigns the same weight to the various EPL sub-indicators. An additional problem is the fact that they concern features of EPL that are similar between countries, while they tend to ignore country-specific regulations. Finally, it is most difficult to measure the degree of enforcement of the norms. It is possible that some countries have rigid norms only softly enforced, while in other apparently flexible countries the norms are enforced very strictly (Boeri 1999).

2 The Optimal Skill Ratio

2.1 Introduction

Before entering into the details of personnel policies, the firm needs to have a general view of the right balance of its workforce. Indeed, choosing the right balance of the workforce is a key pre-requisite for sound personnel management. There are two key dimensions that should be considered: the skill composition of the labour force and the hours/employment trade-off.

Labour is not a homogeneous quantity, and a highly skilled worker is a very different factor of production from an unskilled worker. Highly skilled workers are likely to be more profitable to the firm. But they are also likely to be more costly. A trade-off emerges, and the firm has to find the right balance between cost and productivity. In personnel economics, solving this problem means finding the optimal skill ratio. This chapter shows that the solution to this trade-off requires the analysis of relative costs and relative productivity, where the word relative refers to different skill level. In general, we will see that the best skill composition is not necessarily the cheapest skill composition nor the most productive composition. Technological considerations are also very important. In some firms, only one type of labour will be chosen, while in other firms it will always be optimal to have a positive quantity of both types of workers. This chapter will also give us the possibility of studying the impact on the skill composition of wage compression, an important institutional feature of imperfect labour markets.

Hiring a quantity of labour, irrespective of its skill level, involves a variety of costs, and only some of such costs vary with the hours worked. As a consequence, total labour costs are much larger than the per hour wage cost. Further, some of these costs do not even vary with the number of hours worked. Thus, in real life organization a firm can adjust the quantity of a given type of labour over the hours worked and the number of employees. This is the hours/employment trade-off and will be the focus of the next chapter.

The chapter is organized as follows. Section 2.1 briefly describes the general hiring problem of a firm. Section 2.2 defines some key concepts for describing a firm's hiring behaviour. Section 2.2.1 describes the optimal skill ratio in the case of a technology in which workers are interdependent in the production process while Section 2.2.2 analyses the case of independent workers.

2.2 **A General View on Personnel Policies at the Hiring Stage**

A firm in general wants to maximize profits. Let's imagine for simplicity that the firm is a competitive firm so that the price that the firm charges for its product is fixed at some level. In a short-run dimension, the stock of capital can also be thought of as fixed, so that the scale of operation is given. The key decision concerns the amount of labour to be hired. But labour is a heterogeneous factor of production. The dimension of heterogeneity that is more relevant to the firm is the skill heterogeneity. Some workers are more productive than others. In this chapter we assume that there are only two types of workers: skilled and unskilled. We can think of skilled workers as graduate students and unskilled workers as individuals without a university degree. The firm must decide how much of each type of labour to hire. Further, it has to decide how many hours per week each type of worker should work. Basically, the firm maximization decision can be broken into *three* subsidiary decisions.

1. The firm decides how to produce any given amount of output. In other words, *the firm must decide the skill composition of its workforce.*
2. The firm decides how to combine hours and employment for any given amount of labour. This implies solving the *hours/employment trade-off.*
3. The firm decides how much output to produce.

The key personnel policies at the hiring stage are the first two. In this chapter we analyse the first one. In the next chapter, we analyse the second one. The pricing and quantity decision of the firm problem is certainly a key managerial decision, but is not the topic of personnel economics, while it is the key focus of industrial economics.

2.3 **The Optimal Skill Ratio: Key Concepts**

As we argued above, in this chapter we only focus on the skill combination and we ignore the distinction between hours and employment. This means that the cost of labour we consider is simply the wage to be paid to each employee, without any additional cost. The problem we consider is the following.

The Firm Problem

Let us suppose that we need to produce a given quantity of output $\bar{Y}$.

The firm can potentially use two types of labour for producing any amount of output Y, including the output $\bar{Y}$. The two types of labour are skilled workers and unskilled workers, which can be thought of as graduate workers and non-graduate workers. We indicate with L the quantity of low-skilled workers and with H the quantity of high-skilled workers. The contribution to output stemming from each separate input, holding constant the quantity of other input, is called *marginal productivity*. It is a key concept in most economics as well as in personnel economics. The marginal product of unskilled labour is defined as the change in output resulting from hiring additional workers, holding constant the quantity of other inputs. The formal expression is

$$F_L = \left. \frac{\Delta Y}{\Delta L} \right|_{H=\bar{H}, K=\bar{K}}$$

One additional unskilled worker yields an extra amount of output equal to F_L where the notation makes clear that we are holding fixed the amount of capital and of skilled labour.[1] Similarly one additional unit of skilled labour at constant quantity of unskilled labour yields $F_H = \left. \frac{\Delta Y}{\Delta H} \right|_{L=\bar{L}, K=\bar{K}}$. The only assumption that we make on these two marginal products is that they are *positive*. This means that an additional unit of any type of labour (holding constant the other type) increases total output. It is an obviously reasonable assumption, since it just says that adding more workers to the firm increases output, other things equal.

The salary of each type of worker depends on each skill level. The firm takes as given the wage. The salary of a graduate worker is w_H while the salary of an unskilled worker is w_L. The wage refers to the hourly labour costs. Obviously, $w_H \geq w_L$. Skilled workers are more expensive than unskilled workers.

The firm problem is to choose the skill combination that yields output $\bar{Y}$ and minimizes costs. In other words, the firm must select the combination of H and L that yields the lowest possible labour costs, conditional on producing total output equal to $\bar{Y}$.

[1] More formally, the marginal productivity of unskilled labour can also be thought of as the partial derivative of the production function $Y = F(\bar{K}, L, H)$ with respect to unskilled labour and indicated with $Y_L = \frac{\partial Y}{\partial L} = F_L$.

Our analysis will show that two dimensions are very important. The first one is the relative labour costs, or the ratio of the two wages. The other key dimension will be the relative marginal productivity of the two factors. In addition, careful consideration must be given to the way in which the two types of labour enter the production function, and whether the two factors are complements or substitutes in the production process.

The formal way to think about this problem is assuming that a firm would like to minimize labour costs subject to the constraint that the quantity of output is at least equal to some value $\bar{Y}$. If we let w_H be the skilled wage and w_L the low-skilled wage, the total costs of production are simply given by

$$TC = w_L L + w_H H,$$

where TC is the total labour costs. The curve that describes the combination of skilled and unskilled labour and yields the same amount of cost is called *isocost*. It is easy to study the feature of the isocost in the $H - L$ diagram displayed in Fig. 2.1. The isocost is just a negatively sloped line with the slope equal to the

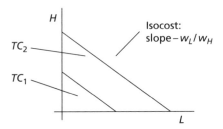

Figure 2.1. The Isocost

wage ratio[1] in absolute value $\frac{w_L}{w_H}$

$$\frac{\Delta H}{\Delta L} = -\frac{w_L}{w_H} \qquad \text{slope of the isocost}$$

Figure 2.1 plots two different isocosts. The curve labelled TC_1 refers to a larger total cost while the curve labelled TC_2 refers to a smaller value of the cost. Note that the two curves are parallel since the relative wage cost is the same in the two curves.

> *The wage skilled premium is the percentage premium required by the market for hiring a skilled worker versus an unskilled worker.*

Given a value w_H and w_L we can write that $w_H = (1+\gamma)w_L$ so that γ *is the skilled premium* required, and the slope of the isocost is simply equal to $\frac{1}{1+\gamma}$.

The firm would clearly like to position itself in the lowest possible isocost, but it has the constraint of producing the quantity of output $\bar{Y}$. A trade-off emerges. To find the formal solution we need to discuss the actual form of the production function. In the general case the relationship between input and output is given by the production function

$$Y = F(\bar{K}, L, H)$$

where $H, L, \bar{K}$ are the inputs and Y is output. The formal problem is to minimize total costs subject to the production constraint

$$Min\ (w_L L + w_H H)$$

$$\text{s.t. } F(\bar{K}, L, H) = \bar{Y}.$$

---

[1] To formally derive the slope of the isocost in the $H - L$ space simply write

$$H = -\frac{w_L}{w_H} L + \frac{TC}{w_H}$$

where $-\frac{w_L}{w_H}$ represents the slope.

As we will see in the rest of the chapter the solution depends on whether the two types of labour are independent in the production process. We analyse two cases. The first one is a case in which the two types of labour are interdependent in the production process, while the second one is a case in which the two factors are independent. The algebraic solution is derived in Appendix 2.1.

2.3.1 SKILLED AND UNSKILLED LABOUR INTERDEPENDENT (INTERIOR SOLUTION)

The first case we analyse is one in which the productivity of one type of labour depends on how many workers of the different types are around. Think of a firm in which the production line requires both engineers (high skilled) and blue collars (low skilled). The idea is that the productivity of a given set of engineers depends on how many blue collars are around. And the reverse is also true. Blue collars are more productive if there are more engineers. Further, no output can be obtained if no engineers and/or blue collars are around. In this case we say that the factors of production are interdependent, or imperfect substitutes.

The formal concept that we use to illustrate the relationship between different input combination and output is the *isoquant*. The isoquant describes the combination of skilled and unskilled labour that yields the same amount of output. Note that the isoquant is a pure *technological* concept, and it has no reference whatsoever to the cost of the two types of labour.

There are three key properties of these constant-output curves which should be familiar from microeconomics:

1. isoquants must be downward sloping;
2. isoquants do not intersect;
3. higher isoquants are associated with higher levels of output.

There is an additional property which depends on the form of the production function. In the case of interdependent production the following feature holds:

4. With interdependent production isoquants are convex to the origin.

Let's discuss these properties with the help of Fig. 2.2. The first property is important and easy to understand. The isoquant must be downward sloping. Let's calculate the slope of the isoquant between points X and Y in Fig. 2.2. In going from point X to point Y, the firm hires an additional ΔL unskilled workers, and each of these workers produces F_L units of output.[2] Hence the

---

[2] The marginal product of L in a production function of the type $Y = F(K, L, H)$ can be indicated either with F_L or with Y_L.

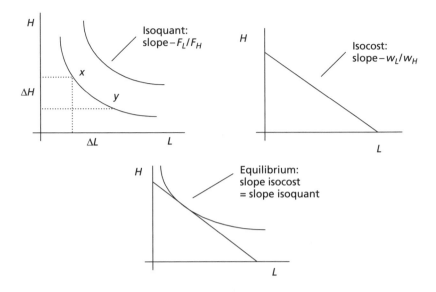

Figure 2.2. The solution to the optimal skill ratio with interdependent production

gain in output is given by the product $\Delta L \times F_L$. In going from point x to point y, however, the firm is also getting rid of ΔH units of skilled labour. Each of these units has a marginal product of F_H. The decrease in output is thus given by $\Delta H \times F_H$. Because output is constant along the isoquant, the gain in output resulting from hiring more skilled workers must be equal to the reduction in output attributable to the reduction in unskilled labour, or

$$\Delta L \times F_L + \Delta H \times F_H = 0$$

Rearranging the terms in the expression yields

$$\left.\frac{\Delta H}{\Delta L}\right|_{Y=\bar{Y}} = -\left.\frac{F_L}{F_H}\right|_{Y=\bar{Y}} \qquad \text{slope of isoquant}$$

The slope of the isoquant is then the negative of the ratio of marginal products. The absolute value of the slope is also called the marginal rate of technical substitution.[3]

---

[3] To derive the slope of the isoquant start from the production function $Y = F(L, H, \bar{K})$ and consider the change in output associated with a change in L and H so that

$$dY = F_L dL + F_H dH$$

Since along the isoquant $dY = 0$ we have that

$$\frac{dH}{dL} = -\frac{F_L}{F_H}.$$

The second property argues that isoquants cannot intersect. This is not surprising, since if they did intersect, a combination of two types of labour yields the same amount of output. Such a property cannot be consistent with the definition of isoquant. The third property says that larger isoquants refer to larger quantity of output. As we move to north-east in the diagram we obtain larger output. Indeed, as we move north-east in the diagram we have a larger amount of input, to which must necessarily correspond larger output (recall that the marginal product is positive).

With interdependent production isoquants are convex to the origin. To understand the convexity part think of how many skilled workers (H) we need in place of unskilled workers (L), and still obtain the same amount of output. The top panel in Fig. 2.2 suggests that the fewer unskilled workers we have relatively to high-skilled workers, the larger this substitution is. Formally, the convexity assumption implies that we have a diminishing marginal rate of technical substitution (or a flatter isoquant) as the firm substitutes unskilled labour for skilled labour.

The firm wants to produce at the lowest possible isocost given the constraint described by the isoquant. The solution is given by a tangency position, where the slope of the isoquant is equal to the slope of the isocost. In other words, the *optimal skill ratio requires that the slope of the isocost is equal to the slope of the isoquant*. Equating the slope of the isoquant to that of the isocost we have

$$\frac{w_L}{w_H} = \frac{F_L}{F_H} \tag{2.1}$$

which is the fundamental condition for determining the skilled combination of the labour force. The solution is clearly illustrated in the bottom panel of Fig. 2.2. The firm could produce the quantity of output $\bar{y}$ with other combinations, but such a choice would yield a larger cost. In other words, the previous condition says that the firm chooses the skill combination so that the *relative marginal product is equal to the relative marginal costs*. The optimal skill composition crucially depends on two ratios: the ratio of marginal productivity and the ratio of wages, and in equilibrium it is obtained by equating the two ratios.

Having determined the optimal skill ratio, we now study what happens if there is a change in the skilled wage premium γ, a parameter that the firm takes as given. Assume that the wage skill premium increases, and assume that the firm needs to produce a quantity indicated by y^*, as indicated in Fig. 2.3. The initial position of the firm is indicated by point A. The increase in the skilled wage induces an anticlockwise shift of the isocost. Following the increase in γ, the original isocost is no longer sufficient to guarantee a production level y^*. This suggests that the output y^* will be more expensive in the aftermath of the increase in γ. But what happen to the optimal skill

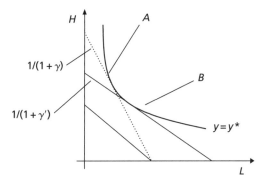

Figure 2.3. The effect of an increase in γ on the optimal skill ratio

ratio? The new equilibrium position will be at point B, a point at which the slope of the new isocost (following the increase in γ) is identical to the slope of the isoquant. The optimal point will correspond to a lower skill ratio, and the firm will tend to substitute low-skilled labour for high-skilled labour. *With interdependent production, an increase (decrease) in the skilled wage premium decreases (increases) the optimal skill ratio.*

The formal proof of this is obtained in the next section, but it can also be seen graphically by the shift of the optimal skill ratio from point A to point B in Fig. 2.3.

Finally note that in deriving the optimal skill ratio, we have not referred to the financial position of the firm, nor whether a firm is making or losing money. So, the optimal skill combination is independent of firm profitability.

The previous remark is important, since it says that the firm should hold on to its optimal skill ratio independently of the current financial conditions. In other words, savings on skilled workers in bad times can just do damage to the firm's profit outlook.

A Formal Example of Interdependent Production: The Cobb–Douglas Production Function

Suppose that the capital stock is equal to 1 and that the production function is $Y = L^\beta H^\alpha$ with $\beta > 0$ and $\alpha > 0$. This implies that the marginal product of labour is $F_L = \frac{\partial Y}{\partial L} = \beta L^{\beta-1} H^\alpha$ while the marginal product of skilled workers is $F_H = \frac{\partial Y}{\partial H} = \alpha L^\beta H^{\alpha-1}$. From these marginal functions, it follows immediately that the marginal product of each type of labour depends on the number of people of the other type that are currently hired. Further, the ratio of the marginal product is

$$\frac{F_L}{F_H} = \frac{\beta L^{\beta-1} H^\alpha}{\alpha L^\beta H^{\alpha-1}}$$

$$\frac{F_L}{F_H} = \frac{\beta H}{\alpha L}$$

and using the key condition one has

$$\frac{w_L}{w_H} = \frac{\beta}{\alpha}\frac{H}{L}$$

so that the optimal ratio is given by

$$\left(\frac{H}{L}\right)^* = \frac{\alpha}{\beta}\frac{w_L}{w_H}$$

Obviously we have $w_H = (1+\gamma)w_L$ so that γ *is the skilled premium* required. It is clear that the optimal skill mix depends on three key parameters: α, β, and γ, as the following equation shows:

$$\left(\frac{H}{L}\right)^* = \frac{\alpha}{\beta(1+\gamma)}$$

The optimal skill ratio increases with α and decreases with γ and β.

Note that in this case we have an interior solution. It is always optimal to use some combination of skilled and unskilled labour regardless of the specific value of γ. Yet, a larger value of γ reduces the optimal skill ratio.

2.3.2 SKILLED AND UNSKILLED LABOUR INDEPENDENT (CORNER SOLUTION)

Suppose that a firm can still produce output with two types of labour, but the production process of each worker is completely independent from how many workers of the other type are around. An example in this dimension could be a firm selling computers, where salespersons can be high skill or low skill. Each seller has some productivity that is independent of the number of other sellers around. For extreme simplicity, let us assume that the productivity of each type of labour is constant so that

$$F_L = a$$

$$F_H = b$$

We will see that in this case only one type of labour is going to be used and the firm will be in a *corner solution*. We typically think that high-skilled workers are more productive, so that $b > a$. This is useful for introducing an important concept, as we do next.

The high-skilled productivity premium is the percentage increase in marginal productivity obtained by hiring a high-skilled worker.

If we say that skilled labour is more productive by δ per cent, then $b = a(1+\delta)$. In other words, δ is the productivity premium. Applying equation 2.1

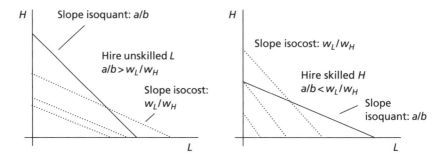

Figure 2.4. Optimal skill ratio with corner solution

would yield $\frac{a}{b} = \frac{w_L}{w_H}$ which is an equation that is independent of both H and L. There is no reason whatsoever why the ratio $\frac{a}{b}$ should be equal to the ratio of $\frac{w_L}{w_H}$. One of the two ratios is larger. We can say that it is optimal to hire *only unskilled labour if and only if*

$$\frac{a}{b} > \frac{w_L}{w_H}$$

This situation is also described in the graphical interpretation of Fig. 2.4, and particularly in the top panel. Note that in this case both the isoquant and the isocost are linear equations, so that in the equilibrium position only one type of labour should be used. This is tectonically defined as a corner solution. In the first panel, it is optimal to hire only unskilled workers, since $\frac{a}{b} > \frac{w_L}{w_H}$. Further elaborating this inequality we can say that unskilled labour should be used if

$$\frac{a}{b} > \frac{w_L}{w_H}$$

$$\frac{1}{(1+\delta)} > \frac{1}{1+\gamma}$$

$$\gamma > \delta$$

In other words, unskilled labour should be used when the wage skill premium is larger than the productivity skill premium. With independent workers, only one type of labour should be used, and the solution is obtained by comparing the value of the skilled wage premium to the productivity premium.

The condition is very intuitive. Suppose that $\delta = 0.05$ and $\gamma = 0.1$, which means that the market requires a premium of 10 per cent for hiring a skilled worker while the productivity premium is only 5 per cent. In this situation, it cannot be optimal to hire skilled workers since the proportional increase in cost is larger than the proportional increase in productivity.

2.3.3 THE EFFECTS OF WAGE COMPRESSION

A key feature of imperfect labour markets is the presence of wage compression across skills. Wage compression refers to a tendency of wages to be equalized across the skill distribution. Such a phenomenon depends on many institutional reasons, and most of them are linked to the unions' desire to have an egalitarian wage policy. We do not want to discuss why such a phenomenon exists. What we are interested in is the consequences of wage compression on the optimal skill ratio.

The presence of wage compression in different countries is clearly visible from Table 2.1. The table reports the relative expected earnings of individuals with different degrees of education in different countries. The expected earning of a worker with below upper secondary education is normalized to 100, and the earning of individuals with higher education is expressed as a multiple of the baseline education. The last column reports the earning ratio of an individual with tertiary education with respect to an individual with below secondary education. Such a ratio is very similar to the skill premium introduced in the text (the concept of γ). The table clearly shows that the ratio changes markedly across countries. Whereas a country such as the United States has a value of γ roughly equal to 3, the same ratio falls to 1.8 in countries such as Germany, and slightly above 2 in countries such as France. Wage compression refers to a reduction of γ for given productivity differences.

We want to understand how the presence of wage compression affects the optimal skill ratio. At the firm level, wage compression can be described as a force that tends to equalize wages across different skill groups. In a world with

Table 2.1. Wage productivity premia in different countries

		Below upper secondary education	Upper secondary education	Tertiary education	Tertiary/below secondary γ
France	males	100	124.08	204.80	2.05
	females	100	136.43	216.53	2.17
Germany	males	100	124.60	181.39	1.81
	females	100	146.86	207.73	2.08
Italy	males	100	188.29	267.09	2.67
	females	100	195.54	229.76	2.30
United Kingdom	males	100	162.81	250.20	2.50
	females	100	140.88	264.02	2.64
United States	males	100	163.88	294.59	2.95
	females	100	173.28	291.82	2.92

Notes: Relative expected earnings of the population with income from employment by education attainment and gender.

Population aged 30–44 below upper secondary=100.

wage compression the wage of skilled and unskilled workers is

$$\tilde{w}_L = w_L(1 + \phi)$$
$$\tilde{w}_H = w_H(1 - \phi)$$

where $\tilde{w}_H$ and $\tilde{w}_L$ refer to the compressed wage and ϕ is the wage compression factor. In the case of independent production, unskilled labour should be used if

$$\frac{a}{b} > \frac{\tilde{w}_L}{\tilde{w}_H}$$
$$\frac{a}{b} > \frac{w_L(1 + \phi)}{w_H(1 - \phi)}$$

Since ϕ increases the right-hand side of this inequality, it is obvious that unskilled labour is less likely to be used the more wages are compressed.[4] Wage compression increases the optimal skill ratio, so that in markets where wages are more compressed firms use technologies that are more skill intensive.

With wage compression, it is possible that a firm that under normal circumstances would hire only unskilled workers will swap the quantity of its workforce and hire only skilled workers. We label this phenomenon *overeducation*, since a given job is filled by individuals that are more qualified than would be the case without wage compression.

2.3.4 INDEPENDENT SKILLED AND UNSKILLED LABOUR INTERACTING WITH COSTLY CAPITAL

In the case of independent production, it is vital to establish whether skilled or unskilled labour should be used. One has just to compare the skilled premium with the productivity premium: unskilled labour should be used as long as $\gamma > \delta$. This rule is not necessarily valid when labour is independent but it interacts with costly capital. Let's say that the production process requires to rent a capital machine at cost C_k. It can well be the case that even if $\gamma > \delta$ (so that unskilled labour should be used) the worker/machine combination that minimizes costs is the one that combines skilled workers with machines. To see this let's define the cost per unit of output of using unskilled labour as

$$\frac{w_L + C_k}{a}$$

where the numerator is the cost of hiring 1 unit of labour with a capital machine that costs C_K while the denominator is the productivity of 1 unit of unskilled

---

[4] Appendix 2.1 derives the consequences of wage compression in the case of interdependent production.

labour. Similar, the cost per unit of output of skilled labour is

$$\frac{w_H + C_k}{b}$$

One answer (which is similar to the rule we used in the previous section) is that skilled labour should be used if the cost per unit of output is lower, so that

$$\frac{w_H + C_k}{b} < \frac{w_L + C_k}{a}$$

Using the fact that $w_H = w_L(1 + \gamma)$ and $b = a(1 + \delta)$ the previous condition is

$$\frac{w_L(1 + \gamma) + C_k}{(1 + \delta)} < w_L + C_k$$

$$w_L(1 + \gamma) + C_k < w_L(1 + \delta) + C_k(1 + \delta)$$

which becomes

$$\delta > \gamma \left[\frac{w_L}{w_L + C_k} \right] \tag{2.2}$$

which is the condition for hiring skilled workers when labour interacts with costly capital. The important thing to notice is that the term in square brackets is less than one, and suggests that it may pay to use skilled workers even when $\delta = \gamma$, since one has to take into consideration costly capital. Let's try to understand the economics of this result. Let's begin with the following:

If capital is not present in the process (so that $C_K = 0$), skilled labour should be used if $\delta > \gamma$.

This simply says that when there is no costly capital the rule is the same as the one analysed in the previous section.

To understand this result, let us define with $\tilde{\gamma}$ the right-hand side of equation so that

$$\tilde{\gamma} = \gamma \left[\frac{w_L}{w_L + C_k} \right]$$

where it is clear that $\tilde{\gamma} < \gamma$ as long as $C_k > 0$. The following gives the condition for hiring skilled labour:

If renting a machine costs $C_k > 0$, skilled labour should be used if $\delta > \tilde{\gamma}$ where $\tilde{\gamma} = \gamma \left[\frac{w_L}{w_L + C_k} \right]$.

How can this result be explained? The intuition is as follows. To obtain one additional unit of output using high-skilled labour requires that $\frac{1}{b}$ more unit of capital is installed, while using unskilled labour requires $\frac{1}{a}$ unit of capital to be used. Since $b > a$ it may pay to use skilled labour and save on costly machinery even if $\gamma > \delta$. This depends on how costly machines are and on how costly unskilled labour is.

Table 2.2. Optimal skill ratio with independent workers and costly capital

		Output/worker	Labour costs	Capital costs	Total costs	Cost/output
Machines A						
	Low-skilled	4	40	6	46	**11.50**
	High-skilled	6	64	6	70	11.67
	Prod. premium	0.5				
Machines B						
	Low-skilled	8	40	10	50	6.25
	High-skilled	12	64	10	74	**6.17**
	Prod. premium	0.5				

Note: Wage rates: $w_l = 40, w_h = 64, \gamma = 0.6$.

Consider the example in which a firm must choose between low- or high-skilled labour with two different technologies which we summarize by their different cost of capital. With the new technology capital is more costly but both skilled and unskilled workers are more productive. Let's see whether the optimal skill choice changes with the new or the old technology. Let $w_L = 40$, $w_H = 64$, and the wage productivity premium γ is 0.6. Output per worker of low-skilled workers is $y_L = 4$ while output per worker of high-skilled workers is $y_H = 6$. If capital is not relevant in the production process, then obviously low-skilled labour should be used. With the old-type technology production requires costly capital ($C_K = 8$), and such cost should be taken into account. Nevertheless, the cost per output of low-skilled labour is still lower ($11.5 < 11.67$) so that unskilled labour should be used even with this capital cost. With the new machine $\tilde{\gamma} = \gamma \left[\frac{w_L}{w_L + C_k} \right] = 0.6 * \left[\frac{40}{40+10} \right] = 0.48$, so that skilled labour should be used since $\delta > \tilde{\gamma}$. Indeed, Table 2.2 shows that high-skilled workers are most cost effective in this case.

☐ APPENDIX 2.1. A FORMAL EXPRESSION OF THE GENERAL PROBLEM

Output at the firm is indicated by Y. Consider two types of labour, high-skilled and low-skilled, which we indicate respectively with H and L. The short-run production function takes the form

$$Y = F(\bar{K}, L, H)$$

where $\bar{K}$ is the fixed amount of capital, L is unskilled labour, and H is skilled labour. Suppose that for each type of labour we have to choose the hours and the number of people so that

$$L = L(E_l, h_l) \qquad H(E_h, h_h)$$

where E_l is the number of low-skilled employees and h_l is the number of hours per unskilled employee. E_h and h_h are similarly defined but with respect to the skilled and unskilled labour. The production function can be written as

$$Y = F(\bar{K}, L(E_l, h_l), H(E_h, h_h))$$

where the total quantity of each type of labour can be obtained by changing either employment or hours. In this chapter the distinction between E_l and h_l (and between E_h and h_h) was ignored, and the focus was on the choice between H and L. In the next chapter the focus is mainly on the distinction between E_l and h_l without considering the distinctions between H and L. This is done for simplicity.

Interdependent Production. The problem in this case is formally studied by setting up a Lagrangian so as to maximize the following function (see Appendix B for a simple explanation of the Langrangian technique)

$$\Lambda = w_L L + w_H H + \lambda[F(\bar{K}, L, H) - \bar{Y}]$$

with respect to L, H, and λ. The first-order conditions read:

$$w_L = \lambda F_L \tag{2.3}$$

$$w_H = \lambda F_H \tag{2.4}$$

$$F(\bar{K}, L, H) = \bar{Y}$$

so that, taking the fraction between the two first-order conditions, one gets:

$$\frac{w_L}{w_H} = \frac{F_L}{F_H} \tag{2.5}$$

which is the key condition for the optimal skill ratio.

Wage Compression with Interdependent Production. Using the wage skill premium factor γ we have:

$$w_H = w_L(1 + \gamma)(1 - \phi),$$

where ϕ is the wage compression factor. To see the effect of wage compression in the case of interior production

$$\left(\frac{H}{L}\right)^* = \frac{\alpha}{\beta} \frac{w_L}{w_H}$$

$$\left(\frac{H}{L}\right)^* = \frac{\alpha}{\beta} \frac{(1 + \phi)}{(1 - \phi)(1 + \gamma)}$$

where it is easy to show that wage compression increases the optimal skilled ratio. To see this note that the partial derivative of $\left(\frac{H}{L}\right)^*$ with respect to ϕ is positive. In formula

$$\frac{\partial \left(\frac{H}{L}\right)^*}{\partial \phi} = \frac{\alpha}{\beta} \frac{1}{(1 + \gamma)} \frac{1}{(1 - \phi)^2} > 0$$

An example of Independent Production. The obvious example is the following production function:

$$Y = [aL + bH]^z$$

where $0 < z < 1$ can be thought of as managerial ability. Indeed, applying the standard rule we have:

$$F_L = azY^{z-1}$$

and

$$F_H = bzY^{z-1}$$

so that the ratio of the marginal product reads

$$\frac{F_L}{F_H} = \frac{a}{b}$$

we typically think that high-skilled labour is more productive than low-skilled labour, so that $b > a$. The case analysed in the text is one in which $z = 1$.

3 The Hours–Employment Trade-Off

3.1 Introduction

In imperfect labour markets, hiring labour involves a variety of costs, and only some of such costs vary with the hours worked. In the previous chapter labour costs were simply defined as the per hour (or per month) wage. In reality, a variety of labour costs exist and most of such costs are independent of the hourly wage cost. Some of these costs are paid only upon hiring, while other costs are paid each month, but are independent of the hours worked. The cost of advertising a vacancy refers to the first type, while paid vacations are an example of the second one. This means that a real life organization can adjust the quantity of labour over two different margins, which are called the extensive margin and the intensive margin. The extensive margin refers to the number of people hired by the firm while the intensive margin refers to the average hours worked per employees. Choosing the right combination between hours per workers and the number of employees means solving the hours–employment trade-off.

Section 3.1 presents a formal, albeit simple, classification of total labour costs. Section 3.2 presents the basic theory of the hours–employment trade-off and derives the firm solution to the trade-off. Section 3.3 explicitly introduces overtime salary into analysis and derives the employment effect of an increase in overtime pay. Section 3.4 presents a case study on the employment effect of an increase in overtime pay, or the effect of a reduction in the normal hours of work. The case study is derived from France in 1982, when the government suddenly decided to reduce the number of hours from 40 to 39. The results of this change are exactly in line with those presented in the theoretical part of the chapter.

3.2 A Formal Classification of Labour Costs

The costs the employer incurs to acquire the services of labour fall into two categories. First, there are fixed costs. These take two forms: (i) non-recurring fixed costs and (ii) recurring fixed costs. Non-recurring costs are also known

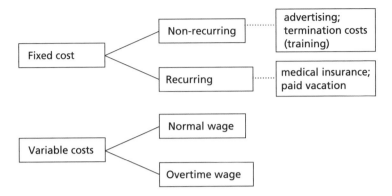

Figure 3.1. Classification of labour costs

as one-off costs, or set-up costs, and are costs that the firm incurs each time it takes on a new worker; recurring fixed costs are paid by the firm on a regular basis, as long as it continues to employ that worker, but do not vary with the number of hours or the intensity with which an employee works. Second there are variable labour costs. These are costs that vary according to the number of hours, and the key distinction is the one between normal wage per hour and overtime. The fact that most forms of employment combine elements of both of these has led to a description of labour as a *quasi-fixed* factor of production. Figure 3.1 reports a diagram with the classification that we just described.

3.2.1 NON-RECURRING FIXED COSTS

Non-recurring fixed costs are paid by the firm once over the employment relationship. The best example of non-recurring fixed costs is the hiring and screening costs that the firm encounters each time it tries to fill a vacancy. These are the costs of advertising a vacancy, and securing and selecting applicants. It is in general very difficult to measure the size of these costs. The best estimate of these costs is the one obtained with Israeli data, and shows that the typical hiring cost is approximately two weeks of paid salary.

An important non-recurring fixed cost is the cost associated with employment protection legislation. These costs can be very large, and are a key feature of imperfect labour markets. They are obviously non-recurring, since they are paid only once. Yet, rather than being paid at the beginning of the employment relationship, they are paid at the end. Further, such costs are not paid if the worker leaves, so that what matters at the time of hiring a worker is the probability of incurring such costs. In any event, employment protection legislation will be analysed in some detail in Chapters 4, 7, and 8. As we will see, the costs associated with employment protection legislation can be very large, and can even reach 20 per cent of monthly wages in some countries.

Another example of a non-recurring fixed cost is the initial expense that the firm faces to train workers. While these costs are certainly fixed, in this book they are considered as investment by firms, and they will be the focus of Chapters 9 and 10.

3.2.2 RECURRING FIXED COSTS

While non-recurring fixed costs are paid only once, there are also important recurring fixed costs. These refer to costs that the employer must regularly pay, independently of the actual hours worked. Employers' contributions to unemployment insurance funds, to health insurance, and to private pension funds are typically paid on a recurring basis, and the level of such payments is often independent of how long or hard the employee works. These contributions are often subject to an upper ceiling and for all those employees earning above the upper ceiling the contributions to such funds are largely independent of the amount they earn. Other examples of recurring but fixed costs are fringe benefits (company cars, mobile phones), the clerical and administrative costs associated with employing labour, and those parts of the personnel and welfare offices that devote themselves to helping existing employees. Most important of all is probably the payment for days that are not worked. Holiday pay, both statutory (public holidays) and negotiated, and sickness pay can be a substantial part of total labour costs.

3.2.3 VARIABLE COSTS

The distinction among variable costs is less well articulated, since such costs are less diverse. Nevertheless, there is a key distinction between standard wages and overtime wages. Such a difference will be also the topic of our case study. In the case of France, an example that we will study in some detail at the end of the chapter, the overtime premium is 25 per cent of the normal wage for the first four hours of overtime, and 50 per cent beyond.

3.3 **A Theory of the Hours–Employment Trade-Off**

3.3.1 THE ISOCOST AND THE TOTAL LABOUR COSTS

In the previous chapter we emphasized the fact that labour is a very heterogeneous factor of production, and skilled and unskilled workers are like two different factors of production. In this chapter we concentrate on the employment–hours trade-off, and for simplicity we assume that there is only one type of labour. Specifically, we let E be the number of people in the firm and h the number of hours per worker.

Let us begin by properly defining E and h. Hours h are measured as hours per unit of time, and the convention in this respect is to measure h as hours per week. E is simply the number of people employed by the firm. As we saw in the previous section labour costs are very diverse. Here we provide a very parsimonious description of total labour costs, and we will (initially) just distinguish between fixed and variable labour costs.

The problem we want to describe is the following.

The firm has to produce a given output quantity $y = \bar{y}$.

The personnel department has to hire a given type of labour. Let's take it that we need to assume skilled labour. The amount of skilled labour hired must be consistent with the output level $y = \bar{y}$.

Hiring skilled workers involves the choice of two quantities: the number of skilled individuals (the extensive margin) and the average hours per worker (the intensive margin).

The aim of the personnel department is to minimize total costs, subject to the constraint represented by the output level.

To solve this problem, let's first think of the total labour costs. There are two dimensions to consider: the number of skilled workers, which we indicate with E, and the number of hours per worker, which we indicate with h. We assume that each worker hired involves a fixed cost equal to F. In this respect, we are just focusing on non-recurring fixed costs. This implies that hiring E workers involves a fixed cost of labour equal to EF, where F is the fixed cost per worker. Let us assume that the wage rate per hour w is initially fixed at w so that the fixed and variable costs can be written as

$$Fixed \text{ Cost} = EF$$

$$Variable \text{ Cost} = Ewh$$

The variable cost is equal to the weekly wage (wh) multiplied by the number of employees. If we indicate with C the total budget allocation then we can write

$$C = EF + Ewh$$

Let's solve the previous condition for E to obtain

$$E = \frac{C}{wh + F}$$

The previous relationship highlights a key trade-off in the firm total costs. There exists a combination of hours (intensive margin) and people (extensive margin) consistent with a given total cost C. In other words, the firm can obtain total costs C by choosing a point over the curve that we label isocost. There are two key features of the isocost that we need to emphasize. First, the isocost is downward sloping. Second, it is non-linear. The bold curve in the chart below describes the relationship. The downward-sloping property of the isocost is not surprising, while the non-linearity is a new feature, and deserves to be discussed. Consider a firm that is hiring many workers, but each worker is working a small number of hours (point X in the figure). Because there are many workers, a small increase in the length of the workweek requires a large reduction in the number of workers to keep costs constant. In contrast, if the firm is hiring few workers, an increase in hours of work need not require a large cut in employment in order to hold costs constant. This means that the isocost will be flatter (point Z in figure 3.2).

How do we describe the output constraint? To answer to this question we need to discuss how hours per worker and employment are combined in the firm so as to obtain a given amount of output. We need again the isoquant introduced in the previous chapter, but this time it refers to a slightly different concept. Suppose that there is a production function that describes how hours per worker and the number of employees are combined so as to obtain a given amount of output in the firm. Let us imagine that a firm can obtain $\bar{y}$ units of output. Such output can be obtained with different combination of hours per worker and number of employees, and all such combinations represent a point of the isoquant. Isoquants have the same features outlined in the previous chapter, and we briefly report them again here.[1]

1. An isoquant must be downward sloping;
2. Different isoquants do not intersect;
3. Higher isoquant labours are associated with higher levels of output;
4. Isoquants are convex to the origin.

At this point we have all the elements for understanding how the firm will operate. The goal is to minimize total costs subject to the isoquant constraint. This means that the firm would like to be in the lowest possible isocost, conditional on the isoquant. The solution is again a tangency condition and it is given by the combination $E^* - h^*$ in Fig. 3.2.

We ask two questions. First, what happens to the employment–hours trade-off if the scale operation increases. Second, what happens to the employment–hours trade-off if the fixed cost of labour increases?

Let's consider first the increase in the scale of operation. This phenomenon can be easily described by an increase in the budget allocation C. The figure describes the upward shift in the budget allocation. Large budget allocation obviously leads to an increase in the number of employees. The effect of hours is less clear, but an obvious feature of average hours per worker observed in real organization is that firms of very different size employ workers for a similar

---

[1] The formal expression of an isolabor is then a function.

$$\bar{y} = f(h, E)$$

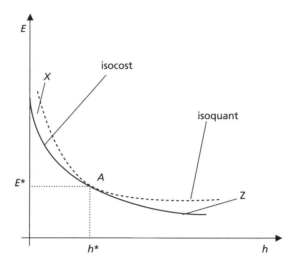

Figure 3.2. The solution to the hours–employment trade-off

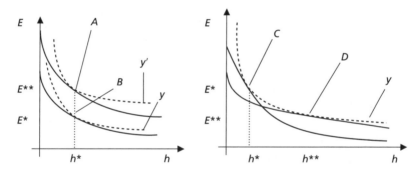

Figure 3.3. The effect of the hours–employment trade-off of an increase in the size of the budget (left panel) and an increase in the fixed cost (right panel)

number of hours per week. The left-hand side of Fig. 3.3, and the formal problem described in Appendix 3.1 captures such real life property:

> *Larger output leads to an increase in the number of employees. Conversely, the choice of hours is independent of output, so that an increase in the budget does not have an impact on the demand for hours.*

This property is empirically consistent with the fact that the average hours per worker is largely independent of the size of the firms, a property that appears empirically true. Next consider the effect of an increase in the fixed cost of hiring labour. The isocost shifts down, and as Fig. 3.3 shows, firms reduce employees and increase hours.

> *An increase in the fixed costs of hiring increases the demand for hours.*

3.3.2 A FORMAL SOLUTION TO THE EMPLOYMENT–HOURS TRADE-OFF

The firm's labour costs are

$$C = E[hw + F]$$

and the production function is

$$y = Eh^\beta \qquad \text{with } \beta < 1$$

The firm wants to minimize costs subject to the constraint that production is equal to a fixed value $\bar{y}$. Forming the Lagrangian one has

$$\Lambda = E[hw + F] + \lambda[\bar{y} - Eh^\beta]$$

whose first-order conditions are

$$wE = \lambda E\beta h^{\beta-1}$$

$$(hw + F) = \lambda h^\beta$$

$$\bar{y} = Eh^\beta$$

The first condition is the derivative of the Lagrangian with respect to h, the second condition is the derivative with respect to E, while the last one is simply the production constraint. Taking the fraction between the two conditions one has

$$\beta h^{-1} = \frac{w}{hw + F}$$

$$\beta hw + \beta F = wh$$

$$h = \frac{\beta F}{w(1 - \beta)}$$

The latter expression gives the hours per worker as a function of the per hour wage and the fixed cost F. To obtain an expression for the number of employees, one can simply substitute the previous expression into the isocost to obtain

$$\bar{y} = E\left[\frac{\beta F}{w(1 - \beta)}\right]^\beta$$

$$E = \bar{y}\left[\frac{\beta F}{w(1 - \beta)}\right]^{-\beta}$$

from which one can immediately see that

$$\frac{\partial \log E}{\partial \log F} = -\beta$$

so that the elasticity of employment to the fixed cost is negative and equal to $-\beta$.

3.4 **The Overtime Premium and the Effects of Reducing the Workweek**

3.4.1 FIRM POSITION WITH THE OVERTIME PREMIUM

In real life organization there is typically a 'normal' number of hours to which the firm pays a base wage. The normal number of hours is set by law or by collective agreements, and it is taken as given by the firm. We indicate with h_o such 'normal' number of hours and with w the corresponding wage.

Firms can choose to employ workers for a larger number of hours $h > h_o$ but such rate requires an overtime wage $\tilde{w} > w$.

Let us assume that the personnel department has a budget allocation equal to C. The existence of the overtime wage implies that the shape of the isocost changes in correspondence to the normal number of hours h_o.

If the firm does not use overtime (i.e. if $h \le h_o$) the isocost is identical to that of the previous section.

$$C = EF + wEh \text{ if } h \le h_o$$

If the firm does use overtime, two different wages apply to the firm: one for normal hours and one for overtime hours. The isocost in this case is equal to

$$C = EF + wEh_o + \tilde{w}E(h - h_o) \text{ if } h > h_o$$

The slope of the isocost changes at the normal hours h_o, with a steeper curvature beyond the normal hours h_o. Figure 3.4 plots the isocost. In correspondence to the normal number of hours the isocost features a kink point.

The isoquant for employees' hours is the same as the one described in the previous section, and the objective of the firm is still to minimize costs subject to the isoquant constraint.

A firm can be in two different positions, depending on whether or not it uses overtime.

Suppose that there are two firms, one that uses overtime and one that does not use overtime. The situation is described in the top panel of Fig. 3.4. The first panel describes a firm that is operating on the 'normal' number of hours, and it positions itself on the kink point of the isocost. The firm in the second panel, conversely, corresponds to a firm that is operating in the overtime range, and positions itself to the right of the kink point h_o.

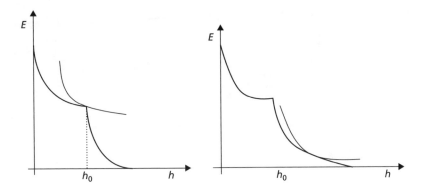

Figure 3.4. Equilibrium position for a firm that uses and does not use overtime

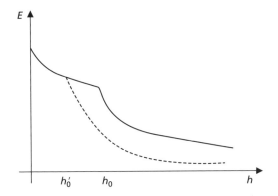

Figure 3.5. The reduction of the normal workweek and the isocost

3.4.2 THE EFFECT OF A REDUCTION IN THE NORMAL WORKWEEK

Let's now consider a reduction in the normal workweek h_0. The first thing to understand is what happens to the isocost when the normal week changes. This is done in Fig. 3.5. Consider a given total cost C. For a number of hours below the new value, the isocost does not change. For values of h above the new minimum the isocost corresponding to C is now lower, since the firm has to pay a larger cost $\tilde{w}$.

Let us first consider a firm that before the change in the normal workweek was working exactly h_0 hours. In the aftermath of the change, such a firm will find itself suddenly in the overtime range. This implies that the wage for the last hour goes up and the isocost, in correspondence to the old normal hours, is now steeper. Such a firm will necessarily reduce the number of employees, and its equilibrium position, as indicated by Fig. 3.6, will shift from point A to point B.

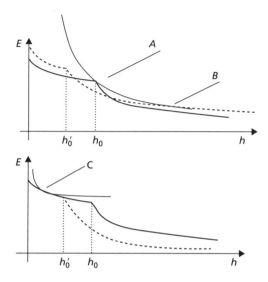

Figure 3.6. The effects of reduction in the normal workweek

Let us now consider a firm that before the overtime change is operating below the normal workweek. In terms of Fig. 3.6, such a firm was operating in point C in the figure. The change in the slope of the isocost involves a part of the constraint that does not affect the position of the firm. This suggests that such a firm will not change its equilibrium position, and will continue to hire the same number of workers for the same workweek.

Combining the results of the two type of firms (described by Fig. 3.6), it is clear that the effect of a reduction in the normal workweek is a reduction in the number of workers hired. The following summarizes the findings:

A reduction in the normal workweek induces a reduction in the number of employees.

The next section analyses a case study on workweek reduction in France, and shows that the theoretical predictions are largely consistent with the empirical evidence.

3.5 **Reducing the Workweek: A Natural Experiment from France**

This section discusses the reduction in the workweek that took place in France in 1982, and shows how our analytical framework is fairly consistent with the empirical evidence.

Table 3.1. France: hours worked 1976–1981

	1976	1977	1978	1979	1980	1981
Fraction of employment Working:						
36 to 39 hours	2.2	2.1	2.5	2.4	2.6	2.4
40 hours	46.6	53.6	56.6	58.6	60.9	65.9
41 to 43 hours	18.8	18.8	19.5	19.3	17.5	15.2
44 hours	4.2	4.4	3.9	2.3	2.7	2.0
45 to 48 hours	28.2	21.1	18.6	17.4	16.4	14.5
Number of observations	5,422.0	6,133.0	6,212.0	6,123.0	6,409.0	6,509.0

Source: Crépon and Kramarz (2002)

The number of hours worked in France strongly decreased during the 1970s, from 48 hours in 1974 to just above 40 hours in 1981 (Table 3.1). Since 1936, the standard workweek in France was 40 hours. The French Socialist government in 1982 reduced the workweek from 40 to 39 hours. In this section we study the effects of such a change on the number of hirings.

François Mitterrand's election in May 1981 induced a sudden decrease of the standard workweek to 39 hours (16 January 1982 ordinance), and the new 39 law was imposed on 1 February 1982. The law mandated a maximum legal workweek of 39 hours, whereas it was 40 hours previously. The overtime regulation did not substantially change: the overtime premium remained 25 per cent for the first four hours (i.e. from 40 to 43 hours), and 50 per cent above. Collective agreements, specifying the terms of application of the decree, ensued in the aftermath of the ordinance, starting with the larger firms in manufacturing industries and spreading to smaller firms and other industries.

It is possible to show that workers directly affected by these changes—those working 40 hours in March 1981 as well as those working overtime at the same date—were more likely to lose their jobs between 1981 and 1982 than those workers not affected by the changes—those working 36 to 39 hours in March 1981. The estimate of the impact of the one-hour reduction of the workweek on employment losses varies between 2 per cent and 4 per cent.

The result is based on a comparison between workers who worked 36 to 39 hours before 1982 and workers who worked exactly 40 hours and those who worked overtime (up to 48 hours). The result shows that workers who were working exactly 40 hours per week in March 1981 as well as workers who were working overtime (41 to 48 hours) per week in March 1981 were less likely to be employed in 1982 than observationally identical workers who, in 1981, were working 36 to 39 hours per week. The analysis uses econometric techniques that allow the scholar to compare changes in labour market position between 1981 to 1982, the period immediately after the implementation of the decree, with those prevailing between 1978 and 1981, before the election of François Mitterrand.

3.6 **Theoretical Predictions and a Natural Experiment**

The theoretical predictions of the Mitterrand policy changes are exactly those analysed in the previous section. Let's think that the standard workweek is $h_o = 40$ and assume that we experience a sudden change to $h'_o = 39$. A key distinction should be made between workers employed in firms that are working 39 hours and workers employed in firms that hire workers for 40 hours. Consider first a firm that before the change is operating with a workweek of 39 hours. What is the impact of the reduction of the workweek for such a firm? If nothing else changes, such a firm should not be affected by the reduction in the normal workweek.

Firms using a workweek of 39 hours before March 1982 should not be affected by the reduction in the workweek. As a consequence, the probability that workers lose their job is independent of the change in the length of the workweek.

Consider now a firm that before the change in working hours is operating with a workweek of exactly 40 hours. Once the change in the workweek is implemented, such a firm will find itself in the overtime range. This induces a shift in the isocosts exactly like that described by Fig. 3.6. Such a firm suddenly finds that the last hour is charged at overtime rate. How should such a firm react to the change? We have learned from the previous section that such a firm should reduce employment (and possibly increase hours).

Firms using a workweek of 40 hours before March 1982 are affected by the change in the hours, and should react by reducing the number of employees. As a consequence, the probability that a worker loses his or her job after the new law should increase.

This example is a wonderful situation for economics, since it can be defined as a natural experiment, exactly like those that are undertaken by the hard science literature. In these situations, we can compare the effect of the policy change on the treatment group with the effect observed on the control group, where the latter type of individuals were not treated by the experiment. In these circumstances we can understand the impact of the policy change by looking at the different response of the two groups.

The treatment we are considering is the reduction in the normal hours of the workweek from 40 to 39 hours. The control group is formed by the individuals that work 36 to 39 hours before the new law is introduced: they are not affected by the treatment. The treatment group are those individuals that were working 40 hours or more before the change. The outcome that we are interested in is the probability of losing a job. For the control group, the probability of losing a job should be independent of the change in the workweek. Conversely, for the treatment group, the probability of losing a job should increase. As a consequence, the difference between the two probabilities should provide an empirical estimate of the size of the impact that we are looking for. If the probability of losing the job for the treatment group increases relatively to the probability of losing the job for the control group, then the impact of the experiment is positive. This is called a natural experiment, and it is a perfect application of our theory. Let's see what the data said in the French case.

3.7 **The Evidence**

Table 3.1 shows the proportion of full-time workers employed 36 to 39 hours within the population of all full-time workers employed 36 to 48 hours in 1981. This fraction is small, 2.4 per cent, but it is increasing across time. The fraction of workers employed 40 hours is also increasing whereas the fraction of over-time workers constantly decreases between 1976 and 1981. Table 3.2 shows the employment to non-employment transition rates for these various cat-egories of workers. Between 1981 and 1982, employment to non-employment transitions are more intense for workers employed 40 hours than for those employed 36 to 39 hours; 6.2 per cent of all workers employed 40 hours in 1981 have no employment in 1982 whereas 3.2 per cent of those employed less than 40 hours are in the same situation, a *difference of three percentage points*.

Let's define with JL_{82}^{40} the probability of a job loss for an individual employed 40 hours in 1982 and with JL_{82}^{36-9} the probability of a job loss for an individual hired 36–9 hours in 1982. In formula, the two expressions read

$$JL_{82}^{40} = \frac{\text{Job losses by 40 hours workers in 1982}}{\text{Number of Workers at 40 hours in 1981}}$$

$$JL_{82}^{36-9} = \frac{\text{Job losses by 36–9 hours workers in 1982}}{\text{Number of Workers at 36–9 hours in 1981}}$$

Table 3.2. Employment losses, by hours, in France

Year t to t + 2	80–2	77–9	78–80	79–81
Job losses of workers employed:				
36 to 39 hours	3.2	3.9	2.7	7.3
40 hours	6.2	4.3	5	5.5
41 to 43 hours	4.6	3.1	3.6	4
44 hours	6	5	2.1	5.8
45 to 48 hours	5.7	4	4	3
Observations	6,509	6,212	6,123	6,409

Source: Crépon and Kramarz (2002)

where JL_{82}^{36-9} is the job loss probability of the control group while JL_{82}^{40} is the job loss probability for the treatment group.

The idea is that the probability of job loss of the treatment group, in excess to the job loss probability of the control group, describes a measure of the impact of the policy change. In formula, a first measure of the potential impact Δ is given by

$$\Delta_{82} = JL_{82}^{40} - JL_{82}^{36-9}$$

Table 3.2 suggests that a simple measure of Δ_{82} is 3 percentage points.

The Formal Evidence

While the estimate of Δ_{82} presented above represents a first important result, there are two other important elements to be taken into account. First, one has to consider the possibility that individuals hired in jobs that require 40 hours are systematically different from individuals hired in jobs that require 36–9 hours. In other words, we need to control for individual characteristics, such as gender, age, education, etc. Second, we need to consider whether the same difference calculated for other years, basically Δ_{79} or Δ_{80}, Δ_{81}, is not statistically different. This is very important, since it would suggest that we are experiencing an effect only in the estimate of Δ_{82}, with no effects on the previous years. This can be done by using regression analysis and individual data. To this end, we introduce the following notation and we label

$$i = \text{all individuals that work at 36,37,38,39 or 40 hours in 1981}$$

$$JL_{82,i} = \begin{cases} 1 & \text{if the worker loses the job in 1982} \\ 0 & \text{otherwise} \end{cases}$$

The key regression is the following

$$JL_{82,i} = Z_{81,i}\beta + \alpha_{81}40h1981 + \varepsilon_{it}$$

where the variable $40h1981$ is a dummy variable that takes a value of 1 if the individual was working 40 hours in 1981. In other words, α_{81} is an estimate of the differences Δ_{82} controlling for individual characteristics. If one wants to introduce also the individual working overtime the regression to be estimated is

$$JL_{82,i} = Z_{81,i}\beta + \alpha_{81}^{40}40h_{81} + \alpha_{81}^{ot}overtimeh_{81} + \varepsilon_{it}$$

The value of α_{81}^{40} is 2.6 per cent, which suggests that the reform increases the chance of losing one's job if working 40 hours by 2.6 percentage points. The coefficient is reported in the first column of Table 3.3. Finally, note that the same regressions calculated for the previous years in which no reform was undertaken are not statistically significant. This can be done by looking at

Table 3.3. Regressions on employment losses

	80–2	77–9	78–80	79–81	Pooled
	1	2	3	4	5
Non-employment at t + 2					
Hours = 40	2.60	−1.26	1.29	−3.85	3.90
standard error	1.44	1.86	1.48	2.30	1.82
41<= hours<= 43	1.32	−2.40	1.06	−5.09	3.49
standard error	1.60	1.91	1.57	2.39	1.97
Hours = 44	2.50	−0.73	−0.32	−4.57	4.20
standard error	2.50	2.35	1.91	2.92	2.88
45<= hours<= 48	2.12	−2.14	1.50	−6.52	4.52
standard error	1.66	1.96	1.61	2.39	2.03

Notes: Regressions for the LFS panels of 77–9, 78–80, 79–81, and 80–2 (linear probability models). The dependent variable is non-employment in the exit year of the panel (79, 80, 81, and 82, respectively)

Independent variables: indicator for the hours categories (only reported coefficients), industry, region (Ile de France or other), skill level (3 categories), sex, diploma (6 categories), experience (4 categories), seniority (4 categories), labour market status (apprentice or not), and hours in first year of the panel strictly below 40 and hours in first year of the panel strictly above 40. The population includes all full-time workers in the private sector working between 36 and 48 hours in the median year of each panel (78, 79, 80, and 81, respectively). Column 1 reports estimates for the panel 80–2, columns 2, 3, and 4 report estimates for the panels 77–9, 78–80, and 79–81 respectively. Column 5 reports pooled estimates where all variables are interacted with the relevant year indicator except for the hours categories for which we introduce pooled coefficients and coefficient specific to year 1981 (panel 80–2). These last coefficients are those reported in column 5 (pooled).
Source: Crépon and Kramarz (2002)

the other columns of Table 3.3 (those labelled 77–9, 78–80, etc.), where the coefficient on 40 hours is not significant.

☐ APPENDIX 3.1. A MORE FORMAL VERSION OF THE HOURS–EMPLOYMENT TRADE-OFF

Initially we assume that if a typical worker is asked to work additional hours, he or she will require a higher wage rate. The firm thus faces the following wage function

$$w = w(h) \qquad w' > 0$$

where the positive slope can be thought of as the result of an upward-sloping labour supply from the worker's standpoint. The firm's labour costs are

$$Labor\ Cost = Ehw(h) + EF$$

where the simple form labour costs $LC = wE$ follows each time we assume that $F = 0$ and $h = 1$ fixed. The production function takes the form as

$$y = E^\alpha h^\beta$$

and the problem can be thought of as one of minimizing total costs subject to a fixed production input $\bar{y}$. Formally, this is equivalent to having

$$Min_{E,h} \quad Ehw(h) + EF$$

$$\text{s.t. } E^\alpha h^\beta = \bar{y}$$

So that forming the Lagrangian one has

$$\Lambda = Ehw(h) + EF - \lambda[E^\alpha h^\beta - \bar{y}]$$

whose first-order conditions are

$$\lambda \alpha E^{\alpha-1} h^\beta = [hw(h) + F]$$

$$\lambda \beta E^\alpha h^{\beta-1} = [Ew(h) + Ehw'(h)]$$

$$E^\alpha h^\beta = \bar{y}$$

Taking the ratio of the first two we obtain

$$\frac{F_E}{F_h} = \frac{MC_E}{MC_h}$$

$$\frac{\alpha E^{\alpha-1} h^\beta}{\beta E^\alpha h^{\beta-1}} = \frac{hw(h) + F}{w(h)E[1 + \frac{h}{w(h)} w'(h)\varepsilon_{w,h}]}$$

$$\frac{\alpha h}{\beta E} = \frac{hw(h) + F}{w(h)E[1 + \varepsilon_{w,h}]}$$

where $\varepsilon_{w,h}$ is the elasticity of $w(h)$ with respect to h.
The general rule is

$$\frac{F_E}{L_h} = \frac{MC_E}{MC_h}$$

where F_E is the marginal increase in output following an increase in total employment while F_h is the marginal increase in output as more hours are worked. An important property follows:

The choice of hours is independent of the scale of operation.

The proof is straightforward from the first-order conditions, since E is immediately removed from the equations so that h is a function of only $\varepsilon_{w,h}$ and F, so that

$$\alpha hw(h)[1 + \varepsilon_{w,h}] = \beta hw(h) + \beta F$$

from which it follows that

$$h = h(F, \varepsilon_{w,h})$$

with

$$\frac{\partial h}{\partial F} > 0$$

$$\frac{\partial h}{\partial \varepsilon_{w,h}} >$$

while from the budget constraint one gets

$$E = \frac{C}{h(\varepsilon, F)w(h) + F}$$

from which it follows that

$$E = E(F, \varepsilon, C)$$

with

$$\frac{\partial E}{\partial F} < 0$$

$$\frac{\partial E}{\partial F} > 0$$

$$\frac{\partial E}{\partial C} > 0$$

The Overtime Premium and the Effects of Reducing the Workweek

If h_s are normal working hours.

$$C = EF + wEh \text{ if } h \leq h_o$$
$$C = EF + wEh_o + \tilde{w}E(h - h_o) \text{ if } h > h_o$$

Let the production function be equal to $y = Eh^\beta$. The firm can be in two possible positions. It uses overtime or it does not use overtime. The two situations are depicted in Fig. 3.4. Let's first study a firm that uses overtime. The formal problem is

$$Min_{h,E} \qquad EF + wEh_o + \tilde{w}E(h - h_o) + \lambda[\bar{y} - Eh^\beta]$$

The first-order conditions are

$$\tilde{w}E = \lambda\beta h^{(\beta-1)}E$$
$$[F + wh_o + \tilde{w}(h - h_o)] = \lambda h^\beta$$

Taking the ratio of the two functions we get

$$\beta h^{-1} = \frac{\tilde{w}}{F + wh_o + \tilde{w}(h - h_o)}$$

$$\beta F + \beta wh_o + \beta \tilde{w}h - \beta \tilde{w}h_o = h\tilde{w}$$

$$h = \frac{\beta F + \beta h_o(w - \tilde{w})}{\tilde{w}(1 - \beta)} \qquad h > h_o$$

Substituting this into the production function and rearranging, the optimal E reads

$$E = \bar{y} \left[\frac{\beta F + \beta h_0 (w - \tilde{w})}{w(1 - \beta)} \right]^{-\beta}$$

A reduction in the normal workweek induces a reduction in the number of employees. To see this simply take the partial derivative of the log to obtain.

$$\frac{\partial \log E}{\partial \log h_0} = -\beta$$

4 Temporary or Permanent?

4.1 Introduction

One of the key issues at the hiring stage concerns the type of contract that should be offered to the firm's workforce. In this chapter, we discuss the key decisions in terms of the length of the contract: open-ended versus fixed-term contract. Alternatively, as such contracts are called in Europe, the firm has to choose between a permanent or a temporary contract. This choice is particularly relevant when two conditions hold. First, employment protection legislation is stringent, and terminating a contract is an expensive activity. Second, uncertainty over business conditions plays an important role. If a contract can be terminated at no cost, the difference between temporary contract and permanent contract is irrelevant. Further, if business conditions do not fluctuate, hiring decisions are not going to be followed by separation decisions, and the type of contract is irrelevant.

In this chapter we assume that terminating a contract involves some costs to the employer and that business conditions can be good or bad. We study three scenarios. First, as a baseline scenario, we consider a firm that can offer only permanent contracts that can never be broken. Business conditions can be good or bad, but employment cannot be adjusted in response to such changes. We study the optimal labour demand in this condition, and we compare it with the employment decision of a firm that is fully flexible, and can hire at will workers on a temporary basis. We find that the rigidity imposed on the firm affects its profitability, but has no impact on the average employment. Indeed, the average employment of the rigid firm is the same as the average employment of a flexible firm.

Second, we consider what happens when a firm has the possibility of combining temporary and permanent contracts. The idea in this scenario is that a buffer of temporary contracts can be used in conjunction with a stock of permanent contracts. We show that under these conditions the constrained firm can do as well as the flexible firm.

Third, we study the buffer stock model under an additional real life phenomenon, namely the fact that hiring a temporary worker requires the use of a costly interim agency. This implies that the cost of temporary workers also includes the mark-up paid to temporary firms. Such a phenomenon will show that the additional cost imposed by the interim agency has important effects on the firm's hiring strategy. We will see that in this scenario a firm can hire an additional amount of permanent workers (with respect to a pure buffer model), just to save on future agency costs.

In real life labour markets, some firms offer temporary contracts while other firms offer permanent contracts. We want to understand how this choice is determined when terminating permanent contracts is not illegal, but requires some costs. We thus study the trade-off between temporary and permanent contracts when labour turnover is costly. We assume that permanent contracts can be terminated at some cost, while temporary contracts can be terminated at no cost. Further, we assume also that workers under temporary contracts have a higher probability of leaving the firm, and their replacement is not necessarily immediate. We will see that under this condition a trade-off emerges, and it is not always optimal to hire under temporary or permanent contracts. A brief look at the evidence completes the chapter.

4.2 Permanent Contracts with Fixed Wages

We make the following assumptions on the environment in which the firm operates.

The production function is described by the following relation

$$Y = A^i \log L,$$

where L represents the quantity of labour employed and Y the output; A_i is the productivity level;

There are business fluctuations in the productivity at the firm; A^i assumes only two values $A^h > A^l$. In every period, there is a probability p that productivity be equal to A^h and a probability $1 - p$ that productivity be equal to A^l; we refer to periods in which the productivity is $A^h = A$ as good times, and periods in which the productivity is equal to A^l as bad times.

The marginal product of the firm is $Y_L = \frac{A^h}{L}$.[1] Fluctuations in A_i are akin to fluctuations in the marginal product.

The wage is fixed and equal to w and the price that the firm charges for simplicity is set equal to 1 and does not change between good and bad times.

The key firm decision is the quantity of labour to be hired.

We consider initially two different scenarios under which the firm operates: the flexible/temporary regime and the rigid regime. In the *flexible regime*, hiring

---

[1] This is obtained by taking the derivative of the production function with respect to L. Notably, $\frac{\partial A^i \log L}{\partial L} = \frac{A^i}{L}$.

and firing can take place at no cost, and the firm can choose its employment level after observing the realization of the value of A. The firm in the flexible regime hires workers on a *temporary basis*. In the *rigid regime*, the firm can only choose the average employment, so that there are only *permanent contracts* that can never be broken. Firms can offer only permanent contracts, and firing is impossible. Once employment is decided it can never be changed.

In the next section we consider an additional regime, mainly the *buffer regime*, which involves the possibility that the firm combines temporary and permanent contracts.

4.2.1 A NUMERICAL EXAMPLE

Before formally solving the problem, let us analyse a numerical example. We assume the following values for the parameters: $w = 1$; $A^h = 10$; $A_l = 4$; and $p = 0.5$.

Let's begin with the *flexible firm*. Such a firm can hire and fire at no cost, and its hiring policy is simply to choose labour so as to maximize profits period by period. In each period, the profits are just the revenues minus costs so that

$$\Pi^F = \begin{cases} 10 \log L - WL & \text{if } A = A^h \\ 4 \log L - WL & \text{if } A = A^l \end{cases}$$

The solution to the firm employment should just be such that the marginal product is equal to the wage in good and bad times, as in a simple and static model of labour demand. Since the wage is 1, the optimal employment is equal to 4 in bad times and 10 in good times. Figure 4.1 also plots the marginal product curve and the wage. Since the probability of having good and bad times is equal to 0.5, the average employment of the flexible firm is simply 7. The firm hires six workers when business conditions improve and fires six workers when business conditions worsen.

Consider now the *rigid* firm. The firm should choose a level of employment that maximizes average profits. Such a level of employment would never be changed. The average profits are

$$\Pi^R = p[A^h \log L - wL] + (1 - p)[A^h \log L - wL]$$
$$\Pi^R = [(1 - p)A^l + pA^h] \log L - wL$$

The value of the profits function Π^R is easily computed in the table, and the optimal employment level corresponds to an employment level equal to 7. Figure 4.2 shows clearly that this is the point at which profits are maximum. We are now in a position to derive three important empirical implications on the effect of the protection regimes.

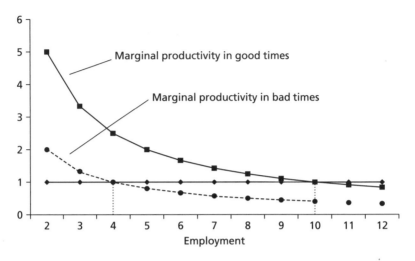

Figure 4.1. Labour demand in good and bad times

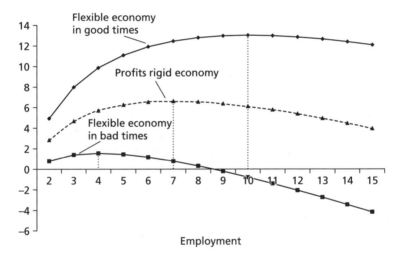

Figure 4.2. Profits in good and bad times

Implication 1: the average employment of the rigid firm is the same as in the flexible firm. In our example, the average employment of both firms is 7.
Implication 2: The volatility of employment is higher for the flexible firm. While employment in the rigid firm is always fixed at 7, the flexible firm hires and fires six workers when the economy switches from good to bad periods, so that obviously its employment is more volatile.
Implication 3: The flexible firm enjoys larger average profits. To compare the profits we need to compare the profits of the rigid economy with the average

Table 4.1. Flexible and rigid regimes

| | Wage | Marginal productivity good times | Marginal productivity bad times | Flexible economy | | Rigid economy average profits |
				Profits good times	Profits bad times	
	2.00	1.00	5.00	2.00	4.93	0.77	2.85
	3.00	1.00	3.33	1.33	7.99	1.39	4.69
L*bad	4.00	1.00	2.50	1.00	9.86	1.55	5.70
	5.00	1.00	2.00	0.80	11.09	1.44	6.27
	6.00	1.00	1.67	0.67	11.92	1.17	6.54
L Rigid	7.00	1.00	1.43	0.57	12.46	0.78	6.62
	8.00	1.00	1.25	0.50	12.79	0.32	6.56
	9.00	1.00	1.11	0.44	12.97	−0.21	6.38
Lgood	10.00	1.00	1.00	0.40	13.03	−0.79	6.12
	11.00	1.00	0.91	0.36	12.98	−1.41	5.79
	12.00	1.00	0.83	0.33	12.85	−2.06	5.39
	13.00	1.00	0.77	0.31	12.65	−2.74	4.95
	14.00	1.00	0.71	0.29	12.39	−3.44	4.47
	15.00	1.00	0.67	0.27	12.08	−4.17	3.96

Notes: Good times shifter $A_h = 10$; bad times shifter $A_l = 4$; wage $w = 1$; probability $p = 0.5$.

profits of the flexible economy. Table 4.2 shows that profits are larger and equal to 7.29 in the flexible case (the average between 13.03 and 1.55), against 6.62 in the rigid case.

Let us now consider the *buffer regime*. The idea is that the firm can hire workers under temporary contracts, and can use a combination of temporary and permanent contracts. A stock of permanent contracts is hired in good and bad times, while temporary workers are used as a buffer stock when conditions improve. Table 4.2 shows that a firm that follows such a policy can reach a level of profits identical to a flexible firm. Basically, the firm has four permanent workers and six temporary workers when conditions improve.

4.2.2 FORMAL DERIVATION

Flexible Firm. Let's consider first the behaviour of the firm if there were no restrictions on the type of contracts. In other words, let's consider the situation when hiring and firing can take place at no cost. Under no constraint, the firm will choose the employment level after observing the productivity level, and it will maximize profits in the following way:

$$\Pi^F = Max_L[A^i \log L - wL]$$

Table 4.2. Profits in various regimes

	Good times	Bad times	Average
Flexible			
Employment	10.00	4.00	7.00
Profits	13.03	1.55	7.29
Rigid			
Employment	7.00	7.00	7.00
Profits	12.46	0.78	6.62
Rigid with temporary			
Permanent employment	4.00	4.00	4.00
Temporary employment	6.00	0.00	3.00
Profits	13.03	1.55	7.29
Rigid with costly interim[a]			
Permanent employment	5.00	5.00	5.00
Interim employment	3.00	0.00	1.50
Profits	12.04	1.44	6.74
Permanent employment	4.00	4.00	4.00
Interim employment	4.00	0.00	2.00
Profits	11.79	1.55	6.67

[a] Mark-up wage equal to 1.25.

which implies, after taking the derivative of the profits with respect to L

$$\frac{A^i}{L} = w \qquad i = h, l,$$

$$L^i = \frac{A_i}{w}$$

$$L = \begin{cases} \frac{A^l}{w} & \text{if } A = A^l \\ \frac{A^h}{w} & \text{if } A = A^h \end{cases}$$

The flexible firm chooses the level of employment after having observed the level of productivity. Since the wage is fixed and equal to w, the flexible firm will fire (hire) $\Delta L = \frac{A^h - A^l}{w}$ when the economy moves from high (low) productivity to low (high) productivity. Because the economy experiences, on average, a fraction p of high productivity periods and a fraction $(1 - p)$ of periods of low productivity, the average employment in the long run will be

$$\bar{L}^F = \frac{(1 - p)A^l + pA^h}{w}$$

Rigid Firm. Let us examine, now, the behaviour of the firm when it is forced to hire only permanent contracts. In other words, an extremely strict employment protection regime is in place, and it is not possible to change employment after productivity changes. In this situation, the best thing the rigid firm can do is to choose the employment that maximizes the expected value of the profits. In formulas, this implies that the employer R will resolve the following problem:

$$\Pi^R = Max_L E \left\{ A^i \log L - wL \right\},$$

where E indicates the expected value of the profits. The being wage fixed, to eliminate the expected value from the previous expression it is sufficient to replace the expected value of production, so that the problem of the employer becomes:

$$\Pi^R = Max_L \left\{ [(1-p)A^l + pA^h] \log L - wL \right\}.$$

The first-order conditions allow us to derive the value of employment in the rigid country R. as

$$\overline{L}^R = \frac{(1-p)A_L + pA_H}{w}$$

The value $\overline{L}^R$ is some average between the level of employment in the flexible country during the expansions and its level during recessions. Moreover, $\overline{L}^R$ coincides with A^l/W if the economy is always in low productivity ($p = 0$). If lay-offs are not allowed, the firm in the rigid regime does not experience any fluctuation as a result of variations in the productivity level.

We are now in a position to derive three important empirical implications on the effect of the protection regimes.

Implication 1: the average employment of the rigid regime is the same as in the flexible regime.
Implication 2:the volatility of employment is higher in the flexible regime.
Implication 3: the firm in the flexible regime is more efficient and makes more profits.

Implication 1 is immediately verified. We have seen that $\overline{L}^R = \overline{L}^F$, or that average employment in the flexible regime is the same as for the firm in the rigid environment. Implication 2 is also easy to show. By construction, in the R economy there are no employment variations, while the F economy fires (hires) $\Delta L = \frac{A^h - A^l}{W}$ labour when the economy moves from high (low) productivity to low (high) productivity. Implication 3 is also easy to demonstrate. It is enough to realize that the employment level chosen by the F employer in each period is the only level that maximizes profits in each period. Consequently, in each period profits are higher in the flexible regime. With the same level of employment, the firm is able to make, on average, a higher level of profits. In other words, the firm in the flexible regime is more efficient.

4.3 **Temporary Contracts as a Buffer Stock**

Let's consider now an environment which is less extreme than the one before. Specifically, let's consider a situation in which a firm can combine permanent and temporary contracts at the same time. The idea is that a stock of permanent contracts can be offered alongside a set of temporary contracts that terminate in bad business conditions. The firm's hiring policy can be described as follows:

$$L = \begin{cases} L^{perm} & \text{if } A = A^l \\ L^{perm} + L^{temp} & \text{if } A = A^h \end{cases}$$

The idea is that the firm can hire a stock of permanent contracts independently of business conditions while it can hire workers under temporary contracts when conditions are good, and dismiss such contracts when conditions are bad. Following the algebra derived in Appendix 4.1, one can show that the stock of permanent workers is equal to employment.

The firm has the following hiring policy:

$$L = \begin{cases} \frac{A^l}{w} & \text{if } A = A^l \\ \frac{A^l}{w} + \frac{A^h - A^l}{w} & \text{if } A = A^h \end{cases}$$

If temporary contracts can be used as a buffer stock, a proper combination of temporary and permanent contracts allows the firm to reach the first best.

These results show that by combining permanent and temporary contracts the firm is able to reach the first best. The stock of permanent contracts is identical to the size of employment in bad times while the stock of temporary contracts acts as a buffer stock that the firm can adjust if conditions change. In this case the stock of workers on permanent contracts does not experience any change in employment status, while temporary contracts are hired and fired at every change in business conditions.

In practice there are three limitations to the policy that we just described:

1. Roll-over of temporary contracts is not always possible. Indeed, if the firm has a sequence of good productivity shocks, it has to roll over temporary contracts for a sequence of periods. And such a policy is not always feasible.
2. Hiring temporary contracts often requires some specific hiring costs. These are particularly relevant if temporary contracts are obtained through interim agencies.
3. Workers under temporary contracts experience high turnover, and are likely to seek permanent job opportunities elsewhere.

In the next section we analyse the role of specific additional costs associated with temporary contracts.

4.4 **The Buffer Stock Model with Interim Costs**

Interim workers are technically defined as workers hired by an interim agency and rented out to a specific firm. From the firm's standpoint, the benefit of hiring workers as interim workers is their inherent flexibility, since such workers are technically hired by the agency. The cost associated with such a policy is the fee that the agency imposes on the firm. In this section we study the role of costly interim contracts in the context of our buffer stock model. We ask what happens to the optimal combination of temporary permanent contracts when the hiring of additional temporary workers requires a fee to be paid to the interim agencies.

Formally, we assume that each worker hired on a temporary basis costs $w(1 + \mu)$ where $\mu > 0$ is the mark-up on the wage (or the fee) to be paid to the interim agency. The firm's hiring policy can still be described by the employment policy of the buffer stock model

$$
L = \begin{cases} L^{perm} & \text{if } A = A^l \\ L^{perm} + L^{interim} & \text{if } A = A^h \end{cases}
$$

where L^{perm} are the permanent workers hired in bad times and $L^{interim}$ are the interim workers hired when conditions turn good. The key question in this context is how the existence of the interim fee modifies the employment position of the firm with respect to a pure buffer stock model with $\mu = 0$.

The firm's position in good business conditions is not difficult to determine, since it is simply obtained by the intersection between the marginal product in good times (when $A = A^h$) and the marginal labour costs, which in this case are equal to $w(1 + \mu)$. The position is described by point C in Fig. 4.3. In good times the firm is hiring less labour than the case of $\mu = 0$, indicated by point B in the figure. This is not surprising, and it is simply linked to the increase in the marginal labour cost.

The determination of employment in bad times is more subtle. In bad times the firm is not going to hire interim workers. This should not be controversial. The difficult question is how many permanent workers should be hired. During bad times the firm knows that good times will eventually come in the future, and that hiring of interim workers involves a mark-up μ on the wage. As a way to partly avoid future hiring costs, the firm may have an incentive to 'overhire' permanent workers in bad times, or in any case to hire more permanent workers than would be the case if μ were zero. Nevertheless, the firm is also aware that permanent workers hired beyond L^L in Fig. 4.3 are associated with some loss, since for such workers the marginal product is lower than the wage. A trade-off emerges in this situation, but it is likely that some overemployment of permanent workers is going to take place. Indeed, the algebra derived in the

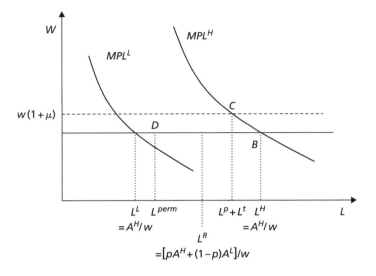

Figure 4.3. Buffer stock model with costly interim workers

Appendix shows that

$$L^{perm}_{(\mu>0)} > L^{perm}_{(\mu=0)}$$

where $L^{perm}_{(\mu=0)}$ corresponds to point L^L in Fig. 4.3 while $L^{perm}_{(\mu>0)}$ corresponds to point D. This overemployment of permanent workers is called *labour hoarding*. A key result is immediately obtained: *The existence of turnover costs (interim wages in these cases) induce labour hoarding of permanent workers in bad times.*

The employment behaviour of the firm can be described as follows

$$L = \begin{cases} \dfrac{A^l}{w-\frac{pw\mu}{1-p}} & \text{if } A = A^l \\[3mm] \dfrac{A_h}{w(1+\mu)} & \text{if } A = A^h \end{cases}$$

From the previous condition one can immediately see that the employment solution collapses to a simple buffer stock model whenever $\mu = 0$. Further, labour hoarding increases with the size of the interim fee: *The larger the interim fee, the larger is labour hoarding.*

To formally establish this point one has simply to differentiate the employment level in bad times with respect to μ, and find that the result is positive.[2]

---

[2] The result yields

$$\frac{\partial}{\partial L} = \frac{A^l pw}{[(1-p)w - pw\mu]^2} > 0$$

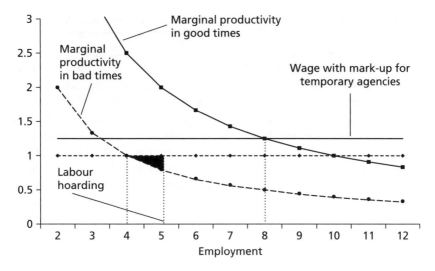

Figure 4.4. Labour hoarding of permanent workers with costly interim

The numerical example in Fig. 4.4 further confirms this point. Using the same numerical assumptions analysed in the previous section, with the additional assumption that the mark-up wage for temporary workers under interim is equal to $\mu = 0.25$, the marginal wage in good times is equal to 1.25, so that the firm should hire eight workers when business conditions are good. The interesting dimension is to study what the optimal employment level is in bad times, and thus the number of permanent and temporary (interim) workers.

4.5 Temporary Contracts with Costly Turnover: Costs and Benefits

The aim of this section is to consider the trade-off between a temporary and a permanent contract when turnover is costly. Turnover costs are the costs associated with the hiring and firing of workers. Turnover costs for workers hired on temporary and permanent contracts are different, in at least two dimensions. First, permanent contracts can be terminated at a cost $-T$ while temporary contracts can be terminated at no cost. In the previous sections we assumed that permanent contracts last forever. Here we assume that a permanent contract can be broken at some cost. Conversely, temporary contracts can be terminated at no cost as the contract expires. Second, workers under temporary contracts have a higher probability of leaving the firm, and their replacement is not necessarily immediate. Under this condition a trade-off emerges, and the firm will choose different types of contracts in different circumstances. The model is described as follows.

There are two periods. A firm has to fill in a vacant job, and there is some positive expected profit associated with the employment relationship. **The key choice of the firm is whether a temporary or a permanent contract should be offered.** A permanent contract in this context is a two-period contract, or a long-term contract, while a temporary contract is a one-period contract. The wage w is the same for both temporary and permanent contracts and it is set outside the firm. This is a reasonable assumption for most imperfect labour markets. The productivity in the first period is fixed at y. When the worker is offered a temporary contract (which lasts one period), the job can terminate at no cost at the beginning of period 2. When the worker is offered a permanent contract (which is basically a two-period contract) the firm can terminate the job at a cost equal to $-T$. The productivity in the second period is random. With probability δ the productivity in the second period is very low and the job needs to be destroyed. With probability $(1 - \delta)$ the productivity in the second period stays at y. Jobs filled by temporary contracts terminate with probability λ, since workers may quit and find another job somewhere else. If the worker leaves, the firm has a chance to find a replacement. However, the firm's ability to replace the worker has some limit, and we assume that there is a positive probability that a replacement is not found. We call q the probability that the firm successfully finds another worker.

We focus on the present discounted value (PDV) of having workers under different types of contract. Let's call J^{perm} the PDV of filling the job with a permanent job. The point of view that we take is the firm's, but the problem is dynamic. The formal expression of J^{perm} reads

$$J^{perm} = y - w + \frac{-\delta T + (1 - \delta)(y - w)}{1 + r},$$

where in the second period, δ is the probability that the job ends because there is a negative productivity shock. If the job is destroyed (at rate δ) the firm needs to pay the cost T. If the job is continued (with probability $1 - \delta$), the firm nets $y - w$ in the second period. The PDV of a vacancy filled with a temporary job is indicated by J^{temp} and its expression reads

$$J^{temp} = y - w + \frac{(1 - \delta)[(1 - \lambda)(y - w) + \lambda q(y - w)]}{1 + r},$$

where the job is continued only if the productivity in the second period remains at y (an event which happens with probability $1 - \delta$). Conditional on the productivity remaining high, and thus the job continuing, two possibilities emerge. If the worker does not leave (which happens with probability $(1 - \lambda)$) production takes place and the firm nets $y - w$. If the worker leaves (which happens with probability λ, the firm nets $y - w$ if and only if the worker is successfully replaced, an event that takes place with probability q.

Let's define the convenience of the firm to offer a permanent contract as

$$\Delta^{perm} = J^{perm} - J^{temp}$$

where Δ is just the net benefit associated with a permanent contract. The decision rule of the firm is very simple: offer permanent contract if and only if $\Delta^{perm} > 0$.

Using the definition of J^{temp} and J^{perm}, one has

$$\Delta^{perm} = \frac{(1 - \delta)(y - w)[\lambda(1 - q)] - \delta T}{1 + r} \qquad (4.1)$$

A few conclusions immediately follow:

Offer a permanent contract if there is no uncertainty $(\delta = 0)$.

This is immediately established by looking at equation 4.1. If $\delta = 0$ $\Delta^{perm} = \frac{(y-w)\lambda(1-q)}{1+r} > 0$. The key benefit of a temporary contract is to avoid firing costs, which are paid conditional on productivity being bad in the second period. As a consequence, when there is no such risk, a permanent contract should be preferred.

Offer a permanent contract if there are no firing costs $(T = 0)$.

This is just a corollary of the previous remark. If there are no firing costs, there are no costs associated with a permanent contract, which basically becomes identical to a temporary contract.

Offer a temporary contract if replacement is immediate $(q = 1)$.

The cost associated with a temporary contract is the risk of forgoing a profitable opportunity in the second period if conditions are good. Such a risk fully depends on the probability of finding a replacement if productivity is high and the worker leaves. Obviously, if another worker is immediately available (an event which implies that $q = 1$) a temporary contract is to be preferred. Formally, one can see that if $q = 1$ $\Delta^{perm} = \frac{-\delta T}{1+r} < 0$.

The role played by other parameters of the model (y, w, r, λ) can also be discussed with a comparative static perspective. The following points are easily established. Offering a permanent contract is more likely when

- profits are higher ($y - w$ is larger);
- probability of quitting is larger;
- interest rate is lower.

To formally establish this result one can differentiate equation 4.1 with respect to the various parameters.[3] The intuition is as follows. Larger net profits $y - w$ increase the benefit of a long-term relationship, and reduce the relative value of firing costs. This suggests that permanent contracts should be more

---

[3] Notable, $\frac{\partial \Delta^{perm}}{\partial (y-w)} = \frac{(1-\delta)\lambda(1-q)]}{1+r} > 0$; $\frac{\partial \Delta^{perm}}{\partial \lambda} = \frac{(1-\delta)(y-w)(1-q)]}{1+r}$; and $\frac{\partial \Delta^{perm}}{\partial r} = -\frac{\Delta^{perm}}{1+r}$.

likely in high-productivity/high-profits jobs. Further, permanent contracts are more likely in situations in which the turnover is higher, since the risk of forgoing profits becomes larger. Finally, larger interest rates reduce the value of future profits, and thus reduce the incentive to offer a permanent contract.

4.6 **A Brief Look at the Evidence**

Temporary contracts are now an important feature of regulated labour markets across the OECD countries in general, and across continental European countries in particular. In 2002, 11 per cent of the total employment stock was held by workers hired under temporary contracts. Such a number is certainly sizeable, but it does not highlight the fact that a larger majority of new jobs are occupied by workers on temporary contracts. This is confirmed by the evidence reported in Table 4.3, where we report the incidence of temporary contracts by different worker characteristics. The incidence of temporary contracts is defined as the share of workers who hold a temporary job conditional on certain observable characteristics, such as gender, education, and the type of job. Table 4.3 clearly shows that young workers are much more likely to hold a temporary contract. One out of four workers aged 15–24 is hired under a

Table 4.3. Incidence of temporary employment in OECD countries

Gender	
Female	12.2
Male	10.5
Age groups	
15–24	25.0
25–54	8.0
55+	9.4
Educational attainment	
Low	15.7
Medium	10.4
High	9.3
Industry	
Agriculture	21.9
Manufacturing	9.6
Service	10.8
Occupation	
White collar	7.7
Pink collar	10.6
Blue collar	9.2
Unskilled	15.3

Source: OECD 2002.

Table 4.4. Status of temporary workers in t and $t + 1$

		Status in 1997			Status in 1999		
	Status in 1996	Permanent	Temporary	Unemployed	Permanent	Temporary	Unemployed
France	Permanent	96.3	1.2	2.6	94.7	1.4	3.9
	Temporary	20.8	56.6	22.5	37.9	41.2	20.9
	Unemployed	9.5	17.2	73.3	20.9	26.2	53.0
Germany	Permanent	92.8	3.3	3.8	92.3	2.5	5.2
	Temporary	40.6	36.4	23.0	53.1	22.7	24.2
	Unemployed	19.7	14.7	65.7	20.7	15.8	63.5
Italy	Permanent	93.1	5.0	1.9	89.3	6.7	4.0
	Temporary	41.3	45.9	12.7	52.2	35.2	12.6
	Unemployed	8.3	9.3	82.4	15.7	17.7	66.6
UK	Permanent	96.4	2.2	1.4	96.5	2.1	1.5
	Temporary	56.1	34.5		67.0	27.0	
	Unemployed	31.4		54.7	46.9		39.3

Source: OECD 2002.

temporary contract, whereas the overall percentage is around 11 per cent. This is consistent with the view that youth workers entering the labour market are offered a temporary contract. The fact that women are, on average, more likely than men to hold a temporary contract is also consistent with this view, since women have less labour market attachment than men.

Looking at other individual characteristics, it is clear that temporary contracts are more likely among individuals with low educational attachment, employed in agriculture, and in unskilled occupations.

An important and interesting dimension to consider is to ask what happens, in a dynamic perspective, to workers hired under temporary contracts. Are such workers likely to transit into permanent jobs, or are they more likely to stay in a temporary contract? Table 4.4 throws some light on this question. The table reports the status of unemployed workers as well as workers hired on temporary and permanent contracts twelve and thirty-six months after the first observations. The evidence refers to different European countries. The table should be read as follows. For each country (say France) the three rows in the table indicate the employed status of workers in 1996; where the employment status can be 'permanent', 'temporary', and 'unemployed' respectively. The columns labelled status in 1997 report the labour market position of such workers twelve months after the first observation, while the columns labelled status in 1999 report the labour market status at a three-year distance.

Let's start with the unemployed workers. In most countries, and France in particular, unemployed workers are much more likely to find a temporary contract than a permanent contract. This is obviously consistent with the idea that labour market entrance takes place through a temporary contract. Looking at the row on temporary contracts, Table 4.4 suggests that workers hired on temporary contracts are much more likely to remain in such a situation than to switch to a job with a permanent contract, even at a distance of three years from the first observation.

☐ APPENDIX 4.1. THE FORMAL DERIVATION OF THE BUFFER STOCK MODEL

The maximization becomes

$$\Pi = p[A_H \log(L^{perm} + L^{temp}) - w(L^{perm} + L^{temp})]$$
$$+ (1-p)[A_L \log L^{perm} - wL^{perm}].$$

The first-order conditions are

$$\frac{\partial \Pi}{\partial L^{perm}} = 0 \qquad \frac{pA_h}{L^{perm} + L^{temp}} + \frac{(1-p)A_l}{L^{perm}} = w$$

$$\frac{\partial \Pi}{\partial L^{temp}} = 0 \qquad \frac{pA_h}{L^{perm} + L^{temp}} = pw$$

From the second equation we get

$$L^{perm} + L^{temp} = \frac{A_h}{w}$$

while substituting this into the first equation

$$\frac{pA_h}{L^{perm} + L^{temp}} + \frac{(1-p)A_l}{L^{perm}} = w$$

$$pw + \frac{(1-p)A_l}{L^{perm}} = w$$

$$L^{perm} = \frac{A_l}{w}$$

so that substituting the expression for L^{perm} we get

$$L^{perm} + L^{temp} = \frac{A_h}{w}$$

$$L^{temp} = \frac{A_h - A_l}{w}$$

☐ APPENDIX 4.2. THE FORMAL DERIVATION OF THE BUFFER STOCK MODEL WITH COSTLY INTERIM AGENCY

The maximization becomes

$$\Pi = p[A_H \log(L^{perm} + L^{temp}) - wL^{perm} - w(1+\mu)L^{temp}]$$
$$+ (1-p)[A_L \log L^{perm} - wL^{perm}].$$

The first-order conditions are

$$\frac{\partial \Pi}{\partial L^{perm}} = 0 \qquad \frac{pA_h}{L^{perm} + L^{temp}} + \frac{(1-p)A_l}{L^{perm}} = w$$

$$\frac{\partial \Pi}{\partial L^{temp}} = 0 \qquad \frac{pA_h}{L^{perm} + L^{temp}} = pw(1+\mu)$$

From the second equation we obtain

$$L^{perm} + L^{temp} = \frac{A_h}{w(1+\mu)} \tag{4.2}$$

while substituting this term in the first equation we get

$$\frac{pA_h w(1+\mu)}{A_h} + \frac{(1-p)A_l}{L^{perm}} = w$$

$$L^{perm} = \frac{A^l}{w - \frac{pw\mu}{1-p}}$$

A key result is immediately obtained.

5 Managing Adverse Selection in Recruiting

5.1 Introduction

Throughout the hiring process, as long as a worker is not fully involved in the firm's activities, the firm is likely to have imperfect information about the worker's productivity. Such information is more likely to be known to the worker. This implies that the hiring process is characterized by an asymmetric information problem, since workers know more about their own ability than the firm does. In the hiring process, the uninformed party is the firm, while the informed party is the worker. This chapter analyses this asymmetric information problem in detail, and studies which personnel policies can partly overcome it.

The firm has a vacant job, and offers the possibility of applying for such a job to a variety of workers. We are in a situation in which the uninformed party (the firm) offers an option to the informed party (the worker). In the economics of imperfect information, each time an uninformed party offers an option to the informed party, the problem of *adverse selection* may arise. We say that a firm has a problem of adverse selection each time the wrong type of workers are attracted to the firm. Dealing with adverse selection in recruiting means finding a set of policies that ensures that only the suitable candidates are attracted to the firm. Dealing with the wrong type of candidates is a very costly and time-consuming process. Conversely, a properly managed hiring strategy can save costly resources.

There are two key ways of dealing with adverse selection in hiring. The first way relies on wage flexibility and on the design of the labour contract. We distinguish two such types of 'contingent' contract: piece rate, and temporary contracts with a probation period. The second way of dealing with adverse selection is the use of credentials (specify workers' characteristics in detail). We briefly describe these mechanisms.

The first part of the chapter introduces wage policies and contingent contracts, and shows how the availability of wage flexibility can help the firm to solve the adverse selection problem in hiring. The idea of a contingent contract is to specify the wage rules of the job in such a way that only the 'right' type of worker is attracted to the job. We highlight these phenomena with two types of contract that we label (i) piece rate and (ii) temporary contract with probation wage.

Piece rate is the simplest contingent contract, with pay that is strictly based on output: the larger the output, the larger the total pay. What the firm must do in this case is to select a wage per piece that will be attractive only to suitable workers. A piece rate solves the adverse selection problem if 'good' candidates are attracted by the firm wage and 'bad' candidates do not apply. The actual implementation of a piece rate requires output to be perfectly measurable. In most professional jobs, notably law firms or consulting firms, output is difficult to measure, and a pure piece rate is a very difficult mechanism to implement. In such cases firms may use probationary periods for dealing with adverse selection. The idea of a probationary period is that firms take 'some time' to learn the ability of the workers. High-ability workers are promoted and tenured, while low-ability workers are dismissed. To deal with adverse selection, the firm has an incentive to reduce the probationary wage (which is paid to both suitable and unsuitable workers) and increase the promotion wage (which is paid only to promoted workers). Under specific circumstances, which depend also on the firm's ability to perfectly monitor 'bad' workers at the end of the probation, this multi-period wage can offer a solution to adverse selection.

In imperfect labour markets, the wage flexibility required to implement contingent contracts is often not available to individual firms. As we have argued several times, a large part of the wage is often decided outside the individual firm. If this is the case, firms cannot rely on sophisticated wage contracts, and other instruments need to be implemented. The chapter considers in some detail the use of credentials, or the possibility of linking the wage offered to the level of education. The idea explored in the second part of the chapter is that education, the most widely used credential, can work as a signal of a candidate's productivity. Firms do not observe ability, but can and do observe whether individuals obtain a degree. If the probability of acquiring the signal (i.e. the probability of graduation) is correlated to the performance on the job, a signalling equilibrium may arise. In such context, firms are willing to pay a wage premium to individuals with a degree. In turn, high-ability individuals have an incentive to undertake the costly signal, in expectation of future wages. In a signalling equilibrium, the credential works and the problem of adverse selection is alleviated.

The chapter proceeds as follows. In section 5.2 we analyse the two contingent contracts: the piece rate and the probationary wage. Section 5.3 analyses credentials, and presents the model of educational signalling in a formal and an informal way.

5.2 **Contingent Contracts**

In this chapter we assume that there are workers that are suitable to the firms and workers that are not suitable. The firm has a vacancy to fill and would like to avoid applications from unsuitable workers. The productivity of each individual is not known to the firm, while it is perfectly known to the worker. The firm only knows that there are suitable and unsuitable candidates, or good and bad workers, but cannot distinguish the two categories before each worker is fully involved in the firm's activity.

How can such a problem be resolved? The idea of a contingent contract is very simple, and is based on writing a contract that is appealing only to the right type of worker. If a contingent contract is successful, the problem of adverse selection is resolved, and only the appropriate worker will come to the firm.

We distinguish between skilled and unskilled workers, where the word skilled is not necessarily synonymous with educational background. Skilled workers are those workers that are perfectly fit for the firm's operation while unskilled workers are those workers that do not perform very well within the firm. There are two types of contract that can potentially be used. The first one is piece rate; the second one is a probationary period. In the next subsection we explore in turn both types of contract.

5.2.1 PIECE RATE AS A CONTINGENT CONTRACT

Piece rate is the most basic form of contingent contract, since pay is strictly on the basis of output. A worker that is paid at piece rate is a worker that is paid proportionally to the amount of output produced.

Let us assume that there are two types of worker, skilled and unskilled, but let us assume that *the firm cannot distinguish between workers who are skilled for the job and workers who are not skilled for the job until they have physically worked with the firm*. Only when prospective candidates are working in the firm is the productivity of each candidate revealed. Conversely, as long as workers are outside the firm there is no way to find out workers' productivity. Can the firm use a compensation package to solve this problem? Yes. The idea is to structure the compensation in a way that is attractive to highly skilled workers but less attractive to unskilled workers.

The output produced by the skilled workers is larger than the output produced by unskilled workers. This is basically a definition of being skilled and unskilled for the job. In other words, let us assume that $y_s > y_u$ where y_s is the output produced by skilled workers and y_u is the output produced by unskilled workers. The firm knows that some workers produce y_s while other workers produce y_u, but can not *ex ante* tell the type of a particular candidate. Before proceeding, let us further assume that skilled and unskilled workers have an outside option, which can be thought of as the value of the best alternative available to the worker outside the firm. Let us indicate with w_u the outside wage of the skilled workers and with w_s the outside wage of the skilled workers. The table below summarizes the notation.

A piece rate is a wage per unit of output. Let us assume that the firm can choose the piece rate. The problem is to select a value of the piece wage w_p so that only skilled workers join. To solve for wage w_p the firm should look at the problem from the point of view of each worker. By properly solving the problem faced by each different worker, the firm can then select the appropriate piece rate.

	Skilled	Unskilled	
outside option	w_s	w_u	
output	y_s	y_u	$y_s > y_u$

We now discuss how the piece wage rate w_p must be selected.

Choose w_p (the piece rate wage) so that

$w_p y_s \geq w_s$ skilled workers join

$w_p y_u \leq w_u$ unskilled workers do not join

This implies that w_p should be such that

$$w_p \geq \frac{w_s}{y_s} \tag{5.1}$$

$$w_p \leq \frac{w_u}{y_u} \tag{5.2}$$

The piece rate wage should be sufficiently high that skilled workers apply but low enough that it does not pay for unskilled workers to apply.

Let's discuss the two conditions of the proposition. We first focus on the skilled workers. The total income obtained by a skilled worker who takes the job is $w_p y_s$, since w_p is the earning per piece and y_s is the total number of pieces produced. If the skilled worker does not work for the firm he or she earns w_s elsewhere. The condition $w_p y_s \geq w_s$ says that the income earned by a skilled worker inside the firm must be larger than the outside wage. The second condition is very similar, but it refers to an unskilled worker. The firm does not want an unskilled worker to apply for the job, and a piece rate that satisfies $w_p y_u \leq w_u$ ensures that the total income earned inside the firm is less than the total income earned outside. w_p solves the adverse selection problem if both conditions are simultaneously satisfied. Figure 5.1 shows how the two conditions can be simultaneous satisfied. On the one hand, the piece rate must be large enough that skilled workers join. On the other hand, the piece rate must be low enough that unskilled workers do not join. Any wage w_p between these two extremes (included in the two dotted regions) will solve the adverse selection problem.

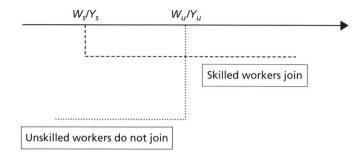

Figure 5.1. Piece rate wage for solving adverse selection in recruitment

Obviously the condition for this scheme to work is that the two regions in Fig. 5.1 do intersect. This is equivalent to saying that the left-hand side of equation (5.1) is smaller than the right-hand side of equation (5.2):

$$\frac{w_s}{y_s} \leq \frac{w_u}{y_u}$$

which can also be written as (inverting the ratio and changing the inequality sign):

$$\frac{y_s}{w_s} \geq \frac{y_u}{w_u}$$

$$\frac{y_s}{y_u} \geq \frac{w_s}{w_u}.$$

The last condition requires that the proportional increase in the productivity of skilled workers is larger than the proportional increase in their respective outside wage. Such a condition is very similar to the condition used for hiring skilled workers in the case of independent production analysed in Chapter 2.[1]

Note that the piece rate is a very simple and effective way to solve the adverse selection problem in hiring. Yet, for it to work at least three key conditions must be satisfied.

1. Wages must be perfectly flexible and the firm must be able to apply different wages to different workers.
2. Workers must correctly estimate their outside option. If they do not do so (i.e. $y_u = y_s$), there is no way you can use piece rate for hiring.
3. Output must be properly measured.

The first condition applies to any contingent contract, not only to piece rate, and it is a serious limit to the use of these schemes in many imperfect labour markets with serious institutional constraints. Similar comments can

---

[1] Note that if $y_s/y_u = 1 + \delta$ and $w_s/w_u = 1 + \gamma$, the condition is analogous to $\delta > \gamma$.

be applied to the second condition. The last condition is probably the most important, and deserves few comments. Pure piece rate is more likely to be applied in occupations in which the job output is easily identified. Obvious examples are sales jobs or basic production activities, such as those found in the garment industry (the case study on team production of Chapter 13 provides such an example), or traditional manufacturing jobs. For professional jobs, such as managing consultants or law firms, piece rates are very difficult to implement. The next section considers an alternative scenario.

Numerical Example

Assume $w_s = 10$, $w_u = 5$, $y_s = 5$, and $y_u = 2$. The conditions for attracting skilled workers require $w_p * 5 \geq 10$, so that $w_p \geq 2$ and simultaneously $w_p * 2 \leq 5$ or a level of w_p that is less than 2.5. This means that a piece wage between 2 and 2.5 would solve the problem. Note that in this case $y_s/y_u = 2.5$ which is greater than $w_s/w_u = 2$, and a piece rate can be found.

5.2.2 TEMPORARY CONTRACT WITH PROBATION WAGE

Consider a situation in which output cannot be properly measured so that a piece rate contract is not really feasible. We assume that wage flexibility is available within the firm, but output is not measurable. There is asymmetric information still present. While workers know their own ability to perform on the job, the firm is able to learn the potential of each worker only after some time.

We assume that the firm is able to assess the productivity of the worker at the end of the first period. The idea here is to offer a temporary contract with a low initial wage, but with a confirmation clause that offers a large wage increase. Good candidates would be attracted by the eventual wage increase, while bad candidates, knowing *ex ante* that they will not be promoted, will prefer to stay away from such a firm.

Contracts of this type are typically envisaged in law firms (or other professional firms) where young lawyers enter the firm with a temporary contract and, once promoted, receive a large wage increase. Indeed, it is very difficult to measure output in law firms, and this scheme seems to be far more appropriate than a piece rate scheme. Such a scheme is also known in the literature as an 'up or out rule' in the sense that young workers either move up the corporate ladder or simply leave the firm.

To make things as simple as possible, we assume that the job (or the worker's career) is described by two periods: a first period in which a temporary contract is offered at a wage w_1, and a second period (when the worker is tenured) in which a tenured wage w_2 is offered. In reality the second period, when the worker is tenured, is much longer than the probationary period. While one can certainly further complicate the problem and take into consideration the length of the second period, in what follows we work with the simplest scheme. There are two types of workers, skilled workers and unskilled workers, where the word skilled refers to the ability of each worker to perform inside the firm. Skilled and unskilled workers have different outside options, which we indicate respectively with w_s and w_u. Finally, we assume that at the end of the first period, the firm is not perfectly able to recognize a skilled worker. Specifically, we assume that there is a probability p that an unskilled worker passes the probationary period and it is tenured inside the firm. There is no discounting of future wages. To summarize, we consider the following definitions

w_s: skilled worker alternative wage
w_u: unskilled worker alternative wage
w_1: probationary wage
w_2: post-probationary wage
p: probability that an unskilled worker passes the probationary stage

The problem of the firm is to select w_1 and w_2 so that only skilled workers join the firm. We first solve the problem in assuming a perfect monitoring technology, so that $p = 0$. In the second part of the section we consider the problem with a positive probability of 'wrong promotion' p.

The Solution with Perfect Monitoring ($p = 0$)

Let us first consider a situation in which the firm is perfectly able to tell whether the worker under temporary contract is fit or not. This is akin to assuming that $p = 0$, so that at the end of the first period the firm has all the information on each worker. To attract skilled workers into the firm we need to set the wage in the two periods so that

$$w_1 + w_2 \geq 2w_s \qquad (5.3)$$

This condition is easy to interpret. It simply says that the total wage earned within the firm by a skilled worker is larger than the cumulative wage earned outside the firm.

To keep unskilled workers out, it is necessary that

$$w_1 + w_u \leq 2w_u \qquad (5.4)$$

The left-hand side is the wage earned inside the firm by the unskilled worker, and it is the sum of the temporary wage earned in the first period plus the wage earned in the second period. Since the worker's contract will not be transformed into a permanent contract, the wage in the second period is the outside wage. The right-hand side is the cumulative wage obtained outside, and it is simply the outside wage for two periods. The latter equation implies that to keep unskilled workers out it suffices to have

$$w_1 \leq w_u$$

or to set a wage under temporary contract lower than the unskilled worker's outside wage. Since the temporary wage will be offered also to permanent workers, the condition (5.3) requires

$$w_2 \geq 2w_s - w_1$$

This condition says that the promotion wage must be larger than the cumulative value of the outside wage ($2w_s$) net of the first period wage. If we satisfy the two constraints with equality (in assuming that skilled workers do not participate if indifferent and skilled workers do participate if indifferent), and we indicate with w_1^* and w_2^*, the solution to this problem reads

$$w_1^* = w_u$$
$$w_2^* = w_s + (w_s - w_u)$$

The idea of the solution is simple. The first period wage should be as low as the outside option of the unskilled workers, so that the job would not be suitable for unskilled workers (who will be fired for sure at the end of the first period). The confirmation wage conversely should be larger than the outside option of the skilled worker. Indeed, in the second period a skilled worker should get his outside wage, plus a compensation premium for the loss of income obtained in the first period. This suggests that the high wage enjoyed by the skilled workers in the second period corresponds to a compensation for their income loss during the first period. Let's define the pre-post probation wage differential Δ as the difference between the wage in the second period and the wage in the second period, so that $\Delta = w_2^* - w_1^*$. The following applies:

The pre-post probation wage differential wage Δ increases with the outside skilled differential $w_s - w_u$.

This is immediately confirmed by substituting in the definition of Δ the expression w_2^* and w_1^*. It follows that $\Delta = 2(w_s - w_u)$. The larger the outside skilled differentials $w_s - w_u$ the larger the compensation that the firm must provide to the skilled worker in the second period.

An extreme form of this type of contract is the *internship*, a type of contract that is often offered to just-graduate students. The idea of an internship is that the worker can work for the firm for wage equal to 0 for an initial short period, and at the end of the internship obtain a large wage as a permanent contract. The firm can then set a first period wage equal to $w_1 = 0$ and a second period wage such that

$$w_2 \geq 2w_s$$

Unskilled workers will not accept the internship, since they know that they will not be promoted, while skilled workers do accept and wait for the large wage increase that comes with promotion.

The situation described is very simple, but it requires the firm to be perfectly able to identify unskilled workers at the end of the temporary contract. Such a condition is not automatically obtained, and it is important to study what happens when the firm errs in the promotion mechanism. This problem is taken up in the next subsection.

The Solution with Imperfect Monitoring ($p < 1$)

We now solve the problem by explicitly considering the case in which the firm does err in the confirmation process, since there is a finite probability that an unskilled worker is promoted. The condition for attracting skilled workers is unchanged and it reads

$$w_1 + w_2 \geq 2w_s \qquad (5.5)$$

where the cumulative wage inside the firm must be larger than the cumulative outside option. The condition for keeping unskilled workers out of the firm is more complicated, since we need to take into account the probability p of a 'wrong promotion'. The formal expression reads

$$w_1 + pw_2 + (1 - p)w_u \leq 2w_u \qquad (5.6)$$

where the left-hand side is the cumulative expected wage inside the firm and the right-hand side is simply the cumulative expected wage outside the firm. The key novelty in equation 5.2 is the wage in the second period, which is obtained as a weighted average between the promotion wage w_2 and the outside wage w_u, with weights equal to the probability of 'wrong promotion' p. Indeed, with probability p the bad worker is promoted and he or she enjoys the second period wage w_2. Conversely, with probability $(1 - p)$ the worker is detected, is fired, and he or she enjoys the outside option w_u.

If we satisfy the two constraints with equality (in assuming that skilled workers do not participate if indifferent and skilled workers do participate if indifferent), and we indicate with w_1^* and w_2^*, from (5.5), it follows that to keep unskilled workers out the maximum unskilled wage is

$$w_1^* = 2w_s - w_2$$

and substituting this into equation (5.2) satisfied with equality one obtains an equation for the minimum unskilled wage w_2^*

$$2w_s - w_2^* + pw_2^* + (1 - p)w_u = 2w_u$$

so that

$$w_2^* = \frac{2w_s - (1+p)w_u}{1-p}$$

from which it follows that the probationary wage is

$$w_1^* = 2w_s - \frac{2w_s - (1+p)w_u}{1-p}$$

$$= \frac{2w_s - 2pw_s - 2w_s + (1+p)w_u}{1-p}$$

$$= \frac{(1+p)w_u - 2pw_s}{1-p}$$

The probationary wage is such that $w_1^* < w_u < w_s$ and $w_2^* > w_s$. In other words the probationary wage requires that the initial wage is lower than the outside unskilled wage while the post-probationary wage is larger than the outside skilled wage.

First let's check that $w_1^* < w_u$. The latter condition is true as long as

$$\frac{(1+p)w_u - 2pw_s}{1-p} < w_u$$

$$(1+p)w_u - 2pw_s < w_u - pw_u$$

$$-2pw_s < -2pw_u$$

$$w_s > w_u \qquad \text{QED}$$

Second, we need to check whether $w_2 > w_s$. The latter condition is true as long as

$$\frac{2w_s - (1+p)w_u}{1-p} > w_s$$

$$2w_s - (1+p)w_u > w_s - pw_s$$

$$w_s > w_u \qquad \text{QED}$$

Let's define the pre-post probationary wage spread as Δ or, in other terms,

$$\Delta = w_2^* - w_1^*$$

$$\Delta = \frac{2w_s - (1+p)w_u}{1-p} - \frac{(1+p)w_u - 2pw_s}{1-p}$$

$$= \frac{2(1+p)(w_s - w_u)}{1-p}$$

As p rises, it is difficult to detect unskilled workers, and a larger spread Δ is needed to keep unskilled workers out.

To see this you need to differentiate Δ with respect to p to yield

$$\frac{\partial \Delta}{\partial p} = \frac{2(w_s - w_u)(1 - p) + 2(1 + p)(w_s - w_u)}{(1 - p)^2} > 0$$

It follows that the wage contract (w_1^*, w_2^*) must simultaneously satisfy

$$w_1^* \leq \frac{(1 + p)w_u - 2pw_s}{1 - p}$$

$$w_2^* \geq 2w_s - w_1^*$$

So that once w_1^* is chosen small enough, one must choose the second period wage accordingly.

While the probationary wage seems a very effective compensation system for solving adverse selection issues, there are some important issues to mention. A potential problem is what is known in the literature as *rat race*, or the fact that effort and ability are likely to be substitutes. Workers put in a lot of effort during probation, so that a firm is likely to observe bad workers working very hard. This problem increases the chance of a mistake. In addition, effort is likely to drop after getting a fixed job.

Numerical Example

Let us assume that $w_u = 2$ and $w_s = 5$ while the probability of passing the test is $p = 0.1$. It is easy to check that the two conditions are

$$w_1^* \leq \frac{1.1 * 2 - 2 * (0.1) * 5}{0.9}$$

$$w_1^* \leq 1.33$$

$$w_2^* \geq 10 - w_1^*$$

so that if we offer $w_1^* = 1.33$ the corresponding $w_2^* = 8.66$. If the first period wage is reduced (let's say to $w_1^* = 1$) the second period wage must be increased to 9.

5.2.3 CONTINGENT CONTRACTS WITH MINIMUM WAGES

The idea of a contingent contract, either a piece rate or a probationary period, is to set initial wages that are so low that the application is unattractive to unsuitable candidates. When a minimum wage is imposed on the firm, it is no longer perfectly obvious that a firm will be able to offer contingent contracts. We now try to understand under which circumstances a contingent contract with minimum wage is a viable option. We analyse this issue in the case of a probationary period, under the assumption that the minimum wage is binding, so that the wage of the first period must be equal to a minimum wage $\bar{w}$. The question we ask is whether it is still possible to have a wage profile $\bar{w}$, w_2 so that unskilled workers do not join the firm. We initially assume that the best alternative option of an unskilled candidate is larger than the minimum wage ($w_u > \bar{w}$) and we analyse the alternative case at the end of this section. What we want to show here is that a probationary scheme will work only if the monitoring technology is sufficiently good, so that the probability of a wrong promotion is sufficiently small. Let's see the key conditions.

To attract skilled workers it is necessary that

$$\bar{w} + w_2 \geq 2w_s$$

where the first period wage w_1 is now identical to the minimum wage $\bar{w}$. To keep unskilled workers out, it is necessary that

$$\bar{w} + pw_2 + (1 - p)w_u \leq 2w_u$$

which is very similar to equation 5.2, with the only key difference being that the first period wage is no longer an endogenous variable of the firm, but it is set equal to $\bar{w}$.

If we satisfy the first constraint with an equals sign (so as to make the skilled workers just indifferent between working for the firm and their outside option), the promotion wage is

$$w_2 = 2w_s - \bar{w}.$$

Substituting this requirement into the second equation we see that the condition is satisfied if

$$p < \frac{w_u - \bar{w}}{2w_s - [w_u + \bar{w}]}$$

from which immediately follows:

1. Only if the risk of wrong promotion (i.e. promoting an unskilled worker) is sufficiently small ($p < p^*$) does a probationary period with minimum wage solve the adverse selection problem, where $p^* = \frac{w_u - \bar{w}}{2w_s - [w_u - \bar{w}]}$.
2. If the outside option of the unskilled worker is exactly equal to the minimum wage $w_u = \bar{w}$, there is no way to use a probationary contract to solve the adverse selection problem.

The last remark shows that $w_u > \bar{w}$ is a necessary condition for the probationary period to work. Indeed, if the outside wage is smaller than the minimum wage, the probationary period requires a negative probability, a situation which is obviously unfeasible (the probability must obviously be between 0 and 1).

It is clear that the existence of a minimum wage greatly diminishes the firm's ability to use the probationary wage as a mechanism for solving the adverse selection problem in the recruiting process. In the next section we study situations in which firms do not use a wage contract but rely on signals and credentials.

5.3 Use of Credentials and the Signalling Model of Education

The idea of a credential is to specify in the job requirement specific conditions that prospective candidates should possess for qualifying for the job. Obvious examples of credentials are college degree, master's, professional certificates. Quite often, in the real world, job advertising explicitly specifies that successful candidates must possess certain credentials, and very often such credentials refer to educational attainments.

In this section we analyse whether the use of credentials can mitigate the adverse selection problem. Our analysis will focus mainly on education as a signal, but it is clear that similar analysis applies to other credentials. The concept we want to stress is the fact that under certain specific conditions a credential can profitably be used to signal a candidate's productivity. When is such signalling likely to work? We will see that two key conditions are necessary:

1. The credential must be correlated with job performance.
2. Obtaining the credential must be relatively easy for well-qualified workers, but difficult for others. In other words the ability to perform well in school and perform on the job are highly correlated (analytically oriented jobs). The idea is that people have private information about their own ability and they know whether the benefit of having the credential is worth its costs.

We now analyse in some details the idea of education signalling.

5.4 Education Signalling

This section studies under which conditions the educational attainment of the candidates may serve to signal unobservable individual ability. In this section we assume that education attainment has no impact on individual ability, and it is not linked to a process of skill acquisition. In reality, skill acquisition is a dimension of the educational experience, and the chapters on training and human capital investment will be fully devoted to such key issues in personnel economics. In this section we are interested in the signalling value of education, and we fully explore such a mechanism.

We thus assume that schooling makes no independent contribution to labour productivity, which is instead determined solely by individual ability. One may reasonably think that under these circumstances prospective employers have no direct interest in the educational attainment of workers, and profit maximizing firms would not be willing to pay a wage premium to workers with more schooling. Things may be very different if individual ability is not observed by employers.

Let's assume that individual ability is invisible to employers, and let us also assume that individual ability is inversely correlated with the cost of schooling. Employers would like to know the ability of potential employees, since more capable employees are more productive inside the firm. Yet, firms are incapable of assessing a worker's ability. The key idea is that firms may be able to fully learn a worker's ability from his or her educational attainment. When such a condition is satisfied we say that the labour market has attained a separating equilibrium.

Let us assume that there are two types of workers, those with high ability and those with low ability. Let us assume that there are 50 per cent of workers that are low ability and 50 per cent of workers that are high ability. The parameter a describes the workers' ability (and their marginal productivity in the workplace), and we assume that

$$a = \begin{cases} a_h & \text{if worker has high ability} \\ a_l & \text{if worker has low ability} \end{cases}$$

Clearly, high-ability individuals are more productive than low-ability individuals so that $a_h > a_l$. Let's consider a situation in which these two different individuals can or cannot take a costly educational attainment. We simply assume that schooling s is a binary variable that can take values 0 or 1, depending on whether the individual decides to acquire education. We should think that $s = 1$ corresponds to having a master's degree while $s = 0$ corresponds to a situation without a master's degree. Undertaking education involves psychological costs, which we assume to be described by this simply relationship

$$c(s = 1, a) = \frac{k}{a}$$

where k is a positive constant. Since a can take only two values, the cost function is equivalent to

$$c(s = 1, a_h) = \frac{k}{a_h} \quad \text{if worker has high ability}$$
$$c(s = 1, a_l) = \frac{k}{a_l} \quad \text{if worker has low ability}$$

The previous conditions imply that high-ability students have lower costs of education, so that

cost of education for low ability > cost of education for high ability

Education attainment is observable to the firms. While firms are not able to offer contracts that are linked to the ability of the candidates, they are able to offer contracts that are linked to the educational attainment. A *separating equilibrium* is a situation in which only high-ability individuals acquire the educational signal and firms offer wage premia to educated individuals. If this situation happens in the marketplace, then the use of credentials acts as a device that solves the adverse selection problems of firms.

To see how a separating equilibrium may emerge suppose that firms expect that only high-ability workers receive education and so they are willing to offer a high wage to a candidate that has attained education. When this is the case high-ability workers may have an incentive to acquire the signal in exchange for future wage gains. Conversely, low-ability workers find such an option too costly, and do not acquire the educational signal.

Figure 5.2 describes a signalling equilibrium. In the horizontal axis there is the education level. Note that only two points are relevant, the origin $s = 0$ and the point $s = 1$, since we are assuming that only two types of education are available in the marketplace. In the vertical axis we report the wage paid for each educational level as well as the cost of education. The wage offered by the firms is $w = a_h$ for individuals with high education and $w = a_l$ for individuals with low education attainment. The upward sloping line reports the cost of education for the two types of workers. Low-ability individuals have a steeper cost function, since acquiring the education signal involves a larger cost.

How will each individual decide whether investing in education is worth the cost? Let's consider low-ability individuals first. If they do not acquire the signal they enjoy a net return equal to the segment Ao in the figure, since point A corresponds to the wage w_l and the cost of education is zero. If they acquire the signal they will get a wage w_h but will have to pay the cost up to point C so that the net value of utility will be equal to the segment BC. Since the segment Ao is larger than BC, low-ability individuals will choose $s = 0$. Let's now consider the high-ability individual. By a similar argument the high-ability individual should compare the segment BD (which is the value when

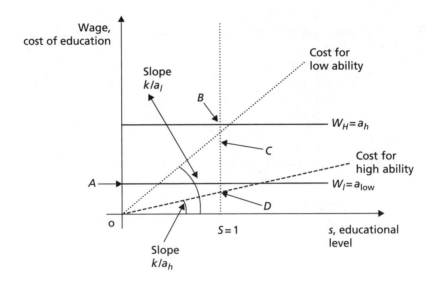

Figure 5.2. Education signalling and a separating equilibrium

he or she acquires education) with the segment Ao. It is clear that high-ability individuals select the education signal. In other words, Fig. 5.2 describes a separating equilibrium. Individuals do acquire the credentials and the firms value such a signal in equilibrium. Under these circumstances the firm is able to fully learn the worker type.

Things can be very different if the firm believes that an individual with a degree has the same chances of being high or low ability. In other words, the firm may expect that the possession of the credentials has no link to the probability of finding a good candidate. Under such circumstances the firm will post only a single wage and there will be no wage premium linked to better educational attainment. This is called a *pooling equilibrium*, a situation that is described in Fig. 5.3. In this situation, both individuals have no incentive to acquire the costly signal, so that both types (high and low) choose not to acquire the education signal. This discussion highlights the fact that firm's beliefs play a key role in shaping the emergence of a separating equilibrium. The next section explicitly considers firm profits and the role played by firm's beliefs.[2]

---

[2] Note further that the nature of the separating equilibrium lends support to the claim that education per se is useless or even pernicious, because it imposes social costs but does not increase total output. Of course such a view is extreme, and education has a lot to do with human capital accumulation, as Chapters 9 and 10 on training will show.

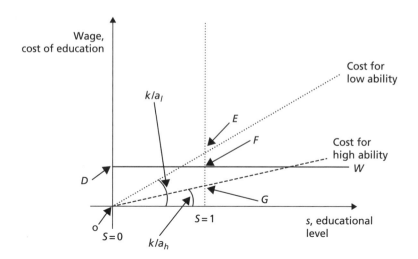

Figure 5.3. Pooling equilibrium (education does not act as a signal)

5.5 **Education Signalling: A Formal Story**

This section provides a formal analysis of the signalling equilibrium described in the previous section. In game theory jargon, signalling is a way for an agent to communicate his type under adverse selection. The idea is that education has no direct effect on a person's ability to be productive, but is useful for signalling his ability to employers. Let half of the workers have the high-ability type less and half of the workers low ability, where ability is a number denoting the dollar value of their output. Employers do not observe the worker's ability, but they do know the distribution of abilities, and they observe the worker's education. To simplify the exposition, we will specify that *the players are one worker and two employers*. The competition of employers will drive profits down to zero, and the worker receives the gains from trade.

The worker must make two choices: the education level and his choice of employer. The employers' strategies are the contracts they offer giving wages as functions of education level. The key to the model is that the signal, education, is less costly for workers with higher ability.

5.6 **Rules of the Game**

Players:

A Worker and two employers

The Order of Play:

1. Nature chooses the worker's ability $a \in \{2, 5.5\}$, the low and high ability each having probability 0.5. In other words $a_l = 2$ and $a_h = 5.5$. *The variable is observed by the worker, but not by the employers.*
2. The worker chooses education level, either no education or education, so that s can take only two values $s \in \{0, 1\}$. Education is observed by both the firms and the workers.
3. Each employer offers a wage contract $w(s)$, specifying the wage to be paid as a function of the educational attainment.
4. The worker accepts a contract, or rejects both of them.
5. Output equals a.

Pay-off:

The worker's utility is his wage minus his cost of education, so that

$$U_w = w - \frac{8s}{a} \qquad \text{if the worker accepts contract } w(s)$$

$$U_w = 0 \qquad \text{if the worker rejects both contracts}$$

The expected profits are output minus wage costs so that

$$\Pi = a - w \qquad \text{for the employer whose contract is accepted}$$

$$\Pi = 0 \qquad \text{for the other employer}$$

There are two equilibria which are of interest, one in which education is not chosen in equilibrium, one in which education is selected only by the high-ability type. We now focus on the two equilibria.

5.7 No Education Equilibrium (Pooling Equilibrium)

The first equilibrium we consider is a no education equilibrium, or a pooling equilibrium in game theory jargon. In such an equilibrium both types (low and high ability) choose no education, and the employer pays a salary which is equal to the average productivity. The idea is that employers believe that an educated worker has the same chance of being either high or low type, so that they do not offer a wage premium to an educated worker. Given the employers' beliefs, it does not pay for the workers to engage in education. Let's first define the average wage as the expected productivity, or as

$$\bar{w} = pa_h + (1 - p)a_l$$

$$\bar{w} = 0.5 * a_h + 0.5 * a_l$$

$$\bar{w} = (2 + 5.5)/2 = 3.75$$

Let's define the employers' beliefs as the probability that the type is low, conditional on being educated as $p(a = Low|s = 1)$, and let us assume that

$$p(a = low|s = 1) = 0.5$$

This means that conditional on having acquired education, the probability of being of low type is the same as that for the population at large.

The no education equilibrium is such that

$$s(low) = s(high) = 0$$
$$w(0) = w(1) = 0.5$$
$$p(a = Low|s = 1) = 0.5$$

This implies that education is useless, since it does not yield any wage premium. In this condition, the model reaches the unsurprising outcome that workers do not bother to acquire unproductive education. Note that under this scenario the beliefs are simple passive conjecture, since $s = 1$ is never observed in equilibrium. It is clear that for the high-ability type it does not make sense for him to educate himself, since the employer would not reward his effort through higher wages. Further, firms make zero expected profits since the average ability is equal to the average wage.

5.8 Education Equilibrium (Separating Equilibrium)

Let us now assume that the employer has a different set of beliefs. In particular, let us assume that the employer believes that a worker who acquires education is a high-ability type, so that

$$p(a = Low|s = 1) = 0$$

This leads to the separating equilibrium for which signalling is best known, in which the high-ability worker acquires education to prove to employers that he really has high ability. The separating equilibrium is such that

$$s(Low) = 0$$
$$s(High) = 1$$
$$w(0) = 2$$
$$w(1) = 5.5$$

How can we check that this is really an equilibrium? We need to check that the separating contract maximizes the utility of the high and low types subject to two constraints:

Participation constraints that the firms can offer the contract without making losses;

Self-selection constraints that the lows are not attracted to the high contract, and the highs are not attracted by the low contract.

The *participation constraints* for the employer requires that

$$w(0) \leq a_L = 2$$
$$w(1) \leq a_H = 5.5$$

but competition between employers makes the expressions above hold as equalities, so that the employers make zero profits.

The *self-selection constraint of the lows* is

$$U_L(s = 0) \geq U_L(s = 1)$$
$$w(0) - 0 \geq w(1) - \frac{8 * 1}{2}$$
$$2 \geq 5.5 - 4$$
$$2 \geq 1.5$$

which is satisfied.

The *self-selection constraint of the highs* is

$$U_H(s = 1) \geq U_H(s = 0)$$
$$w(1) - \frac{8 * 1}{5.5} \geq w(0) - 0$$
$$5.5 - 1.45 \geq 2$$
$$4.05 \geq 2$$

which is also satisfied.

Separation is possible because education is more costly for workers if their ability is lower. If education costs the same for both types of worker, education would not work as a signal, because the low-ability workers would imitate the high-ability workers. The nature of the separating equilibrium lends support to the claim that education per se is useless or even pernicious, because it imposes social costs but does not increase total output.

6 Optimal Compensation Schemes: Foundation

6.1 Introduction

Choosing an appropriate compensation mechanism is probably the core problem of human resource managers, and represents the heart of personnel economics. Loosely speaking good compensation packages must be consistent with profit maximization on the part of firms, but they should also provide workers with the incentives to do as well as possible. If we pay the worker independently of his or her performance, most likely we will not provide him or her with the right incentives to act in the interest of the firm. In the jargon of the economics of imperfect information, the problem with a fully fixed salary is one of moral hazard. The term moral hazard arises in the insurance market and refers to the fact that a person who has insurance coverage will have less incentive to take proper care of insured objects than a person who does not.

Here is an example. A worker who sells computers for a small company has to decide how much effort to put into selling the hardware. The number of computers sold certainly depends on how hard she works, but the total sales will also depend on other factors, like customer willingness to buy computers. Such factors are outside the worker's control. At the end of the month the company will observe the number of computers sold, but will not observe how much effort she put into the task. A very good month's volume of sales can certainly depend on hard work (we will call it effort in this chapter) but can also simply depend on a surge in demand totally unrelated to effort. The question we need to ask is, how much effort will the worker put into her task? Such effort will obviously depend on the structure of compensation. If the worker is paid a fixed salary independent of the computers sold, she is much more likely to take it easy. This is because with a fixed salary the worker is fully insured against changes in the number of computers sold. Indeed, if the pay does not depend on how hard a worker tries, why should she bother to exercise effort? It seems that under straight salary (which corresponds to full insurance) the worker, who in this chapter is called the agent, is doing something that the boss would rather not do. Obviously, it is very difficult for the firm to prove that the worker did not work enough by simply looking at sales, since it is also possible that the low sales were due to low customer demand. This *conflict of interest* is at the heart of the moral hazard problem. What is good for the agent is not (necessarily) good for the principal, and the principal cannot always be on hand to monitor what the agent does.

The only way in which the firm can solve this problem is by choosing an appropriate compensation scheme. Pay for performance, or compensation packages that link the worker's salary to the number of computers sold, are likely to be the solution to the problem. In this chapter we will find that there exists an extreme incentive scheme that is likely to be the solution to our problem. In the extreme scheme the worker ends up making a fixed up-front payment to the firm at the beginning of the month, and thereafter acts as a sort of entrepreneur. In other words, the worker 'buys' the job from the firm, and then acts as a residual claimant on the revenues obtained. This scheme corresponds to a labour contract with a 100 per cent commission rate. The salesman keeps all the revenues from the sales, and pays the firm a fixed fee.

Yet further problems exist. The first problem is whether such a scheme is technically feasible. It is often impossible for the firm to obtain a payment from the worker. Negative payments are simply not allowed. We will see that in this case the firm will have to change its optimal compensation scheme.

Second, the discussion so far has not dealt with an important factor: risk. The worker is likely to be risk averse, and she is likely to prefer income streams that are time invariant to income streams that change dramatically from month to month. We will see that also in this case, the optimal compensation scheme will have to be changed slightly.

We can summarize the problem of the compensation package with the following key questions.

The principal/firm has two problems:

Principal/firm problem Number 1: Of all the possible compensation packages that the principal could offer the agent, which one maximizes the expected profits?

Principal/firm problem Number 2: Once the optimal compensation is found, is it worth hiring the agent?

The worker/agent has two problems

Agent/worker problem Number 1: If the agent accepts the contract and goes to work for this principal, how hard should she work on that job?

Agent/worker problem Number 2: Once she knows how hard it is optimal to work, should she accept such a contract?

6.2 **A Formal Principal–Agent Model**

6.2.1 THE GENERAL SETTING

We assume that the agent is a worker who likes higher income w and dislikes effort. The agent quite likely dislikes income variability, so that at a given average income, she is happier if income is more stable. We take up this issue in section 6.4 of this chapter. In this section we assume for simplicity that the agent is risk neutral and does not worry about income variability.

The job of the agent involves producing a good in quantity x which is sold for a fixed price equal to p. The total revenues generated by the workers are indicated by px, and depend on two key dimensions: *luck and effort.* Greater effort (which we indicate with e) on the part of a worker implies greater output produced and sold x, but larger x can also be the result of good luck or favourite demand conditions. The principal observes only output px and does not know whether the larger output x is the result of luck or the result of effort. Effort e is unobservable, and output x is an imperfect signal of the effort elicited by the agent.

The expected output generated by the worker is denominated by x and depends on luck and effort from the following relationship

$$x = (e + \eta),$$

where e is effort generated by the worker and η is the outcome of a random variable with zero mean ($E(\eta) = 0$) and variance equal to v. Greater effort on the part of the worker implies greater average output $\bar{x}$, but output depends also on other factors, which can be thought of as customer demand, or luck on the part of the worker. These other factors, however, cancel out on average. This means that, on average, output is equal to the effort exercised by the worker so that

$$\bar{x} = E(x) = e$$

In other words, the random components of output are independent of effort, and effort determines average expected output.[1] Given the total revenues, we now specify the compensation package.

---

[1] A more formal way to describe what was said in the text it is to assume that

η is a random variable with zero mean and variance v
x is randomly distributed with mean e and variance equal to v
$x \sim f(x): \bar{x} = e \qquad var(x) = v$

A compensation package offered to the worker is a **wage contract** that specifies a fixed wage component, independent of revenues, and a variable wage component.[2]

We indicate the compensation package with w, where w is a linear function of the revenue produced by the agent. In particular, we let

$$w = \alpha + \beta x$$

$$w = \alpha + \beta(e + \eta)$$

where α and β are two constants. So that the expected value of the compensation is

$$w^e = \alpha + \beta E(x)$$

$$= \alpha + \beta e$$

since $E(\eta) = 0$. Basically a compensation package offered by the principal is a wage contract specifying two constants: α, a fixed wage component, independent of revenues, and β a variable wage component.[3]

It is important to stress the difference between the wage w and its expected value w^e. The compensation wage w depends also on the outcome of the random variable η, while the average compensation w^e depends only on the effort exercised. This makes a lot of sense. One month of high pay can be due to luck, but on average good salaries must be linked to good performance.

One important dimension to emphasize is also that the firm observes the output x but does not observe the effort chosen by the worker. The firm can tell whether output produced was large or low, but it cannot really tell whether a high output was obtained because of high effort or a large realization of η. Such a distinction will turn out to be very important when we consider risk aversion.

There are basically three types of compensation scheme that we consider: fixed compensation schemes, bonus schemes, and franchising schemes.

1. **Purely Input Based Scheme** ($\alpha > 0$ and $\beta = 0$). This scheme is the simplest one, and specifies a fixed payment per unit of time (say a month, or a week, or a day) independently of the output produced and sold. In formula, the compensation package can be written as

$$w = \alpha$$

so that the wage income is completely independent of output.

---

[2] Note that the analysis considers only linear contracts, or contracts in which the wage is a linear transformation of output.

[3] The compensation package has also a variance which is simply given

$$Var(w) = \beta^2 Var(x)$$

$$= \beta^2 v$$

The variance will play an important role when we introduce risk-averse workers.

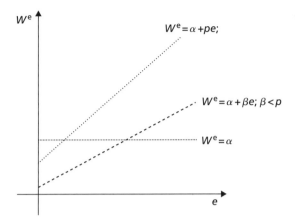

Figure 6.1. Different compensation schemes as worker's constraint

2. **Bonus Scheme** $(0 < \beta < p)$, so that the compensation scheme is made up of a fixed component plus a variable bonus, which is proportional to output. The larger the coefficient β, the larger the sensitivity of the compensation scheme to the revenues obtained.
3. **Franchising Schemes** $(\beta = p; \alpha < 0)$. In this scheme all the extra output is given to the worker, so that he becomes a residual claimant in the project. Under this pay scheme, the agent is an entrepreneur who rents a job, and the firm makes money by choosing the fixed payment α.

The compensation schemes can also be represented graphically by a line in the space $[w^e, e]$, where w^e is the expected wage and e is effort (Fig. 6.1). Each compensation scheme is described by a line in the space $[w^e, e]$, with different schemes being just different lines with different slopes and different intercepts. The intercept corresponds to the fixed part of the compensation while the slope corresponds to the bonus. In Fig. 6.1, the horizontal line is a purely input-based scheme while the two upward-sloping lines are the two incentive schemes, with the slope varying according to the different degree of incentives.

Utility function. We already mentioned that the agent is a worker who likes higher average income w^e but dislikes effort.[4] A *risk-neutral* agent is somebody who does not care about income variability and his utility function is

$$U(w^e, e) = w^e - \delta \frac{e^2}{2}$$

---

[4] As we argued above, we are now sidestepping from risk consideration and we assume that the agent does not care about larger wage variability. We take up this important issue in section 6.4.

where δ is simply a parameter that reflects how much the worker dislikes effort. In the utility function, 1 additional euro of income yields one additional utils, while an additional unit of effort yields a disutility equal to δe. This implies that the marginal utility of income is constant, while the marginal disutility of effort is increasing. At the margin, increasing effort becomes more and more costly to the individual, while additional income yields the same utility level.[5]

Outside option. The agent has always the possibility of turning down the principal's job offer and working at another job (maybe as self-employed) that yields utility level $u \geq 0$.

Firm profits. The principal is a firm that maximizes expected profits. We assume that the principal has only one worker and that there are no other costs beyond labour costs. The expected profits can be written as expected revenues minus expected costs, or

$$E[\Pi] = pE[x] - w^e$$
$$= (p - \beta)e - \alpha$$

where we make use of the definition $w^e = \alpha + \beta e$ and $E[x] = e$. In the previous expression $p - \beta$ is the profit per unit of output sold, $E[x] = e$ is the expected revenues and α represents the fixed cost of the firms, independent of output. Two remarks are in order. First, since $p - \beta$ is the profit per unit of output, the term $(p - \beta)e$ can be thought of as the variable profits of the firm. Second, the fixed cost α can obviously become a fixed revenue, since we argued above that α can be negative.

Indifference Curves

Let's call the indifference curve of the worker the combination of expected income (w^e) and effort (e) that delivers to the individual the same level of utility.[6] (Figure 6.2 reports a family of indifference curves.) There are various properties of these utility functions:

- Indifference curves are upward sloping. Higher effort, which the worker dislikes, must be compensated by higher income in order to remain on the same indifference curve.
- Indifference curves do not intersect. This is true with any indifference curve. If they did intersect, then a unique combination of effort and income would yield two different utility levels, which is obviously not possible.

---

[5] The indifference curves describe the behaviour of the utility function.
[6] The equation of the indifference at utility level $\bar{U}$ for an individual that is risk neutral is

$$E(w) = \delta \frac{e^2}{2} + \bar{U}$$

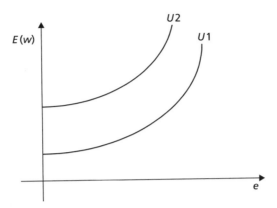

Figure 6.2. Worker's indifference curve

- Indifference curves in the north-west region of the diagram correspond to indifference curves with larger utility levels. In Fig. 6.2, the indifference curve U_2 corresponds to a larger indifference level than the curve labelled U_1.
- The indifference curves are also convex, since more and more effort must be compensated by an ever larger income. This gives the idea that the marginal disutility of work is increasing. Formally, such a property comes from the fact that effort enters the utility function with a square term.

We can also derive the slope of the indifference curve. We need first to define the marginal utility associated with extra income and the marginal utility associated with an extra unit of effort. Our utility function implies that the marginal utility of an extra euro of wage income is 1 (which is exactly what our indifference curve would say), so that

$$MU_w = \frac{\Delta U}{\Delta w^e}\bigg|_{e=\bar{e}} = 1$$

The notation $e = \bar{e}$ in the previous expression simply says that the marginal utility of income is calculated holding constant effort. We can similarly define the marginal (dis)utility of effort as the loss of utility deriving from an extra unit of effort as

$$MU_e = \frac{\Delta U}{\Delta e}\bigg|_{w^e=\bar{w}} = -\delta e$$

so that our utility function implies a marginal disutility that is increasing in effort. In other words, the larger the effort that the worker exercises, the higher the disutility associated with a further increase in effort. Having defined the marginal disutility along an indifference curve the total change in utility must be zero by definition so that

$$\frac{\Delta U}{\Delta e}\bigg|_{E(w)=\bar{w}} \Delta e + \frac{\Delta U}{\Delta E(w)}\bigg|_{e=\bar{e}} \Delta w = 0$$

Rearranging the terms of the previous expression, the slope of the utility function is

$$\frac{\Delta w}{\Delta e} = -\frac{MU_e}{MU_w} = \delta e$$

6.2.2 THE PROBLEM OF A RISK-NEUTRAL AGENT

The agent chooses effort after observing the compensation scheme. The agent faces basically two problems/questions:

Agent Problem Number 1: If I accept the contract and go to work for this principal, what level of effort should I choose?
Answer: I should choose the level of effort e that maximizes my expected utility (a level of effort labelled e^*).
Agent Problem Number 2: If I take the contract and choose the optimal level of effort e^*, I will obtain an expected wage $w^e(e^*)$ that will certainly depend on the effort exercised. Given the effort e^* and the compensation $w^e(e^*)$, the expected utility will be $U(w^e(e^*), e^*)$. Shall I accept such a scheme?
Answer: I will take the principal's offer only if it ensures a utility level which is as high as the outside utility level u.

The Optimal Effort Level: The first problem of the agent

Effort is chosen so as to maximize the agent utility. Let's analyse the level of effort under the various contracts.

Effort under Purely Input Scheme: In the purely input scheme the compensation is $w = \alpha$ so that $w^e = \alpha$. The problem of the worker is to find the highest indifference curve given the constraint represented by the fixed payment. The solution to such a problem is easily obtained graphically. It is clear that the maximum indifference curve is given by the point A in the corner solution in Fig. 6.3, so that the optimal effort is

$$e^*(\text{purely input scheme}) = 0$$

In other words, *when wages are fixed and independent of output, the agent optimally chooses zero effort.*

Effort under the Bonus Contract: In the bonus contract $w = \alpha + \beta x$ so that $w^e = \alpha + \beta e$. The optimal level of effort can be easily analysed graphically, as

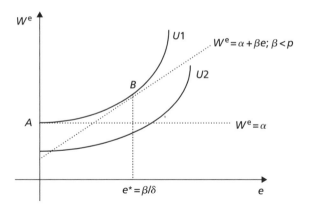

Figure 6.3. The worker problem

the choice of an optimal level of effort on the part of the worker. The worker wants to enjoy the maximum level of utility subject to the budget constraint. The maximum point requires a tangency condition between the indifference curve and the budget constraint. If the budget constraint is horizontal, then clearly the worker maximizes his utility by choosing an optimal level of effort at point A, to which corresponds a zero amount of effort. Conversely, if the budget constraint is the one typical of a bonus scheme, then the optimal position cannot be at zero effort, since the worker can obtain a larger level of utility by choosing a larger amount of effort. The optimal solution of the worker is now at point B, where the level of effort is the one corresponding to the level of effort $e^* = \frac{\beta}{\delta}$. Let's understand why.

The optimal choice of effort is simply given by the tangency between the budget constraint and the indifference curve, so that

$$\text{slope indifference curve} = \text{slope compensation}$$
$$\delta e = \beta$$

The optimal effort choice is typically called the incentive compatibility constraint. As we will see later on, such a condition acts as a constraint on the firm's choice of the optimal compensation package, and should be always taken into account by the firm.

The formal problem of the worker is to maximize utility with respect to e, using the compensation scheme as a constraint

$$Max_e : U(w^e, e) = w^e - \delta \frac{e^2}{2}$$
$$\text{such that } w^e = \alpha + \beta e$$

Substituting the constraint into the utility function, the problem is simply to maximize with respect to effort the following function:

$$Max_e : U(w^e, e) = \alpha + \beta e - \delta \frac{e^2}{2}$$

which implies that the first-order condition is

$$\beta - \delta e = 0$$

so that the optimal effort is

$$e^* = \frac{\beta}{\delta} \qquad \text{(IC: Incentive Compatibility Constraint)}$$

from which two implications immediately follow:

To elicit hard work, workers needs incentive, or a level of $\beta > 0$.

This is immediately verified by looking at the incentive compatibility constraint. The optimal level of effort requires a positive value of β, or a positive component of the bonus scheme.

Effort is maximum under the franchising scheme, i.e. when $\beta = p$.

This result is just a corollary of the previous condition. The maximum level of effort requires the maximum possible level of the bonus scheme, which we know to be $\beta = p$.

Is Participation Convenient? The Second Problem of the Agent

The second problem of the worker is whether participating in the contract is convenient, since the worker can enjoy an outside opportunity that yields expected utility equal to u.

The utility of the agent if she works with the principal is

$$U(w^e, e) = \alpha + \beta e^* - \delta \frac{e^{*2}}{2}$$

where we already know that effort will be chosen optimally at a point in which $e^* = \frac{\beta}{\delta}$. Participation is convenient if and only if the utility obtained by the contract is larger than the outside option. In formula, this is equivalent to

$$U(w^e(e^*), e^*) \geq u \qquad (6.1)$$

where the notation $w(e^*)$ shows that the expected income will depend crucially on the optimal effort e^*. With a general compensation package, the expected income is given by $w^e(e^*) = \alpha + \beta e^*$ which immediately implies that $w^e(e^*) = \alpha + \frac{\beta^2}{\delta}$. The condition 6.1 becomes

$$\alpha + \frac{\beta^2}{\delta} - \delta\frac{\beta^2}{2\delta^2} \geq u$$

so that

$$\alpha + \frac{\beta^2}{2\delta} \geq u \qquad \text{((P) Participation Constraint)}$$

The participation constraint has also a graphical interpretation. The participation constraint requires that at the optimal level of effort the worker enjoys a level of utility which is at least as large as the worker's outside option, which we labelled u. In terms of Fig. 6.3, if we say that the worker can enjoy an outside level of utility equal to $u = U_2$, than at a point such as B, the agent would be better off working for the principal (since the utility level U_1 is larger than the alternative utility level $u = U_2$).

The problem of the agent is now solved and it is fully described by the two constraints IC and P. Having solved the worker's problem, we now turn to the firm's behaviour, taking into account the worker's choices.

6.2.3 THE PROBLEM OF THE PRINCIPAL WITH A RISK-NEUTRAL AGENT

The firm/principal has two problems

Principal Problem Number 1: Of all the possible compensation packages that could be offered to the agent, which is the one that maximizes profits? Answer: The compensation chosen is the one that maximizes expected profits, which implies choosing the level of α and β that maximizes the revenues net of the compensation package.

Principal Problem Number 2: Given the answer to problem 1, is it optimal to hire the agent?
Answer: I should hire the agent as long as profits are positive.

Principal Problem 1: The principal must now choose β and α

The problem of choosing α and β is best solved in two steps. In the first step we consider the choice of α given a generic value of β. In the second step, we choose the optimal level of β, taking explicitly into account the solution to the first step.

Choice of α. Let's first consider the optimal choice of α given β. For given choice of β, the principal will want to pay a salary that ensures that the worker accepts the contract. Alternatively, the firm must choose a level of α so that the worker will choose to work, or so that the participation constraint is satisfied.

The P constraint simply says that the agent will *work for this principal as long as his utility is as high as the outside option.* Thus, the smallest base pay α that the principal can offer, given that she offers β to the worker, and still get the agent to work for her, is the one that makes the agent just indifferent between accepting and rejecting this offer. In other words, the principal will want to choose an α so that the participation constraint (P) is binding:

$$\alpha = u - \frac{\beta^2}{2\delta} \tag{6.2}$$

This condition gives us an important insight. There is a negative relationship between the fixed payment and the bonus scheme: the fixed payment decreases as the bonus scheme increases. There is a lot of intuition here. The principal must provide the worker with a fixed level of utility u. Such a level can be guaranteed with different combinations of fixed pay and bonus component, taking into account that effort will be in any case chosen optimally. The previous expression shows that for very much larger values of the bonus scheme (a larger β), the choice of α can even become negative. In other words, as the bonus scheme increases, the fixed payment can becomes a payment from the worker to the firm.

Choice of β. Let's analyse the profits of the principals as a function of β, given that the agent is offered a level of α indicated above. We know already that the expected profits of the agents are expected revenues minus expected costs or

$$E[\Pi] = px^e - w^e$$
$$= pe - \alpha - \beta e,$$
$$= (p - \beta)e - \alpha$$

Since the agent chooses effort level e^* to maximize his utility and since we know that $e^* = \frac{\beta}{\delta}$, total profits become

$$E[\Pi] = (p - \beta)\frac{\beta}{\delta} - \alpha$$

Profits depend on three terms, and all three terms depend on β. Let's analyse those terms:

1. Firm profit per unit of sale. This is given by the term $p - \beta$. Since β is the bonus component, the firm gets only $p - \beta$ per output sold. A larger β obviously reduces the firm profit per unit of sale.
2. Total quantity sold depends entirely on worker effort, which we know to be equal to $\frac{\beta}{\delta}$. Larger bonus component β implies larger effort and larger quantity.

3. Finally there is the fixed payment α. As we discussed above, notably on equation 6.2 larger β allows the firm to reduce the fixed payment to the worker, which can also become negative as β increases. In such a case the fixed payment becomes a fixed revenue.

The first two elements make the variable part of profits $(p - \beta)\frac{\beta}{\delta}$, while the last term is the fixed part of profits.

$$\text{Total Profits} = \text{Variable Profits} + \text{Fixed Payment (Revenue)}$$

where the term in parentheses reflects the fact that the fixed payment may turn into a positive revenue. The problem of the firm at this point is simply to select the value of β that maximizes profits. We begin the exposition with a numerical example, and we then move to the formal derivation.

A Numerical Example on the choice of β

Let's consider the problem of the firm with the following numerical example. The price that the firm charges is $p = 2$, the outside option u is equal to 0, and $\delta = 1$.

$$\text{Total Profits} = \text{Variable Profits} + \text{Fixed Payment}$$

$$\text{Fixed Payment} = 1 - \frac{\beta^2}{2}$$

$$\text{Variable Profits} = (2 - \beta)\beta$$

The firm must choose the level of β that maximizes total profits. The fixed payment of the worker decreases with β, so that a larger β means that the fixed payments from the worker increase profits. At the same time, a larger β has two effects on the variable profits. On the one hand, a larger β increases the quantity produced. On the other hand a larger β reduces the margin of each quantity since the firm gets only a share equal to $p - \beta$. Indeed, a β equal to p makes the variable profits equal to 0. Table 6.1 calculates all possible values of profits for different values of β. The value of variable profits is maximum when $\beta = 1$ in the figure. But the table shows that $\beta = 1 = \frac{p}{2}$ is not the optimal profits. The firm can do better by further increasing β (and reducing the variable profits) so as to increase the fixed payment. The maximum is clearly reached when $\beta = p$. Figure 6.4 confirms this finding.

Table 6.1. Profits and utility with different bonus schemes

Firm				Worker			
Beta	Var. rev.	Fixed paym.	Profits	Worker's ut.	Fixed paym.	Bonus	Effort cost
0.000	0.000	0.000	0.000	0.000	0.000	0.000	0.000
0.067	0.129	0.002	0.131	0.000	−0.002	0.004	−0.002
0.133	0.249	0.009	0.258	0.000	−0.009	0.018	−0.009
0.200	0.360	0.020	0.380	0.000	−0.020	0.040	−0.020
0.267	0.462	0.036	0.498	0.000	−0.036	0.071	−0.036
0.333	0.556	0.056	0.611	0.000	−0.056	0.111	−0.056
0.400	0.640	0.080	0.720	0.000	−0.080	0.160	−0.080
0.467	0.716	0.109	0.824	0.000	−0.109	0.218	−0.109
0.533	0.782	0.142	0.924	0.000	−0.142	0.284	−0.142
0.600	0.840	0.180	1.020	0.000	−0.180	0.360	−0.180
0.667	0.889	0.222	1.111	0.000	−0.222	0.444	−0.222
0.733	0.929	0.269	1.198	0.000	−0.269	0.538	−0.269
0.800	0.960	0.320	1.280	0.000	−0.320	0.640	−0.320
0.867	0.982	0.376	1.358	0.000	−0.376	0.751	−0.376
0.933	0.996	0.436	1.431	0.000	−0.436	0.871	−0.436
1.000	1.000	0.500	1.500	0.000	−0.500	1.000	−0.500
1.067	0.996	0.569	1.564	0.000	−0.569	1.138	−0.569
1.133	0.982	0.642	1.624	0.000	−0.642	1.284	−0.642
1.200	0.960	0.720	1.680	0.000	−0.720	1.440	−0.720
1.267	0.929	0.802	1.731	0.000	−0.802	1.604	−0.802
1.333	0.889	0.889	1.778	0.000	−0.889	1.778	−0.889
1.400	0.840	0.980	1.820	0.000	−0.980	1.960	−0.980
1.467	0.782	1.076	1.858	0.000	−1.076	2.151	−1.076
1.533	0.716	1.176	1.891	0.000	−1.176	2.351	−1.176
1.600	0.640	1.280	1.920	0.000	−1.280	2.560	−1.280
1.667	0.556	1.389	1.944	0.000	−1.389	2.778	−1.389
1.733	0.462	1.502	1.964	0.000	−1.502	3.004	−1.502
1.800	0.360	1.620	1.980	0.000	−1.620	3.240	−1.620
1.867	0.249	1.742	1.991	0.000	−1.742	3.484	−1.742
1.933	0.129	1.869	1.998	0.000	−1.869	3.738	−1.869
2.000	0.000	2.000	2.000	0.000	−2.000	4.000	−2.000

Notes: Price: $p = 2$; outside options $u = 0$; $\delta = 1$.

The Formal Solution of the Optimal Bonus Scheme

Substituting the value of α expected profits read:

$$E[\Pi] = (p - \beta)e^* - \alpha$$

$$= (p - \beta)\frac{\beta}{\delta} - \left[u - \frac{\beta^2}{2\delta}\right]$$

$$= \frac{p\beta}{\delta} - u + \frac{\beta^2}{2\delta} - \frac{\beta^2}{\delta}$$

$$= \frac{p\beta}{\delta} - u - \frac{\beta^2}{2\delta}$$

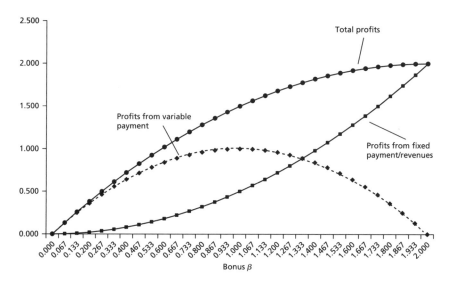

Figure 6.4. Firm profits for different values of the bonus scheme

The principal will maximize profits with respect to β so that the first-order condition solves

$$MaxE[\Pi]_\beta$$

$$\frac{p}{\delta} - \frac{\beta}{\delta} = 0 \qquad (6.3)$$

$$\beta = p \qquad (6.4)$$

which implies that the optimal β is equal to the price. In other words, all the revenues from the sale should go to the worker, and the profits are simply given by the value of α.

With a risk-neutral agent, the optimal commission rate to offer is the franchising commission.

Is the Agent worth enough to the Principal?

The answer to this very last question depends on whether total profits are positive. If total profits are positive, then the Agent is worth enough to the principal. If total profits turn out to be negative, it is better not to offer the contract in the first place.

In light of the optimal β of equation (6.4), the optimal base wage α is

$$\alpha = u - \frac{p^2}{2\delta}$$

from which it follows that the base wage is negative as long as $u = 0$ (the worker is paying for the job). Finally, the net profits of the principal are

$$E[\Pi] = \frac{p\beta}{\delta} - u - \frac{\beta^2}{2\delta}$$

$$= \frac{p^2}{\delta} - u - \frac{p^2}{2\delta}$$

$$= \frac{p^2}{2\delta} - u$$

which are obviously positive as long as

$$u \leq \frac{p^2}{2\delta}.$$

If the latter condition is not satisfied, the principal does not offer the contract to the agent. In other words, the principal has a participation constraint which requires positive expected profits, or $E[\Pi] > 0$.

Summing up

For a risk-neutral agent the optimal compensation scheme of the type $w = \alpha + \beta x$ is such that

$$\beta = p$$

$$\alpha = u - \frac{p^2}{2\delta}$$

and the agent will accept at the utility u. Further, effort is such that

$$e^* = \frac{p}{\delta}$$

The optimal contract is described at point C in Fig. 6.5. The level of utility in equilibrium is exactly equal to that of the outside option, while the incentive

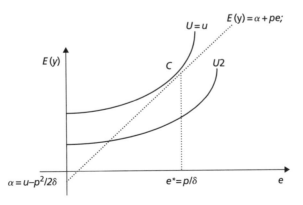

Figure 6.5. The optimal contract

scheme has the slope equal to the price. The optimal effort is chosen at level $e^* = \frac{p}{\delta}$ and the α is negative in the figure, so that the worker buys the job.

6.3 **The Basic Scheme with Non-Negative Payments**

In the rest of this chapter we analyse two important departures from the basic scheme. Both departures are very realistic, and help us to understand why, in real life labour markets, the franchising scheme analysed above is not observed very often. The first departure we analyse is a constraint on the worker's ability to make negative payment to the firm. The second departure (analysed in the next section) deals with risk aversion.

In this section we assume that the worker reservation utility is zero, so that $u = 0$. In this case the optimal franchising scheme would require the worker to make an up-front payment to the firm equal to $p^2/2\delta$. Let us now assume that the worker cannot make any up-front payments to the firm. This is a natural constraint. This situation arises for a number of reasons. First, and most importantly, it is not obvious that a labour contract that imposes a negative up-front payment is at all legal. Second, the worker may not have the resources to obtain such payments and would need to rely on bank credit. In the latter case the worker may be able to borrow some money for the payment, but such borrowing would probably be limited. In any event, we here assume that no borrowing can take place, or that the labour law simply makes such payment undoable. The question is what happens to the optimal scheme in this case.

The existence of a non-negative constraint on α makes it impossible to implement the optimal contract, which we saw was based on having $p = \beta$ and obtaining all the profits from the fixed payment. What should the firm do in this case? It is obvious that in this case the total profits will be just equal to the variable profits,

$$\text{Total Profits} = \text{Variable Profits}$$
$$= (p - \beta)e^*$$
$$= (p - \beta)\frac{\beta}{\delta}$$

and the firm must select the level of β that maximizes variable profits.

We know that the effort chosen by the worker is maximum when $\beta = p$. But we also know that if the firm chooses $\beta = p$, the effort obtained and the quantity produced will be maximum, but profits per unit of sale will be zero. It is clear that in this case the optimal compensation scheme will require lower effort. An important result follows.

When negative payments are not allowed, the optimal compensation is never at the maximum effort, and the firm chooses a level of $\beta < p$.

Let's call $\hat{\beta}$ the level of bonus chosen by the firm when there is a non-negative constraint on α. What will be the optimal level of $\hat{\beta}$ in this case? Let's first look at the numerical example. Figure 6.4 immediately suggests that the optimal $\hat{\beta}$ corresponds to $\beta = 1 = p/2$. Note also that the firm could set a larger $\hat{\beta}$ and still make positive profits, but such profits would be lower.

Let's now formally obtain the optimal $\hat{\beta}$.

$$Max \ (p - \hat{\beta})\frac{\hat{\beta}}{\delta} \qquad when \ \alpha = 0$$

so that the firm chooses $\hat{\beta}$

$$-\frac{\hat{\beta}}{\delta} + \frac{p - \hat{\beta}}{\delta} = 0$$

$$\hat{\beta} = \frac{p}{2}$$

When non-negative payments are ruled out, the optimal commission scheme is the 50 per cent commission rate.

Let's see now what the worker utility is in the case of a full variable payment

$$U(w^e(\hat{\beta}), e^*(\hat{\beta})) = w^e(\hat{\beta}) - \frac{\delta}{2}e^*(\hat{\beta})^2$$

$$= \frac{\hat{\beta}}{\delta}\hat{\beta} - \frac{\hat{\beta}^2}{2\delta}$$

$$= \frac{p^2}{8\delta} > 0$$

where we recall that $u = 0$ in this case. The utility level is strictly positive, and larger than the outside option. In other words, the worker gets a rent, or a value of the utility above the reservation level, as the following remark shows:

When non-negative payments are impossible, the worker gets an extra rent and enjoys a level of utility larger than the reservation value.

It is also clear that the firm reduces its expected profits. In the example in the table the profits of the firms when $\beta = 1$ are much lower than the profits under the first best scheme.

Summing up

For a risk-neutral agent with reservation utility $u = 0$ the optimal compensation scheme with non-negative payments is of the type $w = \beta x$

such that

$$\hat{\beta} = \frac{p}{2}$$

$$\hat{\alpha} = 0$$

Further, effort is chosen so that

$$e^* = \frac{p}{2\delta}$$

The level of utility in equilibrium is strictly larger than the outside option (which was normalized to zero in this case).

6.4 The Basic Scheme when the Agent is Risk Averse

The presence of risk aversion changes the compensation schemes. In the baseline contract, the worker (or the agent) bears all the uncertainty associated with the luck component of output. The firm gets a fixed payment while the worker is obliged to observe fluctuations in her income. When the realization of the luck component is high, the compensation increases, while it falls when the realization of the luck component is low. As long as the worker is risk neutral, she does not care about income variability. This is no longer true in the case of risk aversion. When the worker is risk averse (and the firm risk neutral), the optimal distribution of risk calls for the firm to take up some of the risk. Indeed, as we will see, the optimal compensation implies a reduction in the bonus component and an increase in the fixed payment. In other words, the principal provides some insurance to the agent. Providing insurance, however, has an impact on effort and efficiency, which we know to be maximum under a pure bonus scheme. In other words, the optimal contract under risk aversion is the one that solves this *efficiency/insurance* trade-off.

6.4.1 THE AGENT PREFERENCES

General Agent Preferences. We now assume that the agent likes higher expected wage w^e but he dislikes income variability $Var(w)$. In this section we use a mean-variance utility function, whereby utility increases with the expected value w^e and decreases with the variance of the compensation and with the effort

$$U(w, e) = w^e - \lambda Var(w) - \delta \frac{e^2}{2}$$

The difference between risk aversion and risk neutrality on the agent's preferences is analysed next.

A risk-neutral agent: A risk-neutral agent is somebody who does not care about income variability, as was analysed in the first part of the chapter, so that for a risk-neutral guy $\lambda = 0$ or

$$U(w, e) = w^e - \delta \frac{e^2}{2}$$

$$= \alpha + \beta e - \delta \frac{e^2}{2}$$

Risk-averse guy with mean variance preferences: A risk-averse guy with mean variance preferences is somebody who does care about income variability, so that his utility function is

$$U(w, e) = w^e - \lambda \, Var(w) - \delta \frac{e^2}{2}$$

The larger λ is, the more the worker is averse to income variability.

The linear compensation that we are analysing ($w = \alpha + \beta x$) has a variance that is simply given by $Var(w) = \beta^2 \, Var(x)$. Since the variance of the random variable x is constant and equal to v the variance of the compensation is $Var(w) = \beta^2 v$ so that the utility can be written as

$$U(w, e) = \alpha + \beta e - \lambda \beta^2 v - \delta \frac{e^2}{2}$$

6.4.2 THE PROBLEMS OF THE AGENT

We now solve the two problems of the agents under the case of risk aversion with mean variance preferences. We begin with the choice of effort under the general **bonus contract**: In the bonus contract $w = \alpha + \beta x$ so that $w^e = \alpha + \beta e$ and $Var(w) = \beta^2 v$ and the utility level is

$$Max_e : U(w, e) = \alpha + \beta e - \lambda \beta^2 v - \delta \frac{e^2}{2}$$

which implies that the optimal choice of effort is the condition (IC) above, or that

$$e^* = \frac{\beta}{\delta} \qquad \text{(IC: Incentive Compatibility Constraint)}$$

The choice of the optimal effort does not depend on the presence of risk aversion.

The second problem of the worker is whether participating in the contract is convenient, since the worker can enjoy an outside option which yields expected utility equal to u.

The utility of the agent is

$$U(w, e) = \alpha + \beta e^* - \lambda \beta^2 v - \delta \frac{e^{*2}}{2}$$

since $e^* = \frac{\beta}{\delta}$ it follows that participation is convenient if and only if

$$U(w(e^*), e^*)) \geq u$$

which implies that

$$\alpha + \frac{\beta^2}{\delta} - \frac{\beta^2}{2\delta} - \lambda \beta^2 v \geq u$$

$$\alpha + \frac{\beta^2}{2\delta} - \lambda \beta^2 v \geq u$$

so that

$$\alpha + \beta^2 [\frac{1 - \lambda v 2\delta}{2\delta}] \geq u \qquad \text{((P) Participation Constraint-Risk Aversion)}$$

The presence of risk aversion changes the participation constraint.

The presence of risk aversion makes participation in a bonus scheme a less attractive option to the worker. A bonus scheme is associated with variable wages, since the luck component of the output does affect the worker's utility. As one can see from the participation constraint required, the larger the risk aversion component v, for given β and α, the less likely is participation in the deal. We now move to the problem of the principal.

6.4.3 THE PROBLEM OF THE PRINCIPAL WITH A RISK-AVERSE AGENT: THE OPTIMAL BONUS SCHEME

The principal must now chooses $\tilde{\beta}$ and $\tilde{\alpha}$ where we indicate variables with a $\sim$ symbol to indicate that we are analysing the case of risk aversion.

Choice of $\tilde{\alpha}$. Let's first consider the optimal choice of $\tilde{\alpha}$ given $\tilde{\beta}$. For given choice of $\tilde{\beta}$ the principal will want to pay a salary so that the agent will choose to work. The agent chooses to work for this principal as long as he is just as well off as at his next-base opportunity. Thus, the smallest base pay $\tilde{\alpha}$ that the principal can offer, if she offers $\tilde{\beta}$, and still get the agent to work for her is

$$\tilde{\alpha} + \frac{\tilde{\beta}^2}{2\delta} - \lambda\tilde{\beta}^2 v = u$$

$$\tilde{\alpha} = u - \tilde{\beta}^2 \left[\frac{1 - \lambda v 2\delta}{2\delta} \right]$$

Choice of $\tilde{\beta}$. Let's study the profits of the principal when she offers $\tilde{\beta}$ and the agent is going to work by offering a level of $\tilde{\alpha}$ as indicated above. The expected profits of the agents are

$$E[\Pi] = pE[x] - w^e$$

$$= pe^* - \tilde{\alpha} - \tilde{\beta}e^*$$

$$\text{s.t. } e^* = \frac{\tilde{\beta}}{\delta} \text{ and } \tilde{\alpha} = u - \frac{\tilde{\beta}^2}{2\delta} + \lambda\tilde{\beta}^2 v$$

Substituting the two constraints in the objective functions one has

$$E[\Pi] = \frac{p\tilde{\beta}}{\delta} - u - \frac{\tilde{\beta}^2}{2\delta} - \lambda\tilde{\beta}^2 v$$

The principal will maximize profit with respect to $\tilde{\beta}$ so that the first-order condition solves

$$\frac{p}{\delta} - \frac{\tilde{\beta}}{\delta} - 2\lambda\tilde{\beta}v = 0$$

$$\tilde{\beta} = \frac{p}{1 + 2\lambda\delta v}$$

which implies that the optimal $\tilde{\beta}$ is less than the price (as long as $\lambda > 0$, $v > 0$ and $\delta > 0$).

For a risk averse guy, the optimal commission rate is never the franchising compensation scheme, i.e. $0 < \tilde{\beta} < p$

Summing up

With a risk-averse agent the scheme works as follows

$$\tilde{\beta} = \frac{p}{1 + 2\lambda\delta v}$$

$$\tilde{\alpha} = u - \tilde{\beta}^2 \left[\frac{1 - \lambda v 2\delta}{2\delta} \right]$$

$$\alpha = u - \frac{p^2}{(1 + 2\lambda\delta v)^2} \left[\frac{1 - \lambda v 2\delta}{2\delta} \right]$$

☐ APPENDIX 6.1. WHAT IF THE PRINCIPAL AND THE RISK-AVERSE AGENT COULD CONTRACT ON EFFORT

Let's start by defining the surplus from the deal as the sum of the utility of each party, net of the respective outside option. This is identical to the difference between the revenues from the deal and the workers' cost of eliciting effort. The surplus is then

$$S = (\Pi - 0) + (U - u)$$

$$= pe - w + w - \frac{\delta e^2}{2} - u$$

$$= pe - \frac{\delta e^2}{2} - u$$

and let us assume that the two parties could contract directly on effort, rather than relying on the output x. Let's see what the effort choice is that maximizes the surplus from the job. In other words, the optimal effort is the one that makes the marginal surplus zero (*i.e.* $\frac{\partial S}{\partial e} = 0$). We call the optimal level of effort e^0 and it is easy to see that

$$p - \delta e^0 = 0$$

from which it follows that

$$e^0 = \frac{p}{\delta}$$

The level of effort that maximizes the surplus is $e^0 = p/\delta$.
So that the maximum value of the surplus is (evaluating S at e^0)

$$S(e^0) = \frac{p^2}{\delta} - \frac{\delta p^2}{\delta^2 2} = \frac{p^2}{2\delta}$$

and the job is efficient as long as

$$S(e^0) > 0$$

$$\frac{p^2}{2\delta} > u$$

The analysis above shows clearly that the efficient contract is identical to the contract between the principal and a risk-neutral agent. In other words, with a risk-neutral agent, the franchising payment implements the first best contract.

Thus, in the case of risk neutrality on the part of the agent, there is no cost linked to the impossibility of contracting directly on effort.

The previous expression gives the joint value of the surplus, which still needs to be allocated to the worker and to the firm. The payment w is chosen so that the worker's utility is identical to the outside option $U = u$ so that

$$w = u + \frac{\delta e^{o2}}{2}$$

The worker will receive exactly the utility level u, while the firm will get all the uncertainty and will have a payment equal to the residual value, in other words

$$\Pi(e^o) = \frac{p^2}{2\delta} - u$$

and the deal will be struck as long as

$$\frac{p^2}{2\delta} > u$$

and the principal will get all the risk.

In the case of risk aversion things change, and the solution that we analysed in the text (the one with a bonus scheme that is less than one) does not implement the first best. **What is the cost of being unable to contract on effort?** The cost of being unable to contract on effort is given by the drop in profits with respect to those obtained with the optimal bonus contract. The agent, once he is offered the contract $\tilde{\alpha}$ and $\tilde{\beta}$, gets a level of utility that is equal to its outside payment u. The principal profits under the optimal bonus schemes are

$$\Pi^* = pe^* - (\tilde{\alpha} + \tilde{\beta}e^*)$$

where

$$\tilde{\alpha} = u - \frac{p^2}{(1 + 2\lambda\delta v)^2}\left[\frac{1 - \lambda v 2\delta}{2\delta}\right]$$

$$\tilde{\beta} = \frac{p}{1 + 2\lambda\delta v}$$

$$e^* = \frac{\tilde{\beta}}{\delta}$$

So that profits become

$$\Pi^* = \frac{p\tilde{\beta}}{\delta} - \alpha - \frac{\tilde{\beta}^2}{\delta}$$

$$= \frac{p^2}{1 + 2\lambda\delta v}\frac{1}{\delta} - u + \frac{p^2}{(1 + 2\lambda\delta v)^2}\left[\frac{1 - \lambda v 2\delta}{2\delta}\right] - \frac{p^2}{(1 + 2\lambda\delta v)^2}\frac{1}{\delta}$$

$$= \frac{p^2}{1 + 2\lambda\delta v}\frac{1}{\delta} - u + \frac{p^2}{(1 + 2\lambda\delta v)^2}\left[\frac{-1 - 2\lambda\delta v}{2\delta}\right]$$

$$= \frac{p^2}{2\delta}\left[\frac{1}{1 + 2\lambda\delta v}\right] - u$$

So that the cost of dealing with a risk-averse guy is

$$\Pi^o - \Pi^* = \frac{p^2}{2\delta} - \frac{p^2}{2\delta}\left[\frac{1}{1 + 2\lambda\delta v}\right]$$

$$= \frac{p^2}{2\delta}\left[1 - \frac{1}{1 + 2\lambda\delta v}\right]$$

$$= \frac{p^2}{\delta}\left[\frac{\lambda v}{1 + 2\lambda\delta v}\right]$$

The cost of being unable to contract on effort is equal to zero if $\lambda = 0$ and if $v = 0$.

7 Pay for Performance with Wage Constraints

7.1 **Introduction**

The baseline theory of optimal compensations suggests that properly designed incentive contracts can be very effective in extracting workers' effort. A fixed wage scheme, where compensation is independent of output, does not provide incentives to the worker. As we have seen in the previous chapter, in response to a fixed wage, a utility maximizer worker would choose the minimum amount of effort. Conversely, bonus schemes, where a fixed wage is mixed with a bonus component proportional to output, are a much more effective compensation scheme. We have also seen that as a benchmark limit case, when the worker is risk neutral and no other constraints are binding, the optimal compensation scheme is an extreme bonus scheme, with a negative fixed payment up front and a bonus component identical to the price (we called such a scheme the franchising scheme). In such a setting, production efficiency is maximized and the worker becomes the residual claimant. Yet, we know that such a scheme is hardly attainable in real life labour markets, since it requires the worker to pay for the job.

In real life labour markets and real life organizations, it is very difficult to implement the franchising scheme. Even if agents are risk neutral, payments from the workers to the firms are barely conceivable. The previous chapter has shown that the optimal franchising contract turns into a 50 per cent commission rate as soon as negative payments are not allowed. In such a setting the firms set a base pay equal to zero, and share with the worker the variable outcome.

This chapter looks into compensation behaviour under more realistic wage constraints. For example, firms often have to offer a simple fixed wage independent of performance. Sometimes such a wage can be chosen by the firm and sometimes it is negotiated outside the firm's control, either by a minimum wage constraint or by industry-wide collective agreements. What should the firm do when it is forced to pay a fixed wage, independent of output? How should such a wage be chosen? Is it possible for the firm to obtain the maximum profits when the wage contract must simply be a fixed (positive) wage. The answer is yes, if three conditions hold: (i) the wage level can be optimally chosen by the firm; (ii) a minimum amount of output can be observed and imposed on the employment contract; and (iii) workers are homogeneous vis-à-vis their ability. When one of these conditions breaks, some profits must be given away. This chapter focuses on heterogeneity.

In this chapter we explore in detail the impact on firm performance of worker heterogeneity. We will assume that firms face a variety of workers, and different workers have different attitudes toward efforts. Ability is like a DNA component known to the worker but not known to the firm. We will see that a firm that offers a single wage with a minimum output requirement surrenders some rent to workers, and the most efficient production cannot be realized. Some workers in the firm enjoy a *pure economic rent*, and are strictly better off than their best outside options. This is a situation that probably gets closer to most real life firms. In most firms, workers take it easy and enjoy a specific rent.

The core of the chapter studies how the firm can improve its situation when some of its workers are enjoying a pure economic rent. We basically study the effect of a bonus scheme with a minimum guarantee, or a scheme in which a minimum wage is guaranteed, but if workers do well, they can obtain additional income. We will see that such a scheme is likely to improve productivity vis-à-vis the simple fixed payment with minimum output. We will show that two different effects emerge from such a move: efficiency effects and sorting effects. The *efficiency effects* refer to the improvements in performance and productivity of workers that are already in the firm. The *sorting effects* refer to a change in the composition of the workforce in the firm.

The second part of the chapter shows how a minimum guarantee with bonus scheme worked in a real life case study. We will review the *Safelite* case, a window installer in the United States that introduced a pay for performance scheme with minimum wage guarantee. The case study will clearly show that sizeable sorting and efficiency effects are linked to the changes of remuneration schemes.

7.2 **Heterogeneous Ability: The Set-Up**

The main analytical novelty in this chapter is the emphasis on workers' heterogeneity. To simplify the analysis, *we assume throughout the chapter that individuals are risk neutral and there is no uncertainty.* We will also assume that the firm is producing a homogeneous product whose price is equal to 1.

The quantity of output produced by an individual is indicated by x. The amount of production depends not only on individual effort, but also on individual ability. We assume that individual ability differs across individuals. Specifically, output x is related to ability by the following relationship:

$$x = a + e \qquad (7.1)$$

where a is ability and e is effort. a is a fixed individual parameter *unobservable to the firm* but fully known by the agent. The previous relationship suggests that for a given effort, an individual with larger ability can produce a larger quantity of output. We also assume that the outside option faced by each individual grows with the ability of the agent:

$$\text{outside option} = au$$

so that workers with larger ability have better outside options. This makes sense, since better workers have better outside chances.

Let's see how the preferences and the indifference curve change with ability. The utility function is the same as the one we used in the previous chapter, so that utility depends positively on wage income and negatively on effort.[1] Since output and ability are linked by the relationship $x = a' + e$, the utility function reads for an individual with ability a'

$$U = \left\{ \begin{array}{ll} w & \text{if } x < a' \\ w - \frac{\delta(x-a)^2}{2} & \text{if } x \geq a' \end{array} \right\}$$

To properly understand the utility function introduced above let us study the indifference curve in a space $[x, w]$. An indifference curve in such a setting will refer to all the combinations of x and w that give the same utility to the agent. For this purpose, we need to define the **maximum output at zero effort**.

- Each individual has a maximum output level $\bar{x} = a'$ that he or she can produce without exercising any effort.
- Beyond the zero effort output level $\bar{x} = a'$, individuals need to exercise effort to produce more output.
- Individuals that are more able, have larger output $\bar{x} = a'$.

With respect to the indifference curves in the $[w, x]$ space, the following properties apply

- Indifference curves are flat up to the maximum output at zero effort.
- Indifference curves are upward sloping beyond $\bar{x} = a'$.
- The slope of the indifference curve depends on ability, and less able individuals have steeper indifference curves.

The formal definition of the indifference curve at utility level k for an individual with ability a' is given by the following relationship

$$w = \left\{ \begin{array}{ll} k & \text{if } x < a' \\ k + \frac{\delta(x-a)^2}{2} & \text{if } x \geq a' \end{array} \right\}$$

---

[1] The utility function in the previous chapter was written as $U = w - \frac{\delta e^2}{2}$.

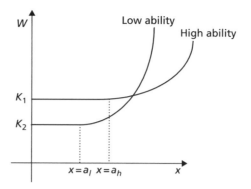

Figure 7.1. Indifference curves with heterogeneous ability

Up to quantity level $x = a'$ the indifference curve is flat. For obtaining further output, effort needs to be exercised and individuals must be compensated with further income. The associated slope[2] is

$$\frac{dw}{dx} = \left\{ \begin{array}{ll} 0 & \text{if } x < a' \\ \delta(x - a') & \text{if } x \geq a' \end{array} \right\}$$

Figure 7.1 presents the indifference curve for two different levels of utility k_1 and k_2 for two different individuals with ability a_l and a_h. The individual with ability a_l has a flat indifference curve up to $x = a_l$ while the individual with ability a_h has indifference curves that are flat up to the point $x = a_h$. Another important dimension to consider is the slope. Consider the point of Fig. 7.1 where the two indifference curves cross.[3] The individual with low ability clearly has a steeper indifference curve. Economically, this means that he or she needs to be compensated with more wages to increase his or her output. This is because more output is more costly (in terms of effort) for the individual with low ability.

---

[2] The formal proof of the indifference curve is given in what follows. Let's recall that, in general, the slope of the indifference curve is given by

$$\frac{\partial U}{\partial w} dw + \frac{\partial U}{\partial x} dx = 0$$

$$\frac{dw}{dx} = -\frac{\frac{\partial U}{\partial x}}{\frac{\partial U}{\partial w}}$$

If x is lower than the zero effort output the slope is zero (since $\frac{\partial U}{\partial x}$), while if x is beyond the zero output level the

$$\frac{dw}{dx} = \left\{ \begin{array}{ll} 0 & \text{if } x < a \\ \delta(x - a) & \text{if } x \geq a \end{array} \right\}$$

[3] The indifference curves for the same individual never cross. Yet, the indifference curves of two *different* individuals can and do cross each other.

7.3 **Fixed Wage with Minimum Output**

Before introducing the effects of heterogeneous ability, we need to understand the behaviour of a firm that pays a fixed wage with minimum output. We begin by assuming that ability is constant.

The idea of a minimum level of output is simply to impose a minimum standard of quantity, so that if a worker does not reach such a minimum standard, the firm is not going to hire the worker, or the employment relationship can be interrupted without cost. In this section we label a job $[w, x_{\min}]$ as a job that pays a fixed wage $\alpha = w$ and requires an output $x_{\min}$.

Appendix 7.1 describes how a minimum output can be chosen optimally, and under which conditions a firm that offers a job $[w, x_{\min}]$ can do as well as a firm that uses the franchising scheme. In practice, a firm that offers a *fixed wage with minimum output* can obtain the same level of profits as an efficient level of output only if various conditions hold. Such conditions are

- There is no uncertainty, so that the output observed reflects the effort exercised.
- There is no heterogeneity in the workforce. In other words, the parameter a is fixed in the population.
- The minimum level of output $x_{\min}$ is chosen by the firm so as to obtain from the worker the efficient level of effort.

Note that when we talk about an efficient level of profits, we mean a level of profits that is as high as the one that would be obtained by a firm that implements the franchising scheme, as indicated by equation 7.2 in Appendix 7.1. Obviously the wage in this setting must be properly chosen by the firm, and the Appendix shows how such a wage can be selected.

Things are more complicated if the wage is completely fixed and outside the firm's control. In this case the firm can hardly make any choice. All it can do is to select a minimum quantity of output $x_{\min}$. In other words, if the wage is completely fixed at $\bar{w}$, all the firm can do is select a quantity so that the worker participation constraint is binding, and operate if profits are positive.

7.4 **Pure Rent: Fixed Wage with Minimum Output and Heterogeneous Ability**

Let's now explicitly introduce heterogeneous ability and let's describe the problem of a firm that $[w, x_{\min}]$ where $x_{\min}$ is some level of output. The firm we are considering pays a fixed wage w regardless of ability, and requires some level of minimum output $x_{\min}$ for working at the firm. Recall that ability is

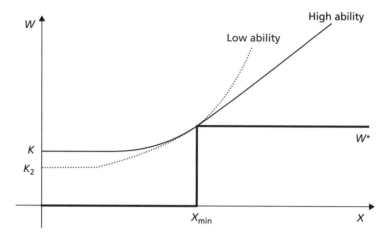

Figure 7.2. Optimal solution with fixed wage and minimum output when ability is heterogeneous

known to the individual but it is not known to the firm. The problem can first be described graphically.

Let us first consider the constraint faced by each worker. The constraint is similar to the linear constraint with the fixed wage that we have analysed in Fig. 6.1, with the only difference that the wage w is obtained only for quantity produced larger than the selected minimum x_{min}. The constraint is thus a *step function*, with the step that corresponds to the point at the minimum output x_{min}.

Given this constraint, it is clear that no employees will ever want to produce more than the minimum required by the firm x_{min}. At the same time, producing less than x_{min} is not allowed. Figure 7.1 presents the indifference curve while Fig. 7.2 describes the equilibrium with minimum output for two individuals with different ability levels. As is clear from the picture, the individual with high ability reaches a utility level k_1 while the individual with low ability reaches a level of utility equal to k_2. Clearly we have $k_1 > k_2$. This makes a lot of sense: an individual with larger ability must exercise less effort to produce an output equal to x_{min} so that he will have a larger level of utility for working at the firm. Yet, there is another key dimension to consider, namely the fact that individuals with larger ability have also larger outside options, and may not find it interesting working in the firm. We need to solve the problem of which worker will self-select for the firm that we are analysing.

The utility for an individual that works for this firm with ability a is

$$U = \begin{cases} w & \text{if } a > x_{min} \\ w - \frac{\delta(x-a)^2}{2} & \text{if } a \leq x_{min} \end{cases}$$

The condition for working at a firm that pays according to the contract $[w, x_{min}]$ is

$$au \leq \begin{array}{ll} w - \frac{\delta(x_{min}-a)^2}{2} & \text{if } a \leq x_{min} \\[6pt] w & \text{if } a > x_{min} \end{array}$$

More able individuals find it easier and easier to produce the minimum amount of output, and thus need to exercise lower and lower effort at the margin. Beyond a level of utility $a = x_{min}$, individuals do not even need to exercise effort to obtain x_{min} and their utility no longer increases. The outside option increases linearly with a. This suggests that the condition above is satisfied for

$$a_l \leq a \leq a_h$$

The solution is clearly described in Fig. 7.3. Individuals with utility level below a_l are characterized by an outside option (the straight line in the figure) that is larger than the utility for working at the firm. Such characteristics hold also for individuals with ability larger than a_h. While individuals in the positions a_l and a_h, the two extremes, are just indifferent and their participation constraint is binding, individuals in between are enjoying a pure economic *rent*. The rent emerges since the firm must obey an egalitarian wage policy.

When a firm pays a job $[w, x_{min}]$ and there is heterogeneity in the population, a subset of workers in the population enjoys a pure surplus by working at the firm.

The result can be summarized by saying that there are three types of worker in the population.

1. Individual workers that are not good enough to work at the firm. Those are the workers for which $a < a_l$;

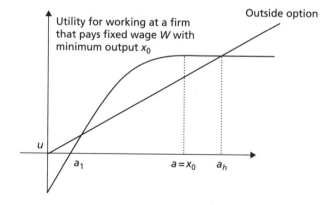

Figure 7.3. Individual self-selection for working at the firm that pays w, x_{min}

2. Individual workers that work at the firm that pays $[w, x_{min}]$ and are those workers for whom $a \in [a_l, a_h]$; Such workers (with the exception of those at the boundaries) enjoy a surplus inside the firm.
3. Individuals workers that are too good to work at the firm, so that $a > a_h$.

7.4.1 A NUMERICAL EXAMPLE

Consider a firm that is forced to pay a fixed wage equal to w to all its workforce. Assume that the utility function is

$$U = \begin{cases} w & \text{if } a \geq x_{min} \\ w - \frac{\delta(x-a)^2}{2} & \text{if } a < x_{min} \end{cases}$$

so that $\delta = 1$. We also assume that $u = 1/2$ and that $\bar{a} = 1$, so that we initially keep ability constant. We label the output associated with the optimal effort x_o and its value is

$$x_o = \bar{a} + e_o$$

$$x_o = \bar{a} + \frac{1}{\delta}$$

$$x_o = 2$$

since $\bar{a} = \delta = 1$. What is the wage that the firm should fix? To find the wage recall that the wage must satisfy

$$w^* = \bar{a}u + \frac{\delta(x_o - \bar{a})^2}{2}$$

$$= \frac{1}{2} + \frac{1}{2} = 1$$

This suggests that when ability is constant and equal to $\bar{a} = 1$ a firm that pays $[w = 1, x_o = 2]$ behaves efficiently. The profits of the firm are $\Pi = \frac{1}{2\delta} + \bar{a}(1 - u) = 1$.

Assume now that workers are heterogeneous and that a is uniformly distributed between $a_{min} = 0$ and $a_{max} = 4$. Let's see which workers will choose to work at this firm that pays $[w^* = 1, x_o = 2]$. The condition is

$$w^* - \frac{\delta(x_o - a)^2}{2} \geq au$$

$$1 - \frac{(2 - a)^2}{2} \geq \frac{a}{2}$$

whose solutions are obtained by the following quadratic equation

$$a^2 - 3a + 2 = 0$$

$$a_l = 1$$

$$a_h = 2$$

Individuals with $a < 1$ are not good enough to work in the firm; individuals with $a > 2$ are too good to work in the firm and will choose their outside option. Individuals in between the two values (a_l, a_h) are enjoying a rent, since they get a utility which is larger than their outside option. In other words, heterogeneity implies that the firm that pays a fixed wage is no longer able to induce all workers to be just to their outside option. Take an individual with ability $a = 3/2$. The utility for working at the firm $w = 1, x_o = 2$ is 7/8 while the outside option is 3/4, so that he is enjoying a rent equal to 1/8. The firm's profits are still 1.

7.5 Performance Pay with a Two-Tier Wage System

Let's consider a firm that is offering a minimum wage with minimum output attached, or a job that pays $[w, x_o]$. We have seen in the previous section that such a firm has to surrender some rent to some individuals, in particular to the individuals that have ability strictly larger than a_l and strictly lower than a_h. What we want to consider is whether the firm may implement a two-tier wage system, or a compensation structure that *guarantees the minimum wage to all the workers and gives the option of having a bonus scheme for some individuals that are particularly productive*. With such a scheme, the basic pay that is offered to each individual is still maintained, while some workers have the option, if they want it, to perform better. Such compensation is for example consistent with a minimum wage to be paid to workers plus a bonus scheme for high-performing workers.

We want to understand what will happen to this firm. In particular, we are interested in two dimensions of the phenomenon that we label incentive effects and sorting effect.

Incentive effects: How will the performance of the individuals who are enjoying a rent with a fixed and egalitarian wage change?
Sorting effects: what will happen to the quality composition of the labour force inside the firm?

Let's consider a firm that is currently paying the following scheme $[\bar{x}, \bar{w}]$ where $\bar{x}$ is the minimum output required and $\bar{w}$ is the fixed wage that is paid

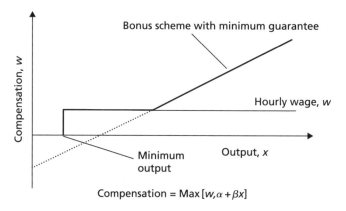

$$\text{Compensation} = \text{Max}\,[w, \alpha + \beta x]$$

Figure 7.4. Bonus scheme with minimum wage guarantee (and minimum output required)

to all workers that produce at least $\bar{x}$. The firm is offering a performance pay w^{pr} that can be described by our general bonus scheme as

$$w^{pr} = \alpha + \beta x$$

where β is the incentive factor ($\beta \leq 1$) and α is the fixed payment for zero output (which we know can be negative). All the individuals that produce more than $\bar{x}$ can be eligible for the performance plan. Figure 7.4 describes the constraints that each worker faces with this scheme. The fixed wage works as a step function exactly like the one we analysed in Fig. 7.2. Yet the figure reports also the constraint of a general bonus scheme, described by an upward-sloping line with intercept equal to α (negative in the figure). The bold lines report the actual compensation. As long as the individual produces the minimum output required, a wage equal to $\bar{w}$ is guaranteed, and only if the pay with the bonus scheme is larger than such value is the bonus scheme effective. In formula, the compensation that we are analysing is described by the following:

$$\text{Compensation} = \begin{cases} 0 & \text{for } x < \bar{x} \\ \text{Max}[\beta x + \alpha, \bar{w}] & \text{for } x > \bar{x} \end{cases}$$

where output $\bar{x}$ is required.

Let's see which individuals would choose to produce under the bonus scheme. We now solve the problem for the quantity x, but we know that there is a one-to-one relationship between effort and output, as described by $x = a + e$. Let's call x^{pr} the quantity of output that maximizes the utility. This means that x^{pr} is the solution to

$$Max_x \qquad U(w^{pr}, x)$$

$$U(w^{pr}, x) = \alpha + \beta x - \frac{\delta(x - a)^2}{2}$$

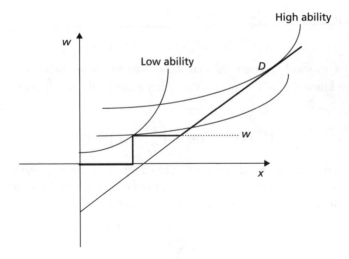

Figure 7.5. Individual optimization with a two-tier system

whose first-order condition implies the following solution

$$x^{pr} = \frac{\beta}{\delta} + a$$

Different individuals with different levels of ability have different preferred quantity x^{pr}. Obviously, an individual who features $x^{pr} < \bar{x}$ would not sell himself into the piece rate scheme but would produce at the minimum required output. The key decision to be taken is for the individuals that under the performance scheme produce an amount of output x^{pr} that is larger than the minimum required output. Assume that there is at least an individual that features $x^{pr} > x^{\min}$. The choice is described by Fig. 7.5. Without the bonus scheme individuals with different levels of utility choose position C, since it does not make any sense to produce more. Things are different if the bonus scheme becomes available. In Fig. 7.5 the low-ability individual chooses to remain at point C, since a move toward the bonus scheme would be associated with a lower indifference curve. Things are different for the high-ability individual, who by moving to point D in the figure increases his or her utility.

7.5.1 THE FORMAL SOLUTION TO THE TWO-TIER WAGE SYSTEM

We want to study how ability influences the decision between the bonus scheme or the fixed wage. An individual with ability level a will choose the bonus scheme if

$$U^{pr}\left(w^{pr}, x^{pr}, a\right) > U(\bar{w}, \bar{x}, a)$$

where we explicitly recognized that utility depends also on the ability level. Since we know that $x^{pr} = \frac{\beta}{\delta} + a$ the utility associated with the performance plan is

$$U^{pr}(w^{pr}, x^{pr}, a) = \left(\frac{\beta^2}{2\delta} + \alpha\right) + \beta a$$

which clearly shows that individuals with larger utility level a get larger utility from the bonus scheme. The utility associated with operating under the minimum guarantee (which corresponds to point C in Fig. 7.5) is

$$U(\bar{w}, \bar{x}, a) = \begin{cases} w & \text{for } a > \bar{x} \\ w - \frac{\delta(\bar{x}-a)^2}{2} & \text{for } a < \bar{x} \end{cases}$$

The previous condition simply says that the utility level associated with the minimum guarantee is at most w. This is not surprising. Very able individuals can obtain the minimum output x without any effort and therefore get a utility equal to w. Conversely, individuals with lower ability need to exercise effort and reach a lower utility. Since the utility with the minimum guarantee has an upper bound level, it is clear that there exists a threshold level $\tilde{a}^+$ such that for all utility levels above the individuals are better off in the bonus scheme. In formula, we can write that

$$U^{pr}(w^{pr}, x^{pr}, a) > U(\bar{w}, \bar{x}, a) \qquad \text{for } a > \tilde{a}^+$$

The situation is clearly described in Fig. 7.6. The horizontal axis reports different utility levels, while the vertical axis reports the utility levels. Let's now focus on the straight line labelled *PPP* and the curved lane labelled Fixed Wage. As one can see, the curved line reaches an upper bound for ability level beyond $a = \bar{x}$ while the line labelled *PPP* is upward sloping. Clearly, individuals beyond $\tilde{a}^+$ are better off in the bonus scheme.

Let's now consider the entire population of individuals with ability that can vary from $a_{\min}$ to $a_{\max}$. In the previous section we established that the population potentially employed by the firm that was paying according to $[\bar{w}, \bar{x}]$ was described by all the individuals that belong to an interval $[a_l, a_h]$ and that with the exception of the individuals on the boundaries, there was a pure economic rent inside the firm. The possibility of producing under the bonus scheme, and the emergence of the threshold $\tilde{a}^+$, modifies the scheme. In particular, the most natural assumption (consistent with Fig. 7.5 and with the case study that will be analysed in the next section) is to have

$$a_l < \tilde{a}^+ < a_h$$

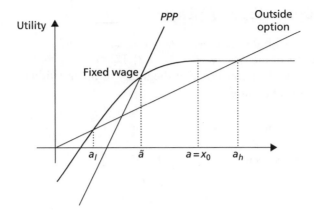

Figure 7.6. Utility levels for different individuals when a bonus scheme is introduced in a firm that was offering a fixed wage with minimum output

The existing workforce is partitioned into various categories, which we analyse next.

1. Individuals with ability level below a_l do not work in the firm.
2. Individuals with ability $a_l \leq a \leq \tilde{a}^+$ operate under the minimum wage guaranteed even if the bonus scheme is available. For these individuals it is too costly, in terms of effort, to produce in the bonus scheme range. Despite the incentive given to them, they would not choose the bonus regime.
3. Individuals with ability $\tilde{a}^+ < a < a_h$ operate under the performance plan if they have the option to do so. These are the individuals that were enjoying a rent under the fixed scheme, but they would respond to the incentive given (we call this the incentive effect).
4. Individuals with ability above a_h are now interested in joining the firm. This shows that the bonus scheme increases the fraction of the workforce for which it is attractive to work at the firm.

From the analysis of these intervals, we can also clearly distinguish between two types of effects associated with the introduction of a bonus scheme: the incentive effect and the sorting effect.

Incentive effects. A minimum wage scheme with a performance option increases productivity of the existing workforce. This is a pure incentive effect, since a given workforce improves its average effort and productivity. *Sorting effect.* A minimum wage scheme with a performance option increases the average ability of the workforce.

7.5.2 TWO-TIER SYSTEM: AN EXAMPLE

Let's continue with the example used before. $a_l = 1$ and $a_h = 2$ and the job at the firm was of the type $[w = 1, x_o = 2]$. Let's assume that $\alpha = -1/4$ and that $\beta = 1$. Let's first consider that the utility of the individual at the lowest minimum output required is

$$U(\bar{w} = 2, \bar{x} = 2, a = 1) = w - \frac{\delta(\bar{x} - a)^2}{2} = \frac{3}{2}$$

while with a bonus scheme (recalling that $x^* = \frac{\beta^*}{\delta} + a$)

$$U^{pr}(w^{pr}, x^{pr}, a) = \left(\frac{\beta^2}{2\delta} + \alpha\right) + \beta a = \frac{1}{2}$$

so that it is clear that at the lowest support of the distribution the individual is better off with the fixed wage. Conversely, for individuals at the upper support $U(\bar{w} = 2, \bar{x} = 2, a = 2) = 2$ while $U^{pr}(w^{pr}, x^{pr}, a = 2) = \frac{9}{4}$ so that individuals at the upper support level prefer the bonus scheme. The individual who is just indifferent is the solution to

$$w - \frac{\delta(\bar{x} - a)^2}{2} = \left(\frac{\beta^2}{2\delta} + \alpha\right) + \beta a$$

which becomes

$$2a^2 - 4a + 1 = 0$$

whose solution above $a_l = 1$ is

$$\tilde{a}^+ = 1 + \sqrt[2]{2}/2$$

so that individuals sort in the following way:

- individuals with ability $a < a_l$ do not join the firm;
- individuals with $a_l < a < \tilde{a}_2^+$ choose minimum;
- individuals between $\tilde{a}_2 < a < a_h$ choose piece rate;
- individuals above a_h are now interested in joining the firm.

Note that this particular type of sorting depends crucially, among other things, on the parameter α which is the implicit cost for the job. The two conditions that we need for this type of sorting are

$$U(a_l, w^*) > U(a_l, PPP)$$
$$U(a_h, PPP) > U(a_l, w^*)$$

The first condition requires α to be sufficiently large while the second condition requires α to be sufficiently low. In other words the implicit cost of the job must be sufficiently high that low-ability individuals do not find it convenient but sufficiently low that some individuals would want to swap to *PPP*.

7.6 **Pay for Performance at Safelite**

Safelite is the largest car windows installer in the United States, and its headquarters is based in Ohio. In 1994, Safelite changed the salary structure of its car window operation. Up to January 1994, the salary structure was based on an hourly rate, which was paid independently of the number of windows installed. Alongside, a minimum amount of production was required in order to continue to be employed at Safelite.

Between 1994 and 1995 the salary structure changed, and it became linked to the number of car windows actually installed. The goal of the firm was to increase productivity without losing any workers.

There were basically two options on the table, which critically depend on the existence of heterogeneity in the workforce.

1. Option number 1 (homogeneous workforce): Safelite may increase the minimum amount of output required by the firm, and leave the salary structure based on an hourly wage (possibly increasing the hourly salary). Our analysis has shown that if individuals are homogeneous, it is possible to increase productivity in this way as long as the initial situation is not the first best efficient. However, if there is heterogeneity in the workforce, an increase in the minimum output leads to undesirable turnover at the firm level.

2. Option number 2: (heterogeneous workforce): Introduce a compensation based on output with minimum guarantee so that more able individuals can work harder without penalizing less able individuals. This is exactly the two-tier compensation scheme that was analysed early in the chapter. Such an option should induce both an incentive effect and a sorting effect.

Safelite implemented option number 2, and introduced a plan that was called PPP (Performance Pay Plan).

Note that Safelite could rely on a very sophisticated and digitally based accountancy system in 1995. Its accounting system allowed management to monitor in real time who installed what component. Since PPP has been introduced over a period of nineteen months across all branches, most workers have been observed under both regimes (fixed time input and PPP). The possibility of observing workers before and after the policy change was introduced is an ideal instrument for studying the effect on individual productivity linked to the introduction of the PPP plan.

Table 7.1 reports some important basic numbers of the case study. The guarantee wage corresponds to $11 per hour. This means that, conditional on a minimum number of windows being installed, a worker was guaranteed a wage equal to $11 per hour. This works as follows: if the weekly pay of a worker turned out to be less than the guarantee, they would be paid the

Table 7.1. Data description for the Safelite case

Data description Variable	Definition	Mean	Standard deviation
PPP dummy	A (dummy) variable equal to 1 if the worker is on PPP during that month	0.53	
Base pay	Hourly wage	$11.48	$2.94
Units-per-worker-per-day	Average number of units of glass installed by the given worker during the month	2.98	1.53
Regular hours	Regular hours worked during the given month	153	41
Overtime hours	Overtime hours during the month	19	19
Pay	Pay actually received in a given month	$2,254	$882
Pay per day	Actual pay per eight hours worked; this differs from PPP pay in that the wage guarantee and other payments are included	$107	$36
Cost per unit	Actual pay for a given worker divided by the number of units installed by that worker	$40	$62

Source: Lazear 2000.

Table 7.2. Basic result for the Safelite case

Variable	Hourly wage		Piece Rate-PPP	
	Mean	Standard dev.	Mean	Standard dev.
Units-per-worker-per-day	2.7	1.42	3.24	1.59
Actual pay	$2,228	$794	$2,283	$950
PPP pay	$1,587	$823	$1,852	$997
Cost per unit	$44.43	$75.55	$35.24	$49.00
Number of observations	13,106		15,246	

Source: Lazear 2000.

guaranteed amount. *Ex post,* many workers ended up in the guarantee range. On average installers were paid about $20 per unit installed. The data are organized as follows. There were 2,755 individuals who worked as installers over the nineteen-month period covered by the data. The unit of analysis is a person month. Each month provides an independent unit of observation. Over the nineteen-month period, there were more than 29,000 observations.

x_{it} = Average numbers of glass units installed by individual i in month t

$i = 1, \ldots, 2{,}775$

$t = 1, \ldots, 19$

Note not all individuals are present in the nineteen months. Some individuals have joined Safelite later than the first month. For example, if individual j has joined Safelite at month 10, he or she will have observation $x_{j1} = ., \ldots x_{j10} = .$ where the dot refers to a missing value (the individual was hired) for that month. Similarly, if individual k leaves Safelite at month 15, he or she will have missing values for the rest of the period. For each individual, it is also possible to know whether he or she was working in the PPP regime or not. Remember that the plan was phased in gradually in different branches, so that for each individual the moment in which the PPP was operating varies.

7.6.1 THEORETICAL PREDICTIONS

The setting of the Safelite changes fits perfectly with the introduction of a two-tier regime, as was discussed in the previous section. There are thus two key theoretical predictions linked to the introduction of the PPP plan.

1. *Incentive effect*: Output (or effort) of the workers should increase (or not fall) as the company moves to a PPP system. Further, if there are able individuals in the workforce, the effort increases (this is an incentive effect).
2. *Sorting effect*: The average quality of the workforce increases (less able individuals stay with the firm, but in addition it is possible to attract better individuals into the firm) (this is a sorting effect).

Average productivity (as a consequence of the two previous effects) should thus increase.

7.6.2 BASIC STATISTICS

Some basic characteristics of the sample are reported in Table 7.1. There are a number of possible productivity measures. The one that most Safelite managers look to is units-per-worker-per-day. This is the total number of glass units per eight-hour day that are installed by a given worker. The units-per-worker-per-day number for each individual observation relates to a given worker in a given month. Thus, units-per-worker-per-day is the average number of units per eight-hour period installed by the given worker during the given month. Means for actual and PPP pay reveal almost nothing about the effects of PPP on performance and sorting. A more direct approach is needed.

7.6.3 BASIC RESULTS

- The key basic results are reported in Table 7.2.
- The average number of windows installed (units-per-worker-per-day) increases by 0.54 units (which corresponds to a 20 per cent increase).
- The variance of individual output increases (standard deviation increases from 1.42 to 1.59).
- labour cost for unit of output falls from $44.43 to $35.24.

The first possible observation of the result could be the following: what about a pure exogenous shift, linked for example to the adverse weather conditions, that increases the demand for windows. At the same time as Safelite introduced the PPP there was an exceptional increase in demand. If this was the case, the basic effect would be the result of the demand pick-up. One way to control for this possible demand effect is to include time dummies in the basic average regression. The results show that productivity (measured as average number of windows installed per day), once time effects are introduced, increases by a remarkable value of 44 per cent!!! This means that if there was a demand effect, such an effect worked in the opposite direction.

In any event, one needs to investigate and rationalize a 44 per cent increase in productivity. This effect can be seen by looking at the results of Table 7.3, in the simplest specification in the first regression. The coefficient on the individual PPP dummy is .368. Evaluated at the mean of the log of units-per-worker-per-day, this coefficient implies that there is a 44 per cent gain in productivity with a move to PPP.

7.6.4 POSSIBLE INTERPRETATIONS

These are our basic interpretations for the observed increase in productivity:

1. incentives: it depends on the pure incentive effect associated with the new plan on the *same* labour force;
2. sorting: it depends on the fact that the average worker is different in the two regimes, and better workers joined Safelite in the PPP regime;
3. Hawthorne effect; it is simply a short-run effect since any change inside an organization leads to an increase in productivity.

We now analyse the three possible explanations.

The Pure Incentive Effect

To obtain an estimate of the pure incentive effect it is necessary to calculate the effect only for the individuals that were operating under both regimes. In other words, one should make the comparison of the productivity change

Table 7.3. Regression results for Safelite cases

Regression	PPP dummy	Tenure	Time since PPP	New hire	R2
1[a]	0.368				0.04
s.d	0.013				
2[b]	0.197				0.73
s.d	0.09				
3[c]	0.202	0.224	0.273		0.76
s.d	0.009	0.058	0.018		
4[d]	0.309	0.424	0.13	0.243	0.06
s.d	0.014	0.019	0.024	0.025	

Notes: Dependent variable: ln (output-per-worker-per-day); observations: 29,837.
[a] Regression 1: Dummies for month and year included.
$lnx_{it} = \delta_t + \gamma PPP_t + \epsilon_{it}$
δ_t are time dummies;
γPPP_{it} is PPP dummy for individual i at time t
ϵ_{it} is a white noise for individual i at time t
[b] Regression 2: Dummies for month and year; worker specific dummies included (2,755 individual workers).
$lnx_{it} = \alpha_i\delta_t + \gamma PPP_t + \epsilon_{it}$
α_i are individual dummies;
Regression 3;
[c] $lnx_{it} = \alpha_i\delta_t + \gamma PPP_t + \phi_1 tenure_{it} + \phi_2 timesincePPP_{it} + \epsilon_{it}$
$tenure_{it}$ is the tenure at Safelite for individual i at time t;
$timesincePPP_{it}$ is the time individual i spent in PPP;
Regression 4;
[d] $lnx_{it} = \alpha_i\delta_t + \gamma PPP_t + \phi_1 tenure_{it} + \phi_2 timesincePPP_{it} + \phi_3 newhire_i + \epsilon_{it}$
$newhire_i$ is dummy if individual i was hired under PPP;
Source: Lazear 2000.

only for those individuals that were operating under both regimes. When one performs such an exercise one finds that the increase in productivity is equal to 22 per cent (which corresponds to 50 per cent of the total increase in productivity).

Hawthorne Effect

The Hawthorne effect is described as the rewards you reap when you pay attention to people. Elton Mayo argued that the mere act of showing people that you are concerned about them usually spurs them to better job performance. Individuals' behaviours may be altered because they know they are being studied; this was first argued in a research project (1927–32) at the Hawthorne Plant of the Western Electric Company in Cicero, Illinois. The research, led by the Harvard professor Elton Mayo, found that regardless of the experimental manipulation implemented, the production of the workers under investigation seemed to improve.

To control for the Hawthorne effect one has to control for the experience of the worker in the firm as well as time since the individual has operated under the PPP regime. Data suggest that the effect actually increases one year after the introduction of the PPP (and if the change was only due to a Hawthorne effect, we should have observed a decline).

Sorting or Learning?

The residual effect could be imputed to a pure sorting effect (better people were employed by the firm), but we have also to consider that experience is very important to the average productivity. One way to go about it is to calculate the effect of the increase in productivity for the individuals hired when the PPP was already introduced. Data suggest that the productivity of the new hires (controlling for tenure or seniority) is much larger. In other words, new hires are more productive.

7.7 **Econometrics**

The econometric model used to estimate the effect of the swap is the following individual-based longitudinal equation

$$\ln x_{it} = \alpha_i + \delta_t + \gamma \, PPP_{it} + \phi_1 \, tenure_{it} + \phi_2 \, timePPP_{it}$$
$$+ \, \phi_3 \, new\_Hire_i + \varepsilon_{it}$$

where $t = 1 \ldots T$ are the nineteen months in which the firm is observed while $i = 1 \ldots I$ are the 3,707 individuals who are observed. The representative individual is the person month.

The dependent variable is $\ln x_{it}$, the log of output per day per person (number of autoglass installed).

α_i are individual fixed effects aimed at capturing a measure of individual ability.

δ_t are time dummies aimed at capturing seasonal effects.

PPP_{it} is an individual dummy that takes a value of 1 if the individual has been in the PPP regime in that particular month. It's the key variable for the analysis of the *incentive effects* (row 2 in the regression table).

$tenure_{it}$ is the control for tenure. It is very important since productivity increases with tenure.

$timePPP_{it}$ is a variable that takes the value of 1 if an individual has been in PPP for 1 year, and 0.5 if for 6 months. It is crucial for the Hawthorne effect.

new_Hire_i is an individual dummy that takes the value of 1 if the individual has been hired after the introduction.

The various regressions in Table 7.3 report the various specifications. The first regression includes only the PPP_{it} dummy and it represents the estimates of the pure *PPP* effect. The coefficient is positive and significant, and evaluated at the mean of the log of units-per-worker-per-day; this coefficient implies that there is a 44 per cent gain in productivity with a move to a *PPP*. Month and year dummies are included in the regression, to account for factors, other than the move to *PPP*, that can have a significant impact on productivity. In the second regression worker-specific dummies are added. When worker dummies are included in the regression, the coefficient drops to .197 from .368. The .197 coefficient is the pure incentive effect that results from switching from hourly wages to piece rates. Evaluated at the means, it implies that a given worker installs 22 per cent more units after the switch to *PPP* than he did before the switch to *PPP*. This estimate controls for month and year effects. Regression 3 controls also for the worker tenure and the time since *PPP*, or the time spent by each individual in the new regime. It shows that there should not be a Hawthorne effect. The regression includes a variable for tenure and also one for time that the worker has been on the PPP programme. The coefficient of .273 on time since tenure coupled with a *PPP* dummy coefficient of .202 means that the initial effect of switching from hourly wage to piece rate is to increase log productivity by .202. After one year on the programme, the increase in log productivity has grown to .475. The Hawthorne effect would imply a negative coefficient on time since *PPP*. If the Hawthorne effect held, then the longer the worker were on the programme, the smaller would be the effect of piece rates on productivity. The reverse happens here. After workers are switched to piece rates, they seem to learn ways to work faster or harder in time. The last row of Table 7.3 provides evidence on the sorting effect, by measuring the output of new workers hired. The variable labelled 'New hire' is a dummy set equal to 1 if the individual was hired after 1 January 1995, by which point almost the entire firm had switched to piecework. The theory predicts that workers hired under the new regime should produce more output than the previously hired employees. Indeed, workers hired under the new regime have log productivity that is .24 greater than those hired under the old regime, given tenure.

7.7.1 OTHER ISSUES

What about quality control? Safelite can fully control the quality of its output, since it is very easy to count the number of windows which return to the dealer because of a faulty installation. In the PPP plan the firm forces the guilty workers to reinstall the faulty glass at their own expense using unpaid time before the order is again reassigned. Actually, after the introduction of the PPP a customer satisfaction survey suggests that there is an increase in customer satisfaction (from 90 to 94 per cent).

☐ APPENDIX 7.1. THE BASIC FRANCHISING SCHEME WITH THE ABILITY PARAMETER

Before entering the analysis of this chapter, we review the optimal franchising scheme when ability is present in the analysis. This is easily done, once we recall from the previous chapter the optimal linear contract $w = \alpha + \beta e$ is described by (replacing u with au)

$$e^* = \frac{\beta}{\delta}$$

$$\alpha = au - \frac{\beta^2}{2\delta}$$

$$\beta = p$$

where α is the fixed payment, β is the bonus scheme, and p is the price of output that in this chapter we fixed at $p = 1$.[4] In light of the optimal scheme, the level of output produced by an individual with ability a is indicated with x^* and reads

$$x^* = a + e^*$$

$$x^* = a + \frac{1}{\delta}.$$

The previous expression shows clearly that a firm that hires a more able individual will produce more output under a franchising scheme which is done for all individuals by a fixed payment plus an extreme bonus scheme. The profits of the firm for an individual with ability a are[5]

$$E[\Pi] = px - w$$

$$= \frac{1}{2\delta} + \bar{a}(1 - u) \qquad (7.2)$$

so that also the firm makes more profits.

---

[4] In the previous chapter we saw that with a compensation equal to $w = a + \beta x$, the optimal amount of effort is $\frac{\beta}{\delta}$. The chapter has also shown that the optimal choice of β from the firm's standpoint is $\beta = p$. Since we set $p = 1$, we have that $\beta = 1$ is the maximum.

[5] The profits are obtained through the following steps

$$E[\Pi] = px - w$$
$$= p(e^* + \bar{a}) - \alpha - \beta e,$$
$$= (p - \beta)e^* + p\bar{a} - \alpha$$
$$= (p - \beta)\frac{\beta}{\delta} + \bar{a} - \left[au - \frac{\beta^2}{2\delta}\right]$$
$$= \frac{1}{2\delta} + \bar{a}(1 - u).$$

☐ APPENDIX 7.2. AN OPTIMAL SCHEME WITH A FIXED WAGE

Suppose now that the only scheme that the firm can implement is a fixed wage scheme, so that the compensation must be equal to a fixed α that cannot vary with output. In other words, the compensation that the firm may offer to its workers is just of the type $w = \alpha$ without any bonus scheme. The firm cannot implement the franchising scheme, since such compensation would require a wage that is negative if no output is produced. Assume that the firm can easily observe output produced, but it cannot observe the ability of the worker. As it will turn out, the heterogeneous ability is very important. To show this we start asking the following question. *What will be the level of efficiency (and of profits) when a firm has to offer a fixed wage?* The answer will depend on two key conditions. What we want to show, as a benchmark case, is that the firm that offers a fixed wage can obtain an efficient level of output if two conditions hold. Such conditions are

- an appropriate minimum level of output x_{min} is chosen by the firm;
- there is no heterogeneity in the workforce. In other words, the workforce is homogeneous.

Note that when we talk about an efficient level of profits, we mean a level of profits that is as high as the one that would be obtained by a firm that implements the franchising scheme, as indicated by equation 7.2.

Let's assume for a moment that both conditions are satisfied. Homogeneous workforce in this chapter means that the parameter a is fixed in the population, so that $a = \bar{a}$, and for technical reasons we also assume that $\bar{a} < 1/\delta$. In other words, all the individuals have the same ability $\bar{a}$. Let's see how the firm can choose a minimum level of output x_{min}. The idea of a minimum level of output is simply to impose a minimum standard of quantity, so that if a worker does not reach such a minimum standard, the firm is not going to hire the worker, or the employment relationship can be interrupted without cost. In this section we label a job $[w, x_{min}]$ as a job that pays a fixed wage $\alpha = w$ and requires an output x_{min}. Let's see how the firm operates. The problem is solved in two steps. The first problem involves the choice of the minimum output x_{min}. The second step involves the choice of the optimal wage w.

It is immediately clear that the first problem, the choice of a minimum quantity x_{min}, has been already solved. With a fixed ability, all the firm should do is to select the minimum output equal to optimal output x^* so that

$$x_{min} = x^*$$

$$x_{min} = \bar{a} + \frac{1}{\delta}$$

The minimum output of the firm should be equal to $x_{min} = \bar{a} + \frac{1}{\delta}$.

The second step involves the choice of the wage, and it requires looking at worker behaviour. Let's begin with a general question. If the firm offers the job $[x_{min}, w]$ which workers will be attracted by such a fixed wage schedule? The utility at the firm that pays

w and requires a minimum level of output x_{min} is

$$U(w, x_{min}) = w - \frac{\delta(x_{min} - \bar{a})^2}{2}$$

In order for the worker to participate in the market we need the level of utility (described by the previous condition) to be larger than the worker outside option:

$$w - \frac{\delta(x_{min} - \bar{a})^2}{2} \geq \bar{a}u$$

The previous condition provides a participation constraint to the firm. Given x_{min}, the firm should choose a level of wage that makes the worker just indifferent between working for the firm and his or her outside option (in other words the participation constraint binds). If we call the optimal wage w^* the problem is solved by

$$x_{min} = \bar{a} + \frac{1}{\delta}$$

$$w^* = \bar{a}u + \frac{\delta(x_{min} - a)^2}{2}$$

The level of profits in this case is[6]

$$\Pi = x_{min} - w^*$$

$$= \frac{1}{2\delta} + \bar{a}(1 - u)$$

One can compare this level of profit with that obtained under a flexible system and one immediately finds that they are the same.

If individuals are homogeneous ($\bar{a}$ is fixed) the efficient level of profits can still be obtained with a fixed wage plus a minimum output guaranteed.

What Happens When the Firm Cannot Choose the Wage?

If the wage is completely fixed and endogenous the firm can hardly make any choice. All it can do is to select a minimum quantity of output x_{min}. The quantity is chosen by

---

[6] The steps of algebra to obtain the results are the following

$$\Pi = x_{min} - w^*$$

$$= \bar{a} + \frac{1}{\delta} - \bar{a}u - \frac{\delta(\bar{a} + \frac{1}{\delta} - \bar{a})^2}{2}$$

$$= \frac{1}{\delta} - \frac{\delta}{2}\frac{1}{\delta^2} - \bar{a}u + \bar{a}$$

$$= \frac{1}{2\delta} + \bar{a}(1 - u)$$

the firm in such a way that the worker participation constraint is binding:

$$Max_{x_{min}} \quad px_{min} - \bar{w}$$

$$s.t. \; \bar{w} - \frac{\delta(x_{min} - \bar{a})^2}{2} \geq au$$

For maximization simply choose an x such that

$$\bar{w} - \frac{\delta(x_{min} - \bar{a})^2}{2} = \bar{a}u$$

And the solution to the quadratic solution gives the minimum output. If profits are positive the firm operates.

If the wage is completely fixed at $\bar{w}$, all the firm can do is select a quantity so that the worker participation constraint is binding, and operate if profits are positive.

A sufficient condition for the minimum level of ability a_l to be found is

$$w - \frac{\delta(x_{min} - a_l)^2}{2} < 0$$

To find the two levels of ability we need to distinguish two cases, which depend on whether $a_h < x_{min}$ or $a_h > x_{min}$. In the first case we need to solve for the following quadratic equation:

$$w - \frac{\delta(x_{min} - a)^2}{2} = au$$

$$\delta a^2 + 2a[u - \delta x_{min}] + \delta x_{min}^2 - 2w = 0$$

whose solutions are

$$a = \frac{(\delta x_{min} - u) \pm \sqrt[2]{u^2 - 2\delta(x_m u - w)}}{\delta}$$

If the largest solution $a_h > x_{min}$ then a_h is obtained as the solution to $a_h = w/u$ so that

$$a_{min} < a_l < x_{min} < a_h < a_{max}.$$

8 Relative Compensation and Efficiency Wage

8.1 Introduction

Piece rates and bonus schemes provide incentives that operate independently of the relationship among co-workers. Specifically, workers need not be working with anyone else to be motivated by a piece rate scheme. Piece rate compensation is based on an individual's *absolute performance* rather than his performance relative to some standard or some other individual. Yet, in reality, most individual motivation is produced not by absolute reward but by a compensation that is based on *relative comparison*. Managerial employees who move up the corporate ladder do so by being better than their peers, not necessarily by being good.

Comparisons are key in determining promotions in private firms. Since promotions carry with them higher salaries, higher status, and perhaps more interesting assignments, workers seek to get promotions. In this process, they exert effort in an attempt to outperform their neighbours. Thus relative compensation can provide an incentive that is as effective as a piece rate or output-based compensation scheme based on individual performance.

There are good reasons why firms may prefer to use relative compensation schemes. The first is that it may be easier to observe relative position than it is to observe absolute position. Second, relative compensation differences out common noise that risk-averse people may not like.

The most extreme form of relative compensation is a pure tournament, a setting in which two workers compete for a promotion, an outcome that can be described in terms of higher salaries. Workers are promoted if they do better than their co-workers. In such a setting, the effort exercised by the workers is proportional to the spread in prize, or to the increase in salary associated with the promotion.

Pure tournaments are just one possible relative compensation scheme. Indeed, the chapter introduces also the concept of a Linear Performance Evaluation (LPE), a situation in which workers receive a salary structure that is the sum of two components: a fixed part plus a bonus (penalty) term, with the bonus term linked to the average performance of the workers. There are differences between LPE and pure tournament, particularly important when players are heterogeneous. In LPE winning by a lot is important, since the larger the victory the larger the increase in salary. In pure tournaments, conversely, all that is important is winning. The implications of the two relative compensation schemes are analysed in the context of a case study of broiler production.

The chapter introduces also the concept of efficiency wage, a compensation scheme whereby firms use salaries to increase workers' effort in the context of imperfect information. In a dynamic context, the efficiency wage mechanism ensures that workers' wages increase with tenure, even when productivity is constant. Upward-sloping wage profiles appear particular relevant in real life labour markets. Further, they form the basis of implicit contract between workers and firms, whereby workers continuously exercise effort in view of future wage increases.

The chapter proceeds as follows. Section 8.2 presents the basis tournament model. Section 8.3 introduces the relative compensation scheme, while sections 8.4 and 8.5 are devoted to the case study of broiler production. Section 8.6 deals with efficiency wages and section 8.7 with the upward-sloping wage profiles.

8.2 **Tournament: A Formal Story**

Relative compensation theory, or tournament theory as it has come to be called, is the theory used to determine the size of a rise associated with a particular promotion. It has four essential features.

1. Prizes are fixed in advance and are independent of absolute performance. The key is just winning the contest, not playing well, and typically the prize awarded is independent of the difference between the two players. In the context of the firm, this means that there are wage slots that are fixed in advance.
2. A player receives the winner's or loser's prize not by being good or bad but by being better than, or worse than, the other player. Again relative performance rather than absolute performance is key.
3. The effort with which the worker pursues the promotion depends on the size of the salary increase that comes with the promotion.
4. It is important to recall that the spread must be large to induce effort, but the average prize money must be sufficiently high to attract workers to come to the firm in the first place. Otherwise, workers will opt to enter some other activity, since participation is not mandatory.

Consider a firm that has only two workers and sets up two jobs: boss and operator. Workers compete against one another with the winner being designated boss and the loser being designated operator. The winner receives wage

W_1, and the loser receives wage W_2. No wages are paid until after the contest is completed. The probability of winning the contest depends on the amount of effort that each individual exerts. Let the two individuals be denoted by j and k.

Output of worker j is denoted by q_j and depends on effort e_j and on luck z so that

$$q_j = e_j - \frac{1}{2}z,$$

where z is a random variable with 0 mean. Similarly, output of worker k is

$$q_k = e_k + \frac{1}{2}z$$

where z can simply be interpreted as relative luck with 0 mean. This implies that expected output for worker j is $E(q_j) = e_j$ while expected output of worker k is equal to $E(q_k) = e_k$. Effort is chosen by the worker and it is not observed by the firm, which observes only output.

We assume that z is uniformly distributed with zero mean over the interval $[-b, b]$. Recall that if a variable is uniformly distributed over the interval $[-b, b]$ the following features hold:

$$E(z) = 0$$

$$Var(z) = \frac{b^2}{3}$$

$$G(x) = P(z \le x) = \frac{x + b}{2b}$$

$$g(x) = \frac{1}{2b}$$

where G is the cumulative distribution function and g is its density function.

Let's define with P the probability of winning the context. For worker j, the probability of winning the context depends on whether his output j is larger than output k, so that

$$P(q_j > q_k) = \text{Pr } ob\left(e_j - \frac{1}{2}z > e_k + \frac{1}{2}z\right)$$

$$= \text{Pr } ob(z < e_j - e_k)$$

$$= G(e_j - e_k)$$

$$= \frac{e_j - e_k + b}{2b}$$

We are now in a position to solve the problem. We do this in two steps. First, we model worker behaviour. Second, we solve for the firm maximization problem, taking worker behaviour into account. The second problem is thus choosing an optimal compensation scheme to maximize profits.

8.2.1 WORKER PROBLEM

The worker utility is the expected wage minus the cost of effort. We assume that the cost of effort is quadratic in effort, while the worker is risk neutral. In other words, if P is the probability of winning the contest the worker's pay-off is

$$U = W_1 P + (1 - P) W_2 - \frac{\delta e_j^2}{2},$$

where δ is the slope of the marginal disutility of effort. The worker chooses e to maximize expected output so that his problem reads

$$\underset{e_j}{Max} \quad W_1 P(q_j > q_k) + [1 - P(q_j > q_k)] W_2 - \frac{\delta e_j^2}{2}$$

Since we know that $P(q_j > q_k) = G(e_j - e_k)$ the problem becomes

$$\underset{e_j}{Max} \quad W_1 G(e_j - e_k) + (1 - G(e_j - e_k)) W_2 - \frac{\delta e_j^2}{2}$$

The *FOC* reads

$$(W_1 - W_2) \frac{\partial G}{\partial e_j} = \delta e_j$$

$$(W_1 - W_2) g(e_j - e_k) = \delta e_j$$

$$\frac{W_1 - W_2}{2b} = \delta e_j$$

where we used the fact that $\frac{\partial G(e_j - e_k)}{\partial e_j} = g(e_j - e_k)$ and that $g(e_j - e_k) = \frac{1}{2b}$ with a uniform distribution.

Note that there is a symmetrical problem for worker k which yields, after a simple and similar simplification,

$$(W_1 - W_2) g(e_j - e_k) = \delta e_k.$$

Since the workers are *ex ante* identical and have identical first-order conditions, there should be a *symmetrical equilibrium in which both workers choose the same level of effort*, so that $e_j = e_k = e^*$. When $e_j = e_k$ the first-order condition becomes

$$(W_1 - W_2) g(0) = \delta e^*$$

Using the fact that the distribution is uniform, so that $g(0) = \frac{1}{2b}$, we obtain the key condition

$$\frac{(W_1 - W_2)}{2b} = \delta e^* \qquad \text{(ICC)}$$

This condition, which determined the optimum amount of effort, acts as an incentive compatibility constraint. From this condition, two important conclusions follow:

Effort is larger the larger the wage spread.

Indeed an increase in the difference $(W_1 - W_2)$ yields an increase in effort.

The more important luck is in determining the outcome, the lower is effort.

To see this recall that the variance of z is $Var(z) = \frac{b^2}{3}$. So the larger b is, the larger is the variance of the luck component. This makes a lot of sense. If most of your output depends on how lucky you are, why should you bother to exercise effort? In production environments where measurements of effort are noisy, large rises must be given in order to offset the tendency by workers to reduce effort.

The worker has also a participation constraint. Note that under the symmetrical Nash equilibrium, each worker has a probability of winning the match equal to $G(0) = 1/2$. This implies that, in equilibrium, a worker's expected utility is

$$U = \frac{W_1 + W_2}{2} - \frac{\delta e^{*2}}{2}$$

and the worker will participate in the match (assuming that the outside option is 0) as long as expected utility is positive, so that

$$\frac{W_1 + W_2}{2} \geq \frac{\delta e^{*2}}{2} \qquad \text{(Participation Constraint)}$$

8.2.2 FIRM PROBLEM

The firm wants to maximize expected profit, or equivalently, profit per worker, since the number of workers hired is assumed exogenous to this problem. Expected output per worker is equal to $E(q) = e^*$ while the average cost of each worker is simply the average prize. This implies that the expected profits of the firm are

$$E[\Pi] = e^* - \frac{W_1 + W_2}{2}$$

The firm tries to maximize profits by choosing W_1 and W_2 subject to the participation constraint. Obviously the firm will set wages low enough to have the participation constraint satisfied with equality. In other words, the firm problem is

$$Max_{W_1, W_2} \quad e^* - \frac{W_1 + W_2}{2}$$

$$\text{s.t.} \quad \frac{W_1 + W_2}{2} = \frac{\delta e^{*2}}{2}$$

which becomes simply

$$\Pi_{W_1, W_2} = e^* - \frac{\delta e^{*2}}{2}$$

So that the first-order condition is

$$\frac{\partial \Pi}{\partial W_1} = \frac{\partial e^*}{\partial W_1} - \delta e^* \frac{\partial e^*}{\partial W_1} = 0$$

$$= \frac{1}{2b\delta} \left[1 - \frac{e^*}{\delta} \right]$$

where we used the fact that $\frac{\partial e^*}{\partial W_1} = \frac{1}{2b\delta}$ from the ICC, which suggests that when wages are chosen optimally

$$e^* = \frac{1}{\delta} \qquad \qquad \text{(efficient effort)}$$

A conclusion immediately follows:

Tournaments elicit the optimal amount of effort.

There are two ways to see this conclusion. First, firms force workers to induce effort up to the point in which the marginal cost of effort (namely δe^*) is equal to the marginal benefit (which is 1). Second, note that this condition is the same condition that appeared in Chapter 6 on optimal wage contracts when $p = 1$. Indeed, with a risk-neutral worker, you recall that the optimal contract requires $\beta = 1$ so that optimal effort is equal to $e^* = \frac{1}{\delta}$. This is the same result that we have now obtained. In other words, a tournament is an optimal compensation package, and satisfies all the conditions of the optimal bonus scheme analysed in Chapter 6 for a risk-neutral worker.

8.2.3 OBTAINING THE WAGES

To obtain the wages, one needs to substitute the optimal level of effort into the incentive compatibility constraint and in the participation constraint, so as to obtain a linear system of two equations in two unknowns. In other words, the system to solve is

$$\frac{W_1 + W_2}{2} = \frac{\delta e^{*2}}{2}$$

$$\frac{(W_1 - W_2)}{2b} = \delta e^*$$

where the optimal level of effort is $e^* = \frac{1}{\delta}$. Using this result we get

$$\frac{W_1 + W_2}{2} = \frac{\delta 1}{\delta^2 2}$$

$$\frac{(W_1 - W_2)}{2b} = 1$$

so that

$$(W_1 + W_2) = \frac{1}{\delta}$$

$$W_1 - W_2 = 2b$$

which gives the final wages and completes the problem

$$W_1 = b + \frac{1}{2\delta}$$

$$W_2 = \frac{1}{2\delta} - b$$

8.2.4 HETEROGENEITY AND RISKY STRATEGIES

If players are not identical there is a problem with tournament, since it becomes very difficult to elicit effort from workers. Because of the natural advantage that more able players possess, both individuals will not work hard enough. The more able worker will tend to shirk since he is likely to win anyway, the less able because he is likely to lose anyway. There is a way to solve this problem. It is called a *handicapping* system. Such a system gives the less able player a head start, so that makes it harder for the more able player to win.

Another feature of tournament with heterogeneous workers is linked to the possibility of choosing strategies that affect not only the average probability of winning, but also its variance. Imagine that two players can choose between two strategies (call the two strategies safe and risky) that offer them the same average probability of winning but have different variance. One can show that with heterogeneous contest, the better individuals will avoid high-risk actions. Choosing the risky actions (high variance) increases the chances of winning the context but also makes it more risky. Since better players are likely to win anyway and winning by little or by a lot makes little difference, this option offers little gain. As a result, more able players will play it safe and choose a low-variance action. The reverse is true for less able players. Since losing by a little or a lot is still losing and this is the likely outcome, expanding the negative tail of the performance distribution has little cost. Less able players should take a chance. Consequently, where tournaments encompass players of unequal ability, *there should be a negative relation between ability and variance of performance.*

8.3 **Linear Performance Evaluation**

To properly understand the role of tournaments and its specificity, particularly with respect to the case studies we will examine, it is important to introduce the concept of Linear Performance Evaluation (LPE). Under LPE players are rewarded on the basis of relative performance, but there are some important differences between a pure tournament and LPE. Suppose that there are many workers and assume that the salary structure is obtained by the sum of two components: a fixed part plus a bonus (penalty) term, with the bonus term linked to the average performance of the workers. If an individual worker produces and performs better than the average, he or she receives an increase in compensation equal to m times the difference between his performance and the average. In formula, such a reward scheme for individual i reads

$$W_i = W + m(e_i - Q) - \frac{\delta e_i^2}{2}$$

where W is the contractually specified reward to a player with average performance, m is the incremental reward (penalty) for above (below) average performance, and Q is the average performance of all players. If individual i views the average performance Q as fixed, he will choose e_i such that

$$m = \delta e_i$$

$$e_i = \frac{m}{\delta}$$

Notice that under LPE effort, and so performance, q_i, depends positively on the incremental reward for better relative performance, m, but is unaffected by the average level of rewards, W. This feature holds for both LPE and tournaments. In dimension LPE looks very much like a tournament.

The key difference between LPE and pure tournament comes about when heterogeneity is relevant. The thing to realize is that in LPE winning by a lot is important, while in pure tournaments all that is important is winning. This implies that, unlike tournaments, LPE provides no incentives for better players to choose conservative strategies and poorer players to choose risky ones, nor does it provide an incentive for organizers to handicap better players. The reason is that under LPE the incremental reward for improved performance is the same whether a player is more able or less able. As a consequence, under LPE there should be no relation between player ability and performance variability nor should there be evidence of handicapping.

8.3.1 INDIRECT EVIDENCE OF RELATIVE COMPENSATION

Some evidence of the importance of relative compensation can be obtained by examining the salary and compensation packages of corporate executives. It seems reasonable to think that top managers' rewards are based upon their own firm's performance relative to that of other firms in the same industry. Several studies provide evidence that firms implicitly reward managers on the basis of relative performance. An important further study is given by Gibbons and Murphy (1992). They show that both compensation of chief executives and the likelihood that they retain their position are related to firm performance relative to industry or relative to market. Thus, it is clear that relative performance matters, and this is an important feature of tournaments.

Further support is found in the examination of the behaviour of professional golfers by Ehrenberg and Bonanno (1990). Using data on professional golf tournaments, the outcome of players' actions and features of the environment such as weather and course rating could be observed. The prediction of tournament theory that is tested is that increases in the differential between prizes provide an incentive for more effort. Richer tournaments should lead to greater effort and better performance (lower scores). The evidence appears consistent with this hypothesis. As prize differentials increase, player performance improves.

8.4 **Evidence on Tournaments in Broiler Production**

We now analyse a case study on relative compensation and tournament based on an explicit business setting. It is the compensation of broiler producers, and it is based on the research carried out by Knoeber and Thruman (1994). Having detailed information on the structure of the tournaments and more than one thousand observations on performance (outcome) reached by different players, three tests can be provided. The first test looks at the effect of a change in the level of prizes holding prize differentials constant. In tournament theory there should be no effect on performance. This is consistent with the discussion outlined above. The second one looks at the relation between the riskiness of performance and player quality (ability). As we argued above, better players should exhibit less variable performance. The third one looks at evidence of handicapping or sorting when tournaments involve players with different abilities. Better players should be handicapped or sorted into more homogeneous tournaments.

8.5 **Broiler Production**

Broiler production is organized by firms called integrators. The integrator hatches baby chicks. However, the integrator does not grow the chicks to broiler size. Rather it contracts with growers to raise the chicks. Baby feed, medical service, and advice are provided by the integrator. Chickens are owned by the integrator. Chicken houses and labour are provided by the grower. The birds are then transported to the integrator's processing plant where they are prepared for the market. The scheme in Fig. 8.1 describes the setting.

The contracts used to compensate growers provide a payment per pound of live broiler produced. This is a piece rate. However, the size of the payment varies among growers and is determined by *relative performance*. Basically the integrator is the firm while the growers are the players. Grower performance is measured by 'settlement cost' per pound of broiler produced. As we will see, the smaller this settlement cost is, the better the grower's productivity and the better the grower's performance of broiler produced. The most common contracts in the broiler industry are LPE contracts, since they reward a grower based upon the strength of his performance relative to the average of other growers. But some contracts look only at performance rankings and so are tournaments in the strict sense. The growers to whom one is compared are

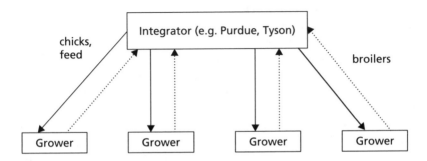

Figure 8.1. Broiler production

those whose flocks are harvested in the same geographical area at nearly the same time.

An important reason for using relative performance schemes to compensate broiler growers is that these schemes automatically difference out the effects of common shocks to grower productivity. Since variations in temperature and the breed of chick delivered by the integrator affect all growers, none must bear the risk of such variation, and contracts are very simple.

The Integrator Data

The data include production information for growers under contract to one integrator from November 1981 to December 1985. There is information on 1,174 flocks produced by 75 growers. The maximum number of flocks produced by any grower over the four-year period was 24. Of the 75 growers, 37 produced 20 or more flocks. For each flock, there is information on placement and harvest dates, number of birds set, and performance by the grower. Performance is measured by settlement cost which is defined as

$$\text{settlement cost} = (\text{chicks} \times 12 + \text{kilocalories} \times 6)/(\text{live pounds})$$

This is a cost-per-live pound measure. Chicks are 'charged' 12 cents apiece and calories (included in the integrator-provided ration) are charged 6 cents per thousand. Settlement cost decreases (so that performance increases) as the number of pounds of chicken produced per chick or per thousand calories increases.

The contract under which broilers were produced changed in June 1984 from a pure tournament (that rewarded growers on the basis of ordinal rank) to an LPE (that rewarded growers on the basis of performance relative to the mean). Prior to 1984 growers whose flocks were harvested within a ten-day period (in the same tournament) were ranked by performance (from smallest to largest settlement cost). The ranking was then divided into quartiles, and per pound payments to growers were determined based upon ranking. Growers received an incremental per pound payment of 0.3 cents as they moved to the next quartile. In the early part of the period the base pay was lowered and ranged from 2.0 cents per pound to 2.45 in 1982. In June 1984 the form of the contracts changed, and LPE was instituted. Now settlement costs were first averaged. Grower pay per pound was then calculated as a base pay of 3.2 cents plus or minus the difference between average settlement cost and the grower's own settlement cost. However a minimum per pound of 2.6 cents was still guaranteed. In November 1984, per pound base pay was raised to 3.4 cents per pound. The pay differential for better performance, however, remained the same. There are basically four compensation regimes over the periods analysed.

The tournament regimes can be expressed as

$$TRN_1 = 2.25 + 0.3[Quart - 1] \qquad \text{from 9-81 to 3-82}$$

$$TRN_2 = 2.7 + 0.3[Quart - 1] \qquad \text{from 3-82 to 6-84}$$

where *Quart* refers to the quartile in which each grower was partitioned. Under the LPE the compensation regime was

$$LPE_1 = Max[3.2 + (\bar{S} - s_i); 2.6] \qquad \text{from 6-84 to 11-84}$$

$$LPE_2 = Max[3.4 + (\bar{S} - s_i); 2.8] \qquad \text{from 11-84 to 12-85}$$

where S refers to average settlement cost while s_i is the settlement of each individual grower. Note that the remuneration increases if the settlement costs are below the average settlement costs. Further, note the existence of a minimum payment guarantee makes the compensation not a pure LPE scheme.

First Prediction: The Effect of Change in Base Pay Holding Differential Constant

The settlement cost, the inverse of growers' performance, is modelled as

$$S_{it} = \mu + \delta_i + \alpha\, days_{it} + \beta\, chicks_{it} + \gamma_1\, TRN_1 + \gamma_2\, TRN_2 + \gamma_3 LPE_1 + \gamma_4 LPE_2$$
$$+ \text{ seasonal effects } + \epsilon_{it}$$

where TRN_1 and TRN_2 refer to the period when pure tournament was in place while LPE_1 and LPE_2 are the periods in which linear relative production was in place. The ideas of these time dummies is to allow for differences in mean performance due to changes in contract structures and level of base pay. The variables *days* and *chicks* are numerical variables and represent the settlement cost effect of longer grow-out periods (days) and larger flocks (chicks). Numeric variables, grow-out length, and chick numbers significantly affect performance. *Days* worsen performance by 0.055 cents per day while an additional 1,000 *chicks* worsen performance by 0.26 cents. The effect of these variables is reasonable, and in line with what intuition would suggest.

The key test about the incentive effect of tournaments is on the period dummies. Recall that periods TRN_1 and TRN_2 were distinguished by different base payment amounts but had identical incremental rewards for moving up the tournament ranks. Similarly periods LPE_1 and LPE_2 had different base periods but the same marginal incentives. Nevertheless, the latter periods were different since payment was determined by LPE rather than by tournament. A test that looks for $\gamma_1 = \gamma_2$ and $\gamma_3 = \gamma_4$ is a test of the constancy of effort (performance) between periods with different absolute levels of payment but constant increments. It is not possible to reject this test, *hence the results suggest that performance is not affected by base pay.*

Another important test is the one that looks whether performance is at all affected by different payment periods. Indeed, mean performance varies across periods, as suggested by the rejection of the test that $\gamma_1 = \gamma_2 = \gamma_3 = \gamma_4$. In other words growers do respond to different payment structures with different levels of effort. Overall, this suggests that incremental rewards, and not absolute levels, determine performance.

Grower Quality and Risk

Tournament theory has interesting predictions when heterogeneous players do not choose only the level of effort but also the risk of the strategy chosen. One way of thinking about the risk of the various strategies is to think that players choose the variability. And theory predicts that a high-quality player will adopt a low-variance strategy to assure his high ranking. Conversely, a low-quality player will adopt a high-variance strategy. Since the data set used contains multiple observations on individual growers (many growers have more than twenty flocks) the settlement regression provides measures of both mean performance and variance. The idea is to interpret the mean performance measure as a proxy for grower quality and investigate the relationship between quality and variability.

Figure 8.2 plots growers' variability against grower quality during the period in which tournaments were used to compensate growers. The measure of variability is σ_i, the sample residual standard deviation for grower i from the settlement cost regression, and each σ_i is calculated only from the flocks grown during the tournament period. The measure of grower quality is the

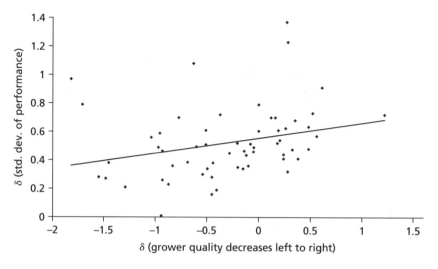

Figure 8.2. Variability of grower performance and grower quality: tournaments

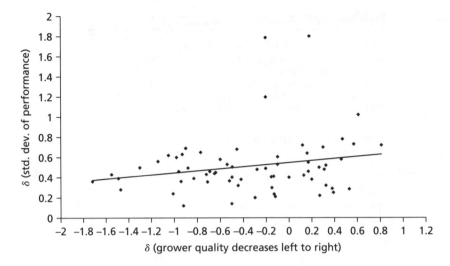

Figure 8.3. Variability of grower performance and grower quality: LPE contracts

estimate of δ_i, the dummy variable coefficient for grower i from the settlement cost regression. Remember that the best growers are those with the lowest settlement cost and the worst are those with the largest. Despite the noise present in Fig. 8.2, it obviously slopes upward. Better growers choose less risky strategies. During the LPE period, growers were paid based on their performance relative to the average of all growers. The reward for improved performance was the same for high-quality and low-quality growers. As a consequence no differential incentive existed for low-quality growers to take risks or for high-quality growers to play safe. In principle, there should be no relation between σ_i and δ_i in the LPE regimes. Nevertheless, in the LPE regime there was a minimum payment provision, so that the per pound payment was truncated from below. The effect of this is to restore the incentive for low-quality growers to take risks. Therefore, low-quality growers did have incentives to adopt high-variance strategies during the LPE regimes, and this seems to be borne out in Fig. 8.3. However, most of the positive relationship seems to be due to the worse growers. To the left of $\delta = -0.4$ the relationship is quite flat while in Fig. 8.2 it is more uniform. This suggests that there was an effect of the minimum payment provision on risk taking by low-quality growers during the LPE period. Nevertheless, there is some qualitative difference in the two regimes.

Handicapping

When players with different qualities interact in tournaments, organizers should try to handicap better players, so that all players have the right incentive

Table 8.1. Regression results for broiler production

Dependent variable: settlement cost (cents/live weight pound)
n=1167; mean=20.8. Estimates: α=0.55 (.008); β=0.26 (0.08)

Test of payment period effects	
1. Mean performance identical between periods TRN1 and TRN2 ($\gamma_1 = \gamma_2$)and periods LPE_1 and LPE_2 ($\gamma_3 = \gamma_4$)	Not rejected
2. Mean performance identical across all periods $\gamma_1 = \gamma_2 = \gamma_3 = \gamma_4$	Rejected
Test of grower heterogeneity:	
3. Growers have identical mean performance ($\delta_1 = \delta_2 = \cdots = \delta_{77}$)	Rejected

to perform. There is no similar reasoning to expect handicapping in an LPE regime, unless there is a minimum payment provision. When a minimum payment provision is in place in an LPE regime, there is some incentive to handicap good players, but such incentives should be lower than in a pure tournament setting. The regressions of Table 8.1 suggest that integrators have two possible ways to handicap players: grow-out length and flock size. Both variables have an unfavourable effect on performance and are controlled by the integrator, and can be used for handicapping players. We show the results with the number of chicks with the following linear model

$$chicks_{it} = \nu + \theta_1 \delta_i + \rho_1 TRN + \gamma_1 \delta_i TRN + \text{ seasonal effects } + \epsilon_{it}$$

where δ_i is the quality variable of grower i and the variable $\delta_i TRN$ looks at the relationship between $chicks_{it}$ and performance under the tournament period. If there is some handicapping we would expect a negative coefficient on δ_i (negative θ_1), with better growers (lower δ_i) being given larger seasonally adjusted flocks. This is because flock size is indeed negatively related to δ_i. Indeed the coefficient θ_1 is negative, and suggests that better growers are given larger flocks. While this is consistent with handicapping it could also simply mean that better growers have more houses. But the key test is on the interaction effect between quality and the tournament periods. Since the incentive to handicap is greater under the TRN regime, one might expect this coefficient to be negative, suggesting that handicapping is stronger under tournaments than under the LPE regime. If a grower is good, it should have more chicks under tournament, so that low delta should be associated with high chicks in the tournament dummy. The coefficient γ_1 is indeed positive.

8.6 Efficiency Wage

The idea behind efficiency wage is that higher wages increase workers' productivity. There are several potential reasons for this phenomenon. In general, higher wages generate greater productivity through a commitment mechanism. For example, the higher the wages are relative to what the worker could get elsewhere, the less likely it is that the worker will quit. Another key reason has to do with supervision. The higher the wage, the larger the cost of being caught shirking. Indeed, employees realize that even though supervision may not be detailed enough to detect shirking with certainty, if they are caught cheating on their promises to work hard and are fired as a result, the loss of a job paying above market wages is costly. As a result a worker may have less incentive to shirk. The idea of high wage as a discipline device is exploited in this section.

The worker's utility depends positively on the compensation received and negatively on the effort exercised. Effort is chosen by the worker and can take two values. For simplicity we assume that e is a binary variable that can take two values $e = \{0, 1\}$. If the worker exercises effort he or she suffers a subjective cost equal to $c/2$ while he or she does not suffer any cost if $e = 0$. If the worker chooses $e = 0$ we say that the worker shirks. The utility function is described as

$$U = compensation - \frac{c}{2}e$$

where *compensation* is the income received by the worker.

The worker has an outside option equal to $u \geq 0$.

The firm worker pair has established a job and produces a labour product equal to y only if the worker exercises effort. If the worker does not exercise effort the value of the labour product is 0.

Effort is observable to the worker but it is not observable to the firm. All the firm can do is monitor the worker. We assume that the monitoring technology is such that the firm has a probability p of finding out whether the worker exercises effort.

If a worker exercises effort and produces the labour product y the firm offers him or her a wage w. The wage w is set unilaterally by the firm.

A worker that is caught shirking is immediately fired and he or she gets the outside wage u.

The compensation of the worker is then simply

$$compensation = \begin{cases} w & \text{if } e = 1 \\ pu + (1 - p)w & \text{if } e = 0 \end{cases}$$

The firm's profits are defined as the difference between the value of the labour product and the wage, and they are positive only if the worker does not shirk. In formula, this is equivalent to

$$\pi = \begin{cases} y - w & \text{if } e = 1 \\ -(1 - p)w & \text{if } e = 0 \end{cases}$$

The firm has a clear interest that the worker does not shirk, since otherwise its profits are going to be negative.

The worker will choose to exercise effort only if the utility with effort is larger than the utility under shirk. This is equivalent to:

$$\left(w - \frac{c}{2}\right) \geq (1 - p)w + pu$$

where the left-hand side is the worker utility if the worker chooses $e = 1$ while the right-hand side is the utility if $e = 0$. Rearranging, the worker will exercise effort if and only if

$$w \geq u + \frac{c}{2p} \qquad \text{(NO SHIRKING)}$$

The previous condition is the fundamental equation of the efficiency wage, since it says that the worker will exercise effort only if the wage is large enough. In this setting, the only instrument that can induce the worker to exercise effort is a high wage. The logic goes as follows. Worker's dislike effort but if they are caught shirking they suffer a penalty equal to the wage loss. As a result, the larger the wage the lower the chance that the worker shirks.

Looking at the firm's profits, it appears that the firm would like to set the lowest possible wage, conditional on the worker choosing $e = 1$. It implies that the optimal wage is the minimum wage that satisfies the no shirking condition, and reads

$$w = u + \frac{c}{2p}$$

The efficiency wage is above the worker's outside option.
The problem solution is the following:

- The worker chooses $e = 1$ and gets a wage equal to $w = u + \frac{c}{2p}$
- The firm profits are $\pi = y - (u + \frac{c}{2p})$ and the job takes place as long as $\pi \geq 0$

From the solution to the model a first conclusion follows:

The efficiency wage increases the more difficult it is monitoring the worker

To establish this conclusion simply note that the lower p is, the larger is the wage. The intuition is that the worker needs to be compensated more the lower the probability of finding out whether he or she is shirking. This suggests that the asymmetric information over effort leads to an increase in wage. To investigate this further we can define the worker surplus as the difference between the utility of the worker and his outside option. The worker surplus is indicated with S_w and its expression reads

$$S_w = U - u.$$

Using the efficiency wage, the total surplus reads

$$S_w = \left(u + \frac{c}{2p}\right) - \frac{c}{2} - u$$

$$S_w = \frac{c(1-p)}{2p}$$

from which a conclusion immediately follows:

The worker enjoys a positive rent as long as $p < 1$.

As we argued above, even though the firm unilaterally sets the wage, the presence of asymmetric information leads to a wage that leads to a pure economic rent, with a utility larger than the outside option.

8.7 Deferred Compensation and Upward-Sloping Wage Profile

We now use the model of the previous section in a dynamic setting. We assume that there are two periods in the worker's career.

The first period corresponds to a period in which the worker is 'young' and the second period corresponds to a period in which the worker is 'old'.

In each period the worker has a utility function that is identical to the utility described in the previous section, and it is the sum of the compensation minus the cost of effort. We label w_y the wage in the first period, when the worker is young, and w_o the wage in the second period, when the worker is old. The cost of effort in each period is $\frac{c}{2}e$. The young worker has a lifetime utility that is given by the sum of the per period utility of the young and the old. In formula, the utility of the young worker is

$$U_y + U_o = \left(w_y - \frac{c}{2}e_y\right) + \left(w_o - \frac{c}{2}e_o\right)$$

where e_o is the effort chosen when the worker is old and e_y that chosen when he is young.

The other assumptions of the model are identical to those of the previous section. In particular, effort is chosen by the worker but it is not observed by the firm, which can monitor, in each period, the worker with a frequency $p < 1$. The worker, if he does not shirk, produces in each period a value of the labour product equal to y. The worker has an outside option in each period equal to u. The problem is described in Fig. 8.4.

The firm sets the wage for the young and the wage for the old, w_y and w_o. One of the key questions we ask in this section is whether w_y is different from w_o and notably whether $w_y < w_o$.

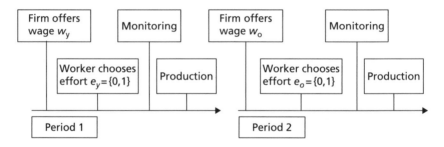

Figure 8.4. Deferred wages

The problem should be solved backwards, starting from period 2 and going backwards to period 1.

In the second period the problem is like a static problem, since there is only one period to go and thereafter the game ends. This suggests that in the second period the problem is identical to the efficiency wage model discussed in the previous paragraph. In formula the wage for the old worker is

$$w_o = u + \frac{c}{2p}$$

The key problem is for the firm to choose the young wage and for the worker to decide whether effort should be chosen or whether shirking is optimal. The firm can take into account the second period wage and knows that in the second period the worker will not shirk and will be paid a wage equal to w_o.

Let's focus on the worker. Suppose that the firm pays a wage w_y (which is still to be determined). The worker will choose to exercise effort if his lifetime utility with effort is larger than the lifetime utility without effort. This is equivalent to

$$\left(w_y - \frac{c}{2}\right) + \left(w_o - \frac{c}{2}\right) \geq (1 - p)\left[w_y + \left(w_o - \frac{c}{2}\right)\right] + p2u$$

The left-hand side of the previous condition is the utility when the worker chooses effort and receives w_y when young and w_o when old. The right-hand side is the utility if the worker shirks in the first period, while he or she will not shirk in the second period, since we have already established this. Rearranging the previous expression one gets

$$(w_y + w_o) \geq \frac{c}{p} - \frac{(1 - p)c}{2p} + 2u$$

and using the solution for the old wage the solution is

$$w_y \geq u + \frac{c}{2p} - \frac{(1 - p)c}{2p} \tag{8.1}$$

The firm's problem is now easy to determine, since the firm will choose the minimum young wage so that the worker does not shirk. This is identical to satisfying equation 8.1 with an equals sign so that

$$w_y = u + \frac{c}{2p} - \frac{(1-p)c}{2p}.$$

The firm defers wages, and offers to the worker an upward-sloping wage profile with $w_y < w_o$.

The proof of the remark is simple, since it follows from a simple comparison of the wage of the young worker and the wage of the old worker. Indeed, $w_y = w_o - ((1-p)c/2p)$.

The reason for the upward-sloping wage profile can be understood by looking at equation (8.1), which represents the no shirking constraint in a dynamic setting. The firm knows that the worker, by shirking, loses not only the wage of the period 1 w_y but also the wage in the old phase. As a result the firm is able to reduce the wage of the young worker. The worker on the job has incentives to work diligently in order to qualify for the wage increase.

9 Training and Human Capital Investment

9.1 Introduction

Lifetime education, as a form of a lifelong process of learning, is a key concept in modern organizations. It is often argued that in a competitive and changing world the only successful firms are those that employ workers that continuously upgrade and adapt their skills. While such a view may look extreme, it is obvious that lifelong learning is a key dimension in all organizations. Just think about how difficult it is for older workers to adapt to a digital economy without the appropriate skills. This means that education, the process of acquiring skills, does not finish with graduation, but it continues throughout the working careers of most workers. And most of such education takes place during the employment relationship, in the form of *training*. In other words, training is a key decision in personnel economics.

The current and the following chapter deal with on-the-job training. In this chapter, the basic models of training are set up. These models are known in the literature as Becker models of training. A common feature of the models of this chapter is the assumption of a perfect labour market. In the following chapter, we will analyse how the training decision changes when the underlying labour market is imperfect.

To understand how economists think about training, it is first necessary to understand how economists think about education in general. The most important view of education is the theory of human capital. Loosely speaking, human capital corresponds to any stock of knowledge or characteristics the worker has (either innate or acquired) that contributes to his or her 'productivity'. This definition is very broad, but it enables us to think not only about the years of schooling, but also about a variety of other characteristics as part of human capital investments. Training done during the employment relationship is one of such characteristics, and it is the core analysis of this chapter.

Before entering into the theory of training, the chapter starts from a simple model of human capital that enables us to understand the individual's decision to acquire education. The human capital approach to education (which is common to this and the following chapter) assumes that acquiring knowledge and education by individuals is a process very similar to the accumulation of physical capital by organization. This is the key concept of the theory of human capital. Education involves first some costs (the investment phase) and some benefits thereafter (mainly in the form of larger future wages). We will see that such a view, extremely influential in the modern economic analysis, delivers a variety of insights into the real life process of skill accumulation.

Human capital investment continues in the aftermath of graduation, through on-the-job training. This is the core part of the chapter. In outlining the basic ideas, the chapter refers to the logical distinction between general training and specific training. General training refers to the acquisition of a set of skills that can be used in each and every organization (or firm) active in the labour market. Specific skills are at the opposite extreme. An investment in specific human capital leads to the accumulation of skills that can be efficiently applied only in the organization in which the worker is currently employed. Such a distinction is very important for understanding the firm and worker decision to engage in the on-the job accumulation of human capital.

In the case of general human capital, as long as the labour market is perfectly competitive and wages fully reflect the marginal product of labour, a firm has no incentive to invest in the general human capital of its workforce. In such a case, the investment incentives rest on the workers, who can optimally undertake the investment by accepting initially lower wages.

In the case of specific human capital, things are more difficult and more complicated, since neither party has an incentive to undertake the entire cost of the investment. Indeed, we will see that the only way by which an opportunity to invest in specific human capital is fully exploited is when both parties share both the costs and the benefits from the investment. Specific human capital creates *firm-specific rents*, and it is the basis for long-term employment relationships.

The chapter proceeds as follows. Section 9.2 presents the baseline model of schooling, human capital investment before the labour market. Section 9.3 defines general and specific investment, while section 9.4 presents a two-period model of general training. Section 9.5 focuses on specific training, and formally defines the concept of a specific rent. Section 9.6 presents some empirical findings on training.

9.2 The Basic Human Capital Model of Schooling

Let's consider an individual who has to decide whether to acquire some level of education. To be specific, let us imagine that we are considering the decision of a just-graduated student to take a degree or not. The individual has already completed secondary education and has to decide whether or not he should continue his investment in education. Formally, we consider an individual who lives two periods and must decide whether or not to acquire education. His utility is given by the difference between the lifetime income and the costs of education. In formula, this utility function reads:

$$U_i = \text{Lifetime income} - \text{costs of education}$$

$$U_i = y_1 + \frac{y_2}{1+r} - e(\gamma + \theta_i)$$

Let's first focus on the lifetime income, which we assume to be just two periods. We let y_1 be the income in the first period while y_2 is the income in the second period. Note that the income of the second period is discounted at the rate of time preference r, which we assume to be identical to market interest rate r. A single unit of income in period 2 (say 1 euro) yields a utility today of just $1/(1+r)$.[1] We next focus on the educational choice, which we label e. Since we are just focusing on the decision to undertake a degree, we assume that the education variable can take only two values. In other words, we assume that an individual can be either educated or not (either he or she has the degree or not), and so $e = \{0, 1\}$. The disutility (or the cost of education) has two components: γ is the tuition fee component while θ_i is the psychological and subjective cost, so that individuals with larger values of θ_i have the largest cost of education.

The income in the first period of life is equal to $y_1 = -\gamma$ if the worker acquired education, while it is equal to the unskilled wage w_u if the worker does not undertake education. In this respect education is a full-time activity. The wage in the second period depends on whether the individual did or did not acquire education in the first period, so that $w_2 = w_s$ (the skilled wage) if the worker acquired education while $w_2 = w_u$ (the unskilled wage) if the worker did not educate himself or herself. The benefits of the education rest with the increase in workers' productivity, reflected in their higher wages.

The education decision is then solved by comparing the lifetime utility of the individual with or without education. In other words, the individual will

---

[1] To understand the discount factor, consider the following experiment. Suppose that the market pays an interest rate equal to r for an investment of 1 euro between the first period and the second period (e.g. one year). This means that 1 euro today will yield to $1(1+r)$ euros tomorrow. Similarly, one can ask what is the value today of 1 euro available in the second period. Call such value x. By definition, it must be true that

$$x(1+r) = 1$$

from which it follows that

$$x = \frac{1}{1+r}$$

In other words, 1 euro available in the second period is equivalent to $1/(1+r)$ euros immediately.

educate himself if

utility with education $\geq$ utility without education

$$-\gamma + \frac{w_s}{1+r} - \theta_i \geq w_u + \frac{w_u}{1+r}$$

which requires

$$(\theta_i + \gamma) + w_u \leq \frac{w_s - w_u}{1+r}$$

Several important insights come from the previous inequalities:

1. The decision of whether or not to acquire human capital is identical to that of acquiring physical capital, and it is governed by a cost–benefit analysis.
2. The cost of education has three components: the direct tuition costs during the education period γ, the opportunity cost of a market wage during the education investment w_u, and the psychological cost θ.
3. The benefits are expressed as net marginal benefits, and they are given by the value of the skilled wage minus the unskilled wage.

Many implications of this simple theory follows.

Not everybody will educate themselves. People who have too large educational costs will choose not to undertake the human capital investment. To see this assume that there is heterogeneity over values of θ_i, a variable that can easily indicate inability, so that more able people are those with lower values of θ_i.[2] It follows that the investment in education will be undertaken only by people with $\theta_i \leq \theta^*$ where θ^* is the individual who is just indifferent to the education investment. The formal expression of θ^* reads

$$\theta^* = -\gamma - w_u + \frac{w_s - w_u}{1+r}$$

The psychological cost for the marginal individual is such that it just offsets the monetary costs (in terms of tuition fees and opportunity cost and the net benefits).

If educational costs increase (an increase in γ) fewer people enter the educational system. To see this note that an increase γ reduces θ^*. If taking a degree is more expensive, fewer people will attend the educational system.

An increase in the interest rate means less schooling. Note that from the role of r it may also follow that there are some people that face very large interest rates independent of ability, and will not acquire education. An additional

---

[2] Assume that θ can take any value between θ_{min} and θ^{max} and there is a continuum of individuals distributed according to the cumulative density function $F(\theta)$ defined over the support $\theta_{min}, \theta^{max}$.

interpretation of the role of financial constraint can come from interpreting θ as the inability to borrow, so that individuals that have more financial constraints have larger θ.

A larger skill premium (i.e. an increase in the difference $w_s - w_u$) means that a larger amount of people will undertake education.

Finally, a note on the timing of the education investment. In this simple model, education will never be taken in the second period, since there is no time to earn back the investment. This implies that education will always be undertaken when people are relatively young.

9.3 General versus Specific Investment

Individuals continue to invest in human capital after the start of employment, and we normally think of such investment as training, provided either by the firm itself on the job, or acquired by the worker (and the firm) through vocational training. While what is learned in school is typically widely usable, what is learned through training is often less general, and can be used only in specific industries or in specific jobs. Further, while the schooling decision is mainly an individual decision, training decisions involve also the firm. Economists typically distinguish between two types of training:

- **firm-specific training:** this provides a worker with firm-specific skills, or skills that will increase his or her productivity only with the current employer;
- **general training:** this type of training will contribute to the worker's general human capital, increasing his or her productivity with a range of employers.

We now present two different models of training, one that focuses on general training and one that focuses on specific training.

9.4 General Training

9.4.1 THE BASIC SET-UP

Consider the following very simple two-period model:

We focus on firms that are formed by single jobs. A firm and a worker are engaged in a production opportunity that we simply call 'job'. The job has been already established. We do not deal here with job creation.

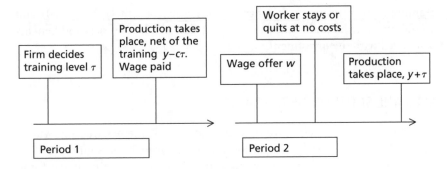

Figure 9.1. A two-period model on general training

In the **first period** there is a level of production equal to y, where y is the value of the marginal product to the firm. In addition, there is a training opportunity in a fixed amount. The training opportunity can either be taken or not. Training is indicated by τ with $\tau = \{0, 1\}$ so that it is equal to 1 if training is undertaken and it is equal to 0 if training does not take place. There are two stages in the first period.

- In the first stage the **firm decides** whether to undertake the training opportunity. Undertaking training costs c, where c is expressed in the same unit of the production. The total costs of training are then $c\tau$.
- In the second stage production takes place, for a value equal to $y - c\tau$.

In the **second period** there are three stages:

- In the first stage the firm makes a take it or leave it wage offer w to the worker, and other firms compete for the worker's labour.
- In the second stage the worker decides whether to quit and work for another firm. We assume that the worker does not incur any cost in the process of changing jobs, so that the labour market is perfectly competitive.
- In the third stage production takes place. At this point the value of output is equal to $y + f\tau$; in other words, if training did take place in the first period ($\tau = 1$) it is equal to $y + f$; if training did not take place ($\tau = 0$), it is equal to zero. We assume that $f > c$.

For simplicity we assume that there is no discounting. Figure 9.1 describes the timing of the game.

9.4.2 THE EFFICIENT LEVEL OF TRAINING

Before proceeding, let's clearly establish that in the model undertaking training is an efficient choice. This is ensured by the fact that $f > c$. Undertaking training is an investment that has a positive net benefit ($f - c > 0$) and would certainly be undertaken by an agent that weighs the costs and benefits associated with the investment.

9.4.3 THE SOLUTION OF THE MODEL

There are two issues. First, we need to understand whether training will be undertaken. Second, and perhaps most important from the personnel economics standpoint, we need to understand who will have the incentive to pay for it.

The model has to be solved backwards, starting from the second period and proceeding backwards to the first one. We begin at the first stage of the second period. In period 2 the level of training has been already decided (whether a positive value or zero). This means that the productivity of the worker will be $y + f$ if training was undertaken ($\tau = 1$) and y otherwise. Suppose for a moment that $\tau = 1$. If the market is competitive and if there are no costs of changing jobs, it is clear that the wage in period 2 must be exactly $y + f$, or the marginal product of labour with training. This is a key condition. As the economists say, 'bygones are bygones', and at $t = 2$, the worker will be trying to obtain the largest possible salary in the marketplace, independently of what was agreed earlier on the financing of the training investment. This is obvious, since any wage smaller than this level would leave the worker with a strong incentive to change job right away. The solution of the second period at time $t = 2$ is then very simple. If training did take place, the worker will accept from the current firm (or from a different firm) only a wage offer equal to $w_1 = y + f$. If training did not take place, the wage would be equal to y, the marginal product of labour without training.

Let's now move back to the first period. Since in the second period the worker will get all the benefits from the investment, the firm will not have the incentive to sponsor the training. The *firm would certainly make a loss on sponsoring training*, since it would incur a certain cost c at time $t = 1$ without incurring any of the benefits at $t = 2$. Hence the firm will not finance the training. But we need also to consider the worker's incentive. Since the worker is the *full residual claimant* of the increase in his or her own productivity, *he or she will have the right incentive to invest.*

How can the worker finance the training? Simply through a wage cut in the first period, so as to compensate the firm for the loss of production during training. This is the key mechanism of the solution and an equilibrium is easily established. The firm will offer to the worker the following package at $t = 1$, $\tau = 1$ and a wage equal to $w_1 = y - c\tau$. In this situation, the worker accepts the deal, since he will get the full wage

$$w_2 = y + f$$

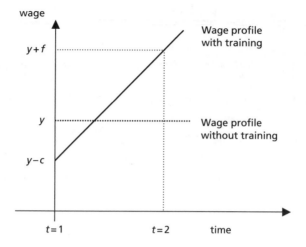

Figure 9.2. Wage tenure profile with general training

in the second period, either from the current or from another employer. The firm makes zero profits, and has no incentive to deviate from such a situation.

To sum up, the equilibrium is described as follows. At time $t = 1$ the firm chooses $\tau = 1$ and offers a wage equal to $w = y - c\tau$. At time $t = 2$ the firm offers a wage $w_1 = y + \tau f$ and the worker accepts. Figure 9.2 plots the solution, with wage on the vertical axis against time on the horizontal axis.

With perfect competition in the labour market, the efficient level of general training will be achieved with firms bearing none of the costs and workers financing training by taking a wage cut in the first period of employment.

Two very important implications follow:

- Human capital investors forgo wages early on in their career in exchange for future wage gains.
- The wage profile becomes positively sloped: workers earn less when they are young but experience makes wages grow.

In section 9.6 we discuss some of the empirical evidence on training.

9.4.4 INVESTMENT IN GENERAL TRAINING: AN EXAMPLE

Let's now consider a worker that is currently paid according to his marginal product, which we set equal to 100 in Table 9.1. The worker is expected to be hired for two years and the interest rate is zero, so that there is no issue of discounting. There is a training opportunity in general skills that involves a loss of productivity at time $t = 1$ of 15, but it generates an increase in productivity

Table 9.1. General and specific training

General training
$y = 100, c = 15, f = 25$

	Marginal prod.		Outside option		Wage		Firm surplus		Worker surplus		Total surplus	
	$\tau = 0$	$\tau = 1$	$\tau = 0$	$\tau = 1$	$\tau = 0$	$\tau = 1$	$\tau = 0$	$\tau = 1$	$\tau = 0$	$\tau = 1$		
$t = 1$	100	85	100	100	100	85	0	0				
$t = 2$	100	125	100	125	100	125	0	0				

Specific training (without sharing)
$y = 100, c = 15, f = 25$

	Marginal prod.		Outside option		Wage		Firm surplus		Worker surplus		Total surplus	
	$s = 0$	$s = 1$	$s = 0$	$s = 1$	$s = 0$	$s = 1$	$s = 0$	$s = 1$	$s = 0$	$s = 1$	$s = 0$	$s = 1$
$t = 1$	100	85	100	100	100	85	0	25	0	-15	0	10
$t = 2$	100	125	100	100	100	100	0	25	0	0	0	25

Specific training (*ex post* sharing)
$y = 100, c = 15, f = 25, \text{beta} = 0.5$

	Marginal prod.		Outside option		Wage		Firm surplus		Worker surplus		Total surplus	
	$s = 0$	$s = 1$	$s = 0$	$s = 1$	$s = 0$	$s = 1$	$s = 0$	$s = 1$	$s = 0$	$s = 1$	$s = 0$	$s = 1$
$t = 1$	100	85	100	100	100	85	0	12.5	0	-2.5	0	10
$t = 2$	100	125	100	100	100	112.5	0	12.5	0	12.5	0	2.5

Specific training (full sharing)
$y = 100, c = 15, f = 25, \text{beta} = 0.5$

	Marginal prod.		Outside option		Wage		Firm surplus		Worker surplus		Total surplus	
	$s = 0$	$s = 1$	$s = 0$	$s = 1$	$s = 0$	$s = 1$	$s = 0$	$s = 1$	$s = 0$	$s = 1$	$s = 0$	$s = 1$
$t = 1$	100	85	100	100	100	92.5	0	5	0	5	0	10
$t = 2$	100	135	100	100	100	117.5	0	12.5	12.5	25		

at time $t = 2$ of 25. The training opportunity is thus efficient. Undertaking training increases the worker's outside option at time $t = 2$ to 125. This means that the worker can obtain in the second period a wage equal to 125, and the firm will not have any incentive to pay for training in the first period. The only equilibrium with training is one in which the worker takes a wage cut at time $t = 1$ equal to 15 and gets a wage equal to 125 in the second period. Table 9.1 confirms this result.

There are several important lessons from this simple example, very similar to the model above. Investing in human capital leads to a reduction in wages early on in the career in exchange for future wage gains. Second, the wage profile becomes positively sloped: workers earn less when they are young but experience (or tenure) makes wages grow, exactly as is implied by this model.

9.5 Firm-Specific Training

The problem of financing general training was that the worker is the residual claimant of the investment and that any firm in the market could benefit from such an investment. We have seen that the equilibrium is one in which the worker takes a wage cut and finances the general training. In the case of firm-specific training the situation is the opposite. The current employer is the only (or probably the main) agent that can benefit from the investment, so there is no competition from other firms to push up the worker's wages. Once the investment is made the current employer is the only buyer of the specific skills, so that the firm becomes 'monopsonistic' vis-à-vis those skills. The problem here is that the worker will not have the right set of incentives to invest, since the firm will get most of the benefits from the investment. As we will see, the solution to the firm-specific training is quite complicated. Let's consider the following problem.

At time $t = 1$, there is a specific training opportunity s that can take two values $s = \{0, 1\}$ $s = 1$ corresponds to a situation in which specific training is undertaken and $s = 0$ when training does not take place. The **worker** decides on s. Undertaking training costs c in terms of forgone production. The marginal product is thus y without training and $y - c$ when training is undertaken.

The wage w_1 in the first period is equal to $y - cs$, so that undertaking training implies obtaining a wage equal to $y - c$.

At time $t = 2$, there are three stages:

- the firm makes a wage offer to the worker;
- the worker decides to accept this wage offer and work for this firm, or take another job without incurring any costs of changing job;
- production takes place and wages are paid. We let the productivity of the worker be $y + fs$.

Since s refers to specific skills, the outside option of the worker at time $t = 2$ is still equal to y.

We also assume that $f > s$; this means that the increase in production is strictly positive and the training opportunity is efficient.

To solve this problem we need to proceed by backward induction. We start from the second period. The worker will accept any wage $w_2 \geq y$ since y represents the worker's outside option. The firm has no incentive to offer any wage larger than the worker's outside option. Knowing this, the firm simply offers $w_2 = y$. We then move to the first period. Given the wage $w_2 = y$ in $t = 2$, in the first period the worker has no investment in specific skills. Undertaking training implies taking a wage cut in the first period which is not going to be followed by a wage gain in the second period. The specific training is not going to be taken, even though the investment opportunity is efficient, since $f > s$.

What is the problem? By investing in firm-specific skills, the worker is increasing the firm's profits, so that the firm would like to encourage the worker to invest. Given the timing of the game, wages are determined by a take it or leave it offer by the firm after the investment has taken place. In this setting, it will always be in the interest of the firm to offer a wage to the worker exactly identical to the outside option. This is known as a *hold-up* problem in economics. In this setting, it is the worker who is held up by the firm. The worker anticipates this hold-up problem and does not invest in his firm-specific skills.

Can the firm have the incentive to pay all the training costs at time $t = 2$ and still offer a wage $w_1 = y$? Such an option would not even work since the firm will make a certain loss at time $t = 1$ and it would not have any guarantee that the worker will stay with the firm in the second period.

9.5.1 SURPLUS AND SPECIFIC RENT

For obtaining a solution, we have first to realize what is so 'specific' about this investment. To do so let's define the concept of surplus, as the difference between the value of the job inside the relationship versus the best alternative option. The formal definition is as follows.

> The worker surplus is the present discounted value of the difference between the wages and the outside option. The firm surplus is the present discounted value of profits (since the firm outside option is normalized to zero).

The present discounted value can be defined at time $t = 1$ and at time $t = 2$. Let's look at the surplus at time $t = 2$. In what follows, we indicate with $S_{w,2}$ and with $S_{f,2}$ the worker (firm) surplus at time $t = 2$, where the notation $S_{w,2}$ ($S_{f,2}$) indicates the worker (firm) surplus at time $t = 2$. The value of the surplus reads

$$S_{w,2} = w_2 - y$$
$$S_{f,2} = y + fs - w_2$$

The worker surplus is just the difference between the wage paid at time $t = 2$ and his or her outside option, which is equal to y. The firm surplus is equal to the marginal product at time $t = 2$, which is now the sum of $y + fs$ net of the wage to be paid to the worker. Without specifying what is the wage that is paid to the worker, it is impossible to argue whether the surplus of each party is positive or not. Nevertheless, no matter how such a wage is determined, once training has taken place, the sum of the two surpluses is a positive amount as long as $s = 1$. Formally

$$S_2 = S_{w,2} + S_{f,2} = fs$$

which is strictly positive if $s = 1$.

Let's now define the surplus at time $t = 1$ as

$$S_{w,1} = (w_1 - y) + (w_2 - y)$$
$$S_{f,1} = (y + fs - w_2) + (y - cs - w_1)$$

Once again, it is not possible to establish the value of the surplus without specifying the wages, but we know that the total surplus at time $t = 1$ is

$$S_1 = S_{w,2} + S_{f,2} = s(f - c)$$

which is strictly positive as long as $s = 1$. We thus have a positive total surplus as long as there is specific training.

> Firm-Specific Rent (or Surplus): A specific rent is a positive surplus that can be exploited only by the current relationship.

From the expression S_1 and S_2 it is easy to establish that firm-specific investment generates firm-specific surplus.

This is immediately established by noting that the expressions S_1 and S_2 are positive as long as $s = 1$. We have now understood that firm-specific training generates firm-specific surplus. The problem is to find an institutional setting that ensures that the surplus is exploited by the firm–worker pair. The next section introduces the concept of rent sharing.

9.5.2 RENT SHARING

A potential solution to the lack of investment in firm-specific skills is rent sharing. Giving some bargaining power to the worker, so that part of the extra profits generated by the specific investment is shared between the two parties, is part of the solution.

Let's modify the game above by assuming that in the final period, rather than the firm making a take it leave it offer, the worker and the firm bargain over the firm-specific surplus generated.

At time $t = 2$, there are three stages:

1. The firm and the worker share the surplus generated by the firm-specific investment, and the worker gets a fraction β of the total surplus in excess of his or her outside option. The bargaining power β is strictly less than 1.
2. The worker decides to accept this wage offer and work for this firm, or take another job without incurring any cost of changing jobs.
3. Production takes place and wages are paid. We let the productivity of the worker be $y + fs$.

This means that in the second period, if there is specific investment, the worker's wage is

$$w_2(s = 1) = y + \beta f$$

which is the sum of the worker's outside option (y) plus a fraction β of the total surplus. The wage in the first period is just the marginal product of the worker, or $w_1 = y - cs$ where s can be zero or one. Given this wage schedule, at time $t = 1$ the worker will choose $s = 1$ if

$$S_{w,1}(s = 1) > S_{w,1}(s = 0)$$

which is equivalent to

$$y - c + y + \beta f > y + y$$

The condition that ensures that the investment is implemented is

$$f > \frac{c}{\beta}$$

Ex post rent sharing ensures that some specific opportunities are undertaken, but does not guarantee that each and every opportunity is undertaken.

Indeed, it is easy to show that as long as $\beta < 1$ it is possible that $f > c$, and yet the investment is not undertaken.

With *ex post* rent sharing firm-specific investment is less than the first best.

The proof of this is easily seen with the help of Fig. 9.3. All the investments that lie above the 45 degree lines are efficient opportunities. Yet, we know that only the investment opportunities that lie above the dotted line $f = c/\beta$ will actually be financed. In Fig. 9.3 investment opportunities such as B and A should be financed while investment opportunities such as C should not be financed. As long as $\beta < 1$ there is always some investment opportunity such as B that is not going to be financed.

Is there a way in which the optimal level of specific human capital can be achieved? A key possibility is a full sharing of cost and benefits, so that the worker and the firm change the organizational system so that not only the benefits are shared, but also the costs. Let's see under what conditions the worker

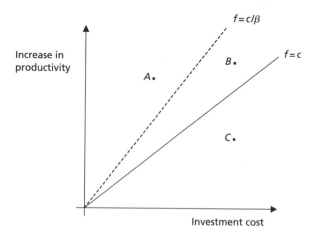

Figure 9.3. Specific investment with *ex post* sharing

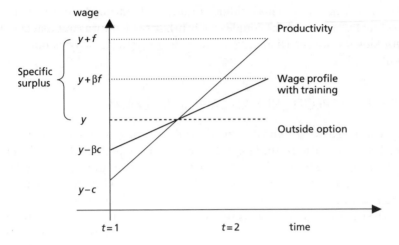

Figure 9.4. Wage tenure profile with firm-specific investment

will invest in training with full sharing, so that the worker pays a fraction β of the costs and gets a fraction β of the revenues. With full sharing, the worker chooses to invest if

$$y + \beta f - y - \beta c > 0$$

which will lead to the worker choosing the investment as long as

$$f > c$$

which is the condition that ensures that the investment is efficient.

One can look at the problem from the firm's standpoint. The firm at time $t = 1$ would like to sponsor training if

$$(1 - \beta)(y + f) - (1 - \beta)(y + c) > 0$$

from which it follows that the firm would choose an amount of training that satisfies $f > c$. An important conclusion follows.

With full sharing of costs and benefits, all profitable specific training opportunities are obtained.

Further note that the wage tenure profile becomes steeper once the specific investment is undertaken.

Note that by splitting costs and benefits, the worker and the firm have an incentive to stay together, so that firm-specific human capital is a good condition for establishing long-run relationships. This suggests that each time parties engage in firm-specific investments, the relationship is going to last longer. Note that these concepts can be applied also outside personnel economics, such as in the economics of family. For two partners, the best example of firm-specific investments is childbirth and child bearing. A child is an invest-ment that is specific to the couple (the firm). Indeed, it turns out that couples with kids last longer (they have a lower divorce rate) exactly as our theory would predict.

9.5.3 FIRM-SPECIFIC HUMAN CAPITAL: AN EXAMPLE

Let's consider a worker who is currently paid according to his marginal product, which we set equal to 100 in Table 9.1. The worker is expected to be hired for two years and the interest rate is zero, so that there is no issue of discounting. There is a training opportunity in specific skills that involves a loss of productivity at time $t = 1$ of 15, but it generates an increase in productivity at time $t = 2$ of 25. The training opportunity is thus efficient. Undertaking training increases the worker's wage at time $t = 2$ to 125, but his outside option remains 100.

We first consider the specific training without any rent sharing. There is a joint surplus equal to 5 at time $t = 1$, but the worker has no incentive to exploit it since his surplus is negative. In such a case all the surplus would go to the firm. Let's first consider the situation with *ex post* sharing, described in the third row of Table 9.1. With $s = 1$ the worker gets a wage cut at $t = 1$ equal to 15 against an increase in benefit at time $t = 2$ equal to 12.5. This implies that the benefit at time $t = 1$ is negative if $s = 1$. As a result, the worker will choose not to incur the specific investment. This is also consistent with the exposition given above, since $f = 25$ is lower than $c/\beta = 30$.

Let's now consider the situation with *ex ante* and *ex post* sharing. By sharing the costs and benefits, the worker surplus at time $t = 1$ is positive and equal to 2.5. This means that the worker will undertake the investment. The equilibrium is such that the worker takes a wage cut at time $t = 1$ equal to 7.5 and gets a wage increase equal to 12.5 in the second period. Table 9.1 confirms this result.

9.6 **Some Evidence on Training**

There are two main themes in the empirical literature on training. The first theme refers to the incidence of training across different dimensions, and the second is the relation between training and wages. We briefly review these two themes.

A common finding is that younger, better educated, and male workers are more likely to participate in training. The finding that training decreases with age is certainly consistent with the human capital investment theory: the pay-off period shortens with age and so will training rates. The second finding is that better-educated workers participate more in training than less-educated workers. This suggests that the marginal revenues to training are higher for

more skilled workers and/or that their marginal costs are lower. Most studies find also that women receive less training than their male counterparts.
The most common argument points to the lower labour force attachment of
women, which may cause employers to invest less. Gender differences might
also come about because women hold jobs that require less training, for which
there is some evidence. Training rates are also found to increase with firm size.
Perhaps the main explanation is economies of scale in training provision from
which larger firms benefit.

Human capital theory predicts upward-sloping productivity profiles. Wage
profiles are assumed to proxy these productivity profiles. The problem, however, is that there are many other theories, besides human capital, that predict
upward-sloping wage profiles and as such it is hard to argue that this is a defin-
itive test. One would like to know to what extent wage growth correlates with
productivity growth, but the literature has not found an obvious test for such
a prediction.

It is practically very difficult to distinguish between firm-specific and general
training, since in real life most training opportunities contain a combination
of the two. In this respect, the results reviewed in this section apply to both
types of investment. Yet, one can find a range of examples for which the
baseline theory of general training appears to provide a good description.
These include some of the historical apprenticeship programmes where young
individuals worked for very low wages and then graduated to become master
craftsmen; pilots who work for the Navy or the Air Force for low wages, and
then obtain much higher wages working for private sector airlines; securities
brokers, often highly qualified individuals with MBA degrees, working at a
pay level close to the minimum wage until they receive their professional
certification; or even academics taking an assistant professor job at Harvard
despite the higher salaries in other departments.

☐ APPENDIX 9.1. GENERAL TRAINING

The Basic Set-up

We now consider a generalization of the simple model proposed in the main chapter.
Consider the following very simple two-period model:

In the first period there is level of production equal to y. There are two stages:

1. The **firm decides** the level of training τ incurring the cost $c(\tau)$, where $c(\tau)$ reads

$$c(\tau) = \frac{c\tau^2}{2}$$

and c is a positive constant. We are assuming that training can be simply measured
through the variable τ.

2. Production takes place, for a value equal to $y - c(\tau)$.

In the second period there are three stages:

1. The firm makes a take it or leave it wage offer w to the worker, and other firms compete for the worker's labour.
2. The worker decides whether to quit and work for another firm. We assume that the worker does not incur any cost in the process of changing jobs, so that the labour market is perfectly competitive.
3. Production takes place. At this point the value of output is equal to $y + f(\tau)$ where $f(\tau)$ reads

$$f(\tau) = a\tau - \frac{b\tau^2}{2}$$

and a and b are positive constants.

For simplicity we assume that there is no discounting.

The Efficient Level of Training

Before proceeding, let's first establish what is the efficient level of training. It is simply the level of training that maximizes the difference between training benefits and training costs.

$$Max_\tau \qquad f(\tau) - c(\tau)$$

In such a case, training should be undertaken as long as the marginal benefit is equal to the marginal cost. In other words, the level of training τ^* should be chosen so that

$$c'(\tau^*) = f'(\tau)$$

where $c'(\tau) = c\tau$ and $f'(\tau) = a - b\tau$ so that the optimal level of training solves

$$c\tau = a - b\tau$$

$$\tau^* = \frac{a}{b + c}$$

The Solution of the Model

There are now two important issues to solve. First, we need to understand whether the efficient level of training is going to be achieved, and second and probably most important from the personnel economics standpoint, we need to understand who will have the incentive for paying it.

The model has to be solved backwards. At $t = 2$, the worker will be trying to obtain the largest possible salary in the marketplace. The solution of the second period at time $t = 2$ is then very simple. The worker will accept from the current firm (or from a different firm) only a training opportunity that guarantee a wage $w_2 = y + f(\tau)$ somewhere in the market, where τ is the level of training.

Let's now move back to the first period. Since in the final period the worker will get all the benefits from the investment, it is clear that the firm will not have the incentive to sponsor the training. The *firm would certainly make a loss on the training*, since it would incur a certain cost at time $t = 1$ without incurring the benefits. Since the worker is the *full residual claimant* of the increase in his or her own productivity, he or she will have the right incentive to invest. The firm will then offer to the worker the following package at $t = 0$, level of training $\tau^* = a/(b+c)$ and wage equal to $w_0 = y - c(\tau^*)$. In this situation, the worker accepts the deal, since he will get the full wage

$$w_1 = y + f(\tau^*)$$

in the second period, either from the current or from another employer.[3]

□ APPENDIX 9.2. FIRM-SPECIFIC TRAINING

Let's consider this problem:

- At time $t = 1$, the worker decides how much to invest in firm-specific skills, denoted by s at the cost $c(s) = cs^2/2$.
- At time $t = 2$, the firm makes a wage offer to the worker.
- The worker decides to accept this wage offer and work for this firm, or take another job.
- Production takes place and wages are paid. We let the productivity of the worker be $y + f(s)$, where $f(s) = a - (bs^2/2)$.
- Since s refers to specific skills, the outside option of the worker is still y.

To solve this problem we need to proceed by backwards induction. The worker will accept any wage $w_1 \geq y$ since y represents the worker's outside option. Knowing this, the firm simply offers $w_1 = y$. Then, given this wage $w_1 = y$, in the previous period the worker makes no investment in specific skills, even though there is an efficient level of investment that satisfies $c'(s) = f'(s)$ so that

$$a - bs^* = cs^*$$

$$s^* = \frac{a}{b+c}$$

The problem is the sharing of the specific investment and the fact that the worker is held up by the firm. The partial solution to the underinvestment in firm-specific skills is rent sharing. Let's modify the game above by assuming that in the final period, rather than the firm making a take it leave it offer, the worker and the firm bargain over the firm-specific surplus so that the worker's wage in the first period is

$$w_1(s) = y + \beta f(s)$$

[3] To understand why offering exactly τ^* is the equilibrium one would need to consider the alternative policy of offering any $\tau \neq \tau^*$. For being in equilibrium, we have to be in a situation in which no unilateral deviation increases profits. Let's see whether there are possible deviations when the training investment is $\tau \neq \tau^*$. In that case the worker's income would be lower, since by definition $y - c(\tau^*) + y + f(\tau^*) > y - c(\tau) + y + f(\tau)$. In this case a firm offering to the worker $y_0 - c(\tau^*) - \epsilon$ in the first period would attract the worker and make positive profits. This implies that there is a profitable deviation from the policy of offering $\tau \neq \tau^*$, so that we cannot be in equilibrium.

where β is the worker's bargaining power. Given this wage, at time $t = 0$ the worker will choose s so as to maximize with respect to s

$$y + \beta f(s) - c(s)$$

which gives the investment

$$\beta f'(\hat{s}) = c'(s)$$
$$\beta a - \beta b \hat{s} = c \hat{s}$$

which yields the investment level

$$\hat{s} = \frac{\beta a}{\beta b + c}$$

which is a positive amount.

Rent sharing induces a positive amount of investment in firm-specific skills, and partly solves the underinvestment problem.

Yet, it is easy to show that as long as $\beta < 1$, the amount of investment is less than the efficient level.

With *ex post* rent sharing firm-specific investment is less than the first best.

Is there a way in which the optimal level of specific human capital can be achieved? The only way is a full sharing of cost and benefits, so that the worker and the firm change the organizational system in such a way that not only the benefits are shared, but also the costs. Let's see what is the amount of training that the worker will choose with full sharing, so that the worker pays a fraction β of the costs and gets a fraction β of the revenues. With full sharing, the worker chooses an amount s^w such that he or she maximizes with respect to s^w

$$y_1 + \beta f(s^w) - \beta \gamma(s^w)$$

which will lead the worker to choose the investment such that

$$\beta f'(s^w) - \beta \gamma'(s^w) = 0$$

from which it immediately follows that $s^w = s^*$. Let's see now what level of training is going to be chosen by the firm. The firm at time 0 would like to sponsor an amount of training that maximizes with respect to s^f

$$(1 - \beta)f(s^f) - (1 - \beta)\gamma(s^w)$$

from which it follows that the firm would choose an amount of training that satisfies

$$(1 - \beta)f'(s^w) = (1 - \beta)\gamma'(s^w)$$

from which it follows that $s^f = s^*$. An important conclusion follows:

With full sharing of costs and benefits, the efficient amount of training is obtained. This is true, since, as we saw above, with full sharing $s^f = s^w = s^* = \frac{a}{b+c}$.

10 Training Investment in Imperfect Labour Markets

10.1 Introduction

The general conclusion of the baseline model of training (or the Becker model as it is known in the literature) developed in the previous chapter is that there will be no firm-sponsored investment in *general training*. This conclusion follows from the assumption that the labour market is competitive, so the firm will never be able to recoup its training expenditures in general skills later during the employment relationship.

In real life labour markets, and particularly in imperfect labour markets, there are many instances in which firms bear a significant fraction (sometimes all) of the costs of general training investments.

The chapter explores the key dimensions of firm-sponsored general training. We will see that in imperfect labour markets, where specific rents are pervasive, it may well be the case that firms undertake some investment in general training. Such a result crucially depends on the existence of an imperfect labour market, in the sense that wages paid to workers are higher than the corresponding outside option. Yet, such a condition is not sufficient to guarantee firm-sponsored training. Beyond market imperfection, firm-sponsored training requires skill wage compression. The intuition of this key result is that with wage compressions firms make greater profits from better-trained workers, and have an incentive to increase the skills of their workforce.

A first piece of evidence comes from the German apprenticeship system. Apprenticeship training in Germany is largely general. Firms training apprentices have to follow a prescribed curriculum, and apprentices take a rigorous outside exam in their area of expertise at the end of the apprenticeship. The industry or crafts chambers certify whether firms fulfil the requirements to train apprentices adequately, while works councils in the firms monitor the training and resolve grievances. At least in certain technical and business occupations, the training curricula limit the firms' choices over the training content fairly severely. Estimates of the net cost of apprenticeship programmes to employers in Germany indicate that firms bear a significant financial burden associated with these training investments. The net costs of apprenticeship training may be as high as 4,000 euros per worker.

Another interesting example comes from the recent growth sector of the USA, the temporary help industry, and this chapter also presents a case study. The temporary help firms provide workers to various employers on short-term contracts, and receive a fraction of the workers' wages as commission. The majority of temporary workers are in clerical and secretarial jobs. These occupations require some basic computer, typing, and other clerical skills, which temporary help firms often provide before the worker is assigned to an employer. Workers are under no contractual obligation to the temporary help firm after this training programme. Most large temporary help firms offer such training to all willing individuals. As training prepares the workers for a range of assignments, it is almost completely general. Although workers taking part in the training programmes do not get paid, all the monetary costs of training are borne by the temporary help firms, giving us a clear example of firm-sponsored general training.

There are also many examples of firms that send their employees to college, MBA, or literacy programs, and problem-solving courses, and pay for the expenses, while the wages of workers who take up these benefits are not reduced. In addition, many large companies, such as consulting firms, offer training programmes to college graduates involving general skills. These employers typically pay substantial salaries and bear the full monetary costs of training, even during periods of full-time classroom training.

The chapter proceeds as follows. Section 10.2 presents the baseline model of training in imperfect labour markets, in a simple set-up that assumes that the worker has no possibility of financing general training. Section 10.3 extends the baseline model, assumes that both the firm and the worker can finance the training, and studies under what conditions firm-sponsored training emerges in equilibrium. Section 10.4 presents the case study of the US temporary help industry, where firm-sponsored general training seems pervasive.

10.2 Firm-Sponsored Training: The Baseline Case

10.2.1 THE SET-UP

Consider the following two-period model.

In period 1, the **firm decides** whether or not to invest in the general training of the worker. The variable τ can take on only two values: $\tau = 0$ or $\tau = 1$, where $\tau = 1$ corresponds to a situation in which training is undertaken. The structure of the problem is reported in Table 10.1.

There is no discounting, and all agents are risk neutral.

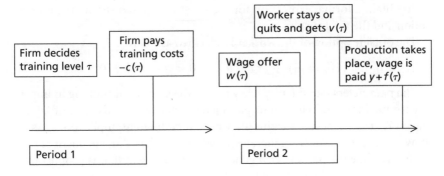

Figure 10.1. A two period model of firm-sponsored general training

If the firm undertakes training in period 1 it incurs a cost c. There is no production in the first period.

In period 2 there are three stages:

1. At the beginning of the period the worker receives a wage offer $w(\tau)$, where the notation $w(\tau)$ explicitly refers to the possibility that the wage depends on the availability of training.
2. The worker decides to stay or quit. The labour market is imperfect and the outside option is lower than the marginal product. In particular, the outside option v is lower than the corresponding wage so that

$$v(\tau) < w(\tau) \qquad \forall \tau$$

The previous condition ensures that the worker has some costs of changing jobs, even when there is no training. As we describe below, the wage is obtained through a simple rent sharing.
3. If the worker stays with the firm production takes place and the wage is paid. The value of the marginal productivity is $y + f\tau$.

Assume that all *training is technologically general* in the sense that the marginal product is $y + f\tau$ in all firms.

f is greater than c, which ensures that undertaking training is potentially an efficient opportunity.

As we argued above, the labour market is imperfect, and the value of the outside option is less than the wage. Assume now that wages are obtained by rent splitting, and the worker gets his outside option plus a fraction β of the total surplus. This is equivalent to assuming that the wage $w(\tau)$ reads

$$w(\tau) = v(\tau) + \beta S(\tau)$$

where $v(t)$ is the outside option of the worker and $S(\tau)$ is the total firm-specific surplus.

To obtain a formal expression for the wage we need to specify the outside option and the total surplus.

The outside option of the worker is specified as follows:

$$v(\tau) = a[y + f\tau] - b \qquad 0 < a < 1; \; b > 0$$

The parameters a and b play a key role in the analysis of training in imperfect labour markets. While both parameters refer to the existence of labour market rents and specific surplus, they have very different implications. As we show next, the parameter b generates a specific rent that is independent of productivity, while the parameter a generates a specific rent that is proportional to the marginal productivity on the job.

Let's now consider the surplus.

If we indicate with $S_f(\tau)$ and $S_w(\tau)$ the firm and the worker surplus at time $t = 2$, and with $w(\tau)$ the wage, the expression of the total surplus $S(\tau)$ is

$$S_f(\tau) = y + f\tau - w(\tau)$$
$$S_w(\tau) = w(\tau) - v(\tau)$$
$$S(\tau) = y + f\tau - v(\tau)$$
$$S(\tau) = (1 - a)(y + f\tau) + b$$

The surplus is positive as long as $a < 1$ and/or $b > 0$. We will see below that the two types of imperfections generate very different implications. What is crucial to our analysis is that the parameter b generates a specific rent that is independent of productivity $y + f\tau$, while the parameter a generates a specific rent that is proportional to the marginal productivity on the job.

10.2.2 THE SOLUTION

The key decision is the training decision.

At time $t = 1$, the firm decides to undertake training if and only if the firm surplus (or the firm profits) net of the training costs at time $t = 1$ is greater with training

$$S_f(\tau = 1) - c\tau > S_f(\tau = 0)$$

which is equivalent to

$$y + f - w(\tau = 1) - c > y - w(\tau = 0)$$

or to

$$f > c + \Delta w \qquad (10.1)$$

where $\Delta w = w(\tau = 1) - w(\tau = 0)$ is the increase in wage associated with training. Equation (10.1) is a key condition for firm-sponsored training in imperfect labour markets. It says that the firm will finance training if the increase in the marginal product (hence in revenue) associated with training is larger than the cost of training augmented by the increase in wage. This condition implies that if the wage increase associated with training is equal to the increase in the marginal product (hence $\Delta w = f$) there is no way in which firm-sponsored training can arise in equilibrium. This is exactly what happens in the case of a perfect labour market. Conversely, if there is no increase in wage (hence $\Delta w = 0$) then firm sponsoring of general training may arise. To obtain a solution we need to calculate the increase in wage.

Using the definition of the surplus, the wage with and without training is

$$w(\tau = 1) = a(y + f) - b + \beta[(1 - a)(y + f) + b]$$
$$w(\tau = 0) = ay - b + \beta[(1 - a)y + b]$$

so that the increase in wage associated with training is

$$\Delta w = f[\beta + a(1 - \beta)]$$

The previous condition shows that the increase in wage is proportional to f, but it is less than f as long as $a < 1$. The parameter a shows that the key condition for general training is *wage compression*. The smaller a is, the more compressed are the wages, since the wage difference across different skill levels is larger the smaller a is. Condition (10.1) is thus identical to

$$f > c + f[\beta + a(1 - \beta)]$$

so that the final key condition is

$$f[1 - a](1 - \beta) > c \qquad (10.2)$$

Several important conclusions follow:

If labour markets are perfect, firms never finance general training.

This is easily established. Markets are perfect if $a = 1$ and $b = 0$. It is clear that if $a = 1$ firm-sponsored training never takes place. Note that the parameter b does not enter in the condition (10.2). Another important conclusion immediately follows:

If labour markets are imperfect but wages are not compressed firms do not finance general training.

This implies that if $b > 0$, a condition that ensures that labour markets are imperfect, firm-sponsored training does not arise. In other words, the key condition for firm-sponsored training is wage compression, as the next and last conclusion shows:

If labour markets are imperfect and wages are compressed, financing of general training is possible.

If a is sufficiently low it is possible that a firm may sponsor general training, as equation (10.2) shows.

A numerical example is the following. Suppose that $f = 35$, $c = 15$, and $\beta = 0.5$. The key condition for firm-sponsored training is, from equation (10.2),

$$\frac{7}{6}(1 - a) > 1$$

which is satisfied only if $a < 1/7$. This suggests that as long as wages are compressed but $a > 1/7$ firm-sponsored training does not arise.

10.3 A More General Framework

In the previous section we studied a model in which workers could not finance the general training. The model in this sense was very specific, particularly when we know from the theory of training in perfect labour markets that workers in general have an incentive to take wage cuts and finance general training. We thus now study a more complicated version of the model in which both the workers and the firm can finance general training. In addition, we assume that the variable τ can take on a continuous value.

Consider the following two-period model.

In period 1, the worker and/or the employer choose how much to invest in the worker's general human capital, τ. There is no production in the first period.

In period 2, the worker either quits or stays with the firm and produces output $y = f(\tau)$, where $f(\tau)$ is simply a linear function of τ so that

$$y = \delta\tau$$

where δ is the marginal benefit of training. If the worker stays he is also paid a wage rate, $w(\tau)$, as a function of his skill level (training) τ, or he quits and obtains an outside wage. If the worker quits he or she obtains an outside wage $v(\tau)$. The cost of acquiring τ units of skill is described as a function $c(\tau)$, which is strictly increasing and convex, and reads:

$$c(\tau) = \frac{c\tau^2}{2}$$

There is no discounting, and all agents are risk neutral. Assume that all training is technologically general in the sense that $f(\tau)$ is the same in all firms. If a worker leaves his original firm he will earn $v(\tau)$ in the outside labour market. Suppose $v(\tau) < f(\tau)$. That is, despite the fact that τ is general human capital, when the worker separates from the firm, he will get a lower wage than his marginal product in the current firm. As in the model above, the expression for the outside option is written as

$$v(\tau) = af(\tau) - b \qquad a \leq 1 \text{ and } 0 \leq b \leq 1$$

The fact that $v(\tau) < f(\tau)$ or that $b > 0$ implies that there is a surplus that the firm and the worker can share when they are together. The total surplus is $S(\tau) = f(\tau) - v(\tau)$. Let us suppose that this surplus will be divided by Nash bargaining, which gives the wage of the worker as:

$$w(\tau) = v(\tau) + \beta[f(\tau) - v(\tau)]$$
$$= af(\tau) - b + \beta[f(\tau) - af(\tau) + b]$$
$$w(\tau) = [a + \beta(1 - a)]\delta\tau - b(1 - \beta)$$

where $\beta \in [0, 1]$ is the bargaining power of the worker. Note that the equilibrium wage rate $w(\tau)$ is independent of $c(\tau)$: the level of training is chosen first, and then the worker and the firm bargain over the wage rate. At this point the training costs are already sunk, and do not feature in the bargaining calculations. As is typically the case with sunk costs, bygones are bygones.

Assume that τ is determined by the investments of the firm and the worker, who independently choose their contribution, c_w and c_f, and the total amount of training τ is given by $c(\tau) = c_w + c_f$. Assume that \$1 investment by the worker costs \$$p$ where $p \geq 1$. When $p = 1$, the worker has access to perfect credit markets and when $p \to \infty$, the worker is severely constrained and cannot invest at all.

More explicitly, the timing of events is:

1. In the first period the worker and the firm simultaneously decide their contributions to training expenses, c_w and c_f. The worker receives an amount of training τ such that $c(\tau) = c_w + c_f$.
2. At the beginning of the second period the firm and the worker bargain over the wage for the second period, $w(\tau)$, where the threat point of the worker is the outside wage, $v(\tau)$, and the threat point of the firm is not to produce.
3. Production takes place.

Given this set-up, the contributions to training expenses c_w and c_f will be determined non-cooperatively. More specifically, the firm chooses c_f to maximize profits:

$$\pi(\tau) = f(\tau) - w(\tau) - c_f = (1 - \beta)[f(\tau) - v(\tau)] - c_f$$
$$\pi(\tau) = (1 - \beta)[(1 - a)f(\tau)] - \frac{c\tau^2}{2}$$

subject to $c(\tau) = c_w + c_f$. The first-order condition is

$$(1 - \beta)(1 - a)f'(\tau) = c\tau_f \qquad (10.3)$$

$$(1 - \beta)(1 - a)\delta = c\tau_f$$

the worker chooses c_w to maximize utility:

$$u(\tau) = w(\tau) - pc_w = \beta f(\tau) + (1 - \beta)v(\tau) - pc_w$$

$$[a + \beta(1 - a)]f'(\tau) = pc\tau_w$$

$$[a + \beta(1 - a)]\delta = pc\tau_w \qquad (10.4)$$

subject to the same constraint.

Let's start considering the case of $p \to \infty$, so that the worker is severely credit constrained and cannot pay for the training.

$b = 0$ and $a = 1$ is a perfect labour market. In this case there is no firm-sponsored training. The result of no firm-sponsored investment in general training by the firm obtains when $f(\tau) = v(\tau)$, which is the case of a perfectly competitive labour market. Equation (10.3) implies that $\tau_f = 0$, so when workers receive their full marginal product in the outside labour market, the firm will never pay for training.

$a = 1$ and $b > 0$. One may think that the key condition is to have a labour market imperfection with an outside wage that is less than the productivity of the worker, that is $v(\tau) < f(\tau)$. Is it enough to ensure firm-sponsored investments in training? The answer is no. To see this, first consider the case with no wage compression, that is, the case in which a marginal increase in skills is valued appropriately in the outside market. Mathematically this corresponds to $a = 1$ and $b > 0$, or to a case of an imperfect labour market without wage compression. In this case firm-sponsored training does not happen. Indeed b does not enter the determination of the equation. For firm-sponsored training to happen it is not sufficient that markets are imperfect.

$a < 1$. The key condition for firm-sponsored training is that $a < 1$. This is the definition of *wage compression*. When $v'(\tau) < f'(\tau)$ it is clear that the firm may be willing to invest in the general training of the worker. The simplest way to see this is again to take the case of severe credit constraints on the worker, that is, $p \to \infty$, so that the worker cannot invest in training. Then, $a < 1$ is sufficient to induce the firm to invest in training. This shows the importance of wage compression for firm-sponsored training. The intuition is simple: wage compression in the outside market translates into wage compression inside the firm, i.e. it implies $w'(\tau) < f'(\tau)$. As a result, the firm makes greater profits from a more skilled (trained) worker, and has an incentive to increase the skills of the worker.

To clarify this point further, Fig. 10.2 draws the marginal benefit and the marginal cost of training with and without wage compression. When $a = 1$

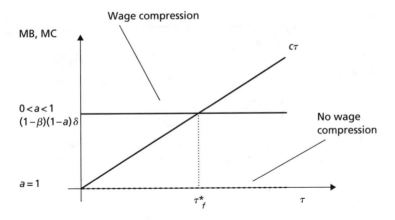

Figure 10.2. Marginal benefit and marginal cost of training to the firm with and without wage compression

there is no wage compression and the marginal benefit is along the horizontal axis. In this case there is no incentive from the firm to sponsor training and $\tau^* = 0$ will be chosen. A competitive labour market obviously implies this outcome. Conversely, when $0 < a < 1$ the marginal benefits cross the marginal costs at a positive amount and the firm is willing to sponsor general training. The intuition is that when there is wage compression and $a < 1$ the firm makes more profits from more skilled workers, and is willing to invest in the general skills of its employees.

Consider now a situation in which p is finite so that there is a solution to both τ_w and τ_f. Let τ_w be the level of training that satisfies (10.4), and τ_f be the solution to (10.3). It is then clear that if $\tau_w > \tau_f$, the worker will bear all the cost of training. And if $\tau_f > \tau_w$, then the firm will bear all the cost of training (despite the fact that the worker may have access to perfect capital markets, i.e. $p = 1$).

A decrease in a is equivalent to a decrease in the price of skill in the outside market, and would also tilt the wage function inside the firm, $w(\tau)$, decreasing the relative wages of more skilled workers because of bargaining between the firm and the worker, with the outside wage $v(\tau)$ as the threat point of the worker. Starting from $a = 1$ and $p < \infty$, a point at which the worker makes all investments, a decrease in a leads to less investment in training, as is clear from equation (10.4) and Fig. 10.3. This is simply an application of the Becker reasoning; without any wage compression, the worker is the one receiving all the benefits and bearing all the costs, and a decline in the returns to training will reduce his investments. As the parameter a declines further, we will eventually reach the point where $\tau_w = \tau_f$. Now the firm starts paying for training, and a further decrease in a increases investment in general training (from (10.3)).

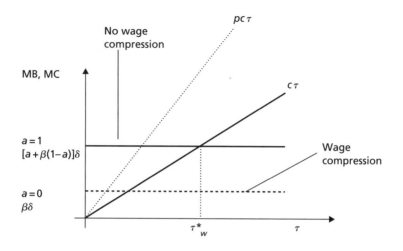

Figure 10.3. Worker financing of general training with imperfect labor markets

Therefore, there is a *U-shaped* relation between the skill premium and training, so starting from a compressed wage structure, a further decrease in the skill premium may increase training.

Changes in labour market institutions, such as the minimum wage, will also affect the amount of training in this economy. To see the impact of a minimum wage, consider the case with $a = 1$ and $b > 0$. The wage is then $w(\tau) = -b(1-\beta) + \delta\tau$. We have already established that in such a case there should not be firm-sponsored training. Yet, for very low values of τ such a wage can even be negative. Suppose that there is a minimum wage $\bar{w}$ that is binding for values of τ lower than $\bar{\tau}$. In other words, the wage is

$$w(\tau) = \begin{cases} \bar{w} & \text{if } \tau \leq \bar{\tau} \\ -b(1-\beta) + \delta\tau & \text{if } \tau > \bar{\tau} \end{cases}$$

In this situation firm-sponsored training may arise, as indicated in Fig. 10.4. Imposing a minimum wage distorts the wage structure and encourages the firm to invest in skills up to $\bar{\tau}$, as long as $c(\bar{\tau})$ is not too high. This is because the firm makes higher profits from workers with skills $\bar{\tau}$ than workers with skills $\tau = 0$. This is an interesting comparative static result, since the standard Becker model with competitive labour markets implies that minimum wages should always reduce training. The reason for this is straightforward. Workers take wage cuts to finance their general skills training, and minimum wages will prevent these wage cuts, thus reducing training. Therefore, an empirical investigation of the relationship between minimum wage changes and worker training is a way of finding out whether the Becker channel or the wage compression channel is

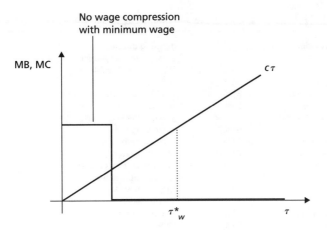

Figure 10.4. Firm-sponsored training with a minimum wage

more important. Empirical evidence suggests that higher minimum wages are typically associated with more training for low-skill workers.

10.4 **Firm-Sponsored Training in Temporary Help Firms**

The temporary help service (THS) industry supplies its workers to client sites on an as-needed basis, charging the client an hourly fee that typically exceeds the wage paid to the THS worker by 35 to 65 per cent. David Autor has used the case study of the THS industry as a well-documented example of employer-financed general training. In this section we review such a case study.

THS employment grew rapidly throughout the 1990s, accounting for about 10 per cent of net US employment growth over the decade. As of 2001, approximately 1 in 35 US workers was an employee of the THS industry. Further, given turnover rates exceeding 350 per cent, the industry's point in time employment is likely to substantially understate the number of workers who have contact with it annually. Up to the mid-1990s, the job skills required by THS firms (primarily clerical) were essentially static without any signific-ant amount of training. Things changed with the proliferation of workplace computing technology that generated demand for new and rapidly shifting expertise that could be mastered quickly. As is documented in Table 10.1, from the mid-1990s training is a pervasive industry feature. Of 1,002 US THS estab-lishments surveyed by the Bureau of Labor Statistics (BLS) in 1994, 78 per cent offered some form of skills training, and 65 per cent provided computer skills training. (Computerized tutorials are the most common form of instruction

Table 10.1. Skills training: prevalence and policies at US temporary help agencies

Training provided		Training policies	
All skills training		*(multiple policies possible)*	
Any	78%	'Up-front': All/Volunteers	
White-collar workers	56%	trained	66%
Clerical/sales workers	81%	Establishment selects	
Blue-collar workers	59%	trainees	34%
Computer skills training		Client requests and pays	36%
Any	65%	No training	22%
White-collar workers	27%	Training methods used	
Clerical/sales workers	74%	(if training given)	
Blue-collar workers	14%	*(multiple methods possible)*	
'Soft' skills training		Computer-based tutorials	82%
Any	70%	Classroom work, lectures	45%
White-collar workers	52%	Written self-study materials	52%
Clerical/sales workers	70%	Audiovisual presentations	47%
Blue-collar workers	58%	Other	14%

Detailed training subject frequencies by major occupation group				
	Any	White collar	Clerical/sales	Blue collar
Word processing	63%	23%	75%	13%
Data entry	58%	19%	69%	11%
Computer programming languages	22%	12%	23%	1%
Customer service	41%	27%	47%	12%
Workplace rules/on-job conduct	66%	55%	68%	60%
Interview and résumé development skills	30%	31%	32%	13%
Communications skills	14%	15%	14%	10%

(82 per cent), while 52 per cent of establishments provide workbook exercises and 45 per cent provide classroom-based training.)

Almost without exception, training is given prior to or between assignments *during unpaid hours* with all fixed and marginal costs paid by the THS firm. It is reported that 44 per cent of all skills training is given 'up front' to allow workers to qualify for their first assignments. Trainees are not contractually bound to take or retain a job assignment afterwards, nor would such a contract be enforceable. While THS firms are prone to overstate the efficacy and depth of their training, evidence of its value is found in the fact that several leading firms sell the same training software and courses to corporate customers that they provide for free to their workers.

These basic facts run counter to the baseline human capital model of training outlined in the previous chapter. In the competitive case analysed by Becker, workers pay for general skills training by accepting a wage below their marginal product during training. The threat of poaching or hold-up ensures that workers earn their full post-training marginal product, and hence up-front general skills training should never be provided by the employer. By contrast, the case study under scrutiny reveals that THS firms routinely provide training up front during unpaid hours, and hence the opportunity for workers to offset costs through a contemporaneously lower training wage is essentially non-existent.

David Autor (2001) used a unique survey for analysing the relationships among wages, training, and competition at temporary help establishments.[1] Conducted in 1994, the survey enumerates employment, wages, training offerings, and training policies at 1,033 temporary help establishments in 104 Metropolitan Statistical Areas (MSAs). The sample comprises an estimated 19 per cent of all THS establishments employing twenty or more temporary workers in 1994 and 34 per cent of all THS employment. One of the questions in the survey was whether establishments offer skills training to each 'collar' in eight subject categories: word processing, data entry, computer programming languages, workplace rules and on-the-job conduct, customer service skills, interview and résumé development skills, communications skills, and other. The core of the regression analysis that follows relies on computer skills because they are well defined, hold market value, and clearly constitute general skills training.

10.4.1 THE EVIDENCE: WAGES AND TRAINING IN THE THS INDUSTRY

In the baseline model of training, wages should be higher in establishments that provide general training. Since training is general, the worker is the residual claimant of the training provided, and he or she should obtain a wage gain in the aftermath of training. Table 10.2 reports a bivariate comparison of mean log wages at training and non-training establishments in the nine major occupational groups in the sample (three in white collar, two in clerical/sales, four in blue collar). The comparison is striking. In eight of nine occupations, mean wages are lower at training establishments, with an average occupational wage difference of minus 6.4 log points. Since workers receive training during non-work hours, the wage differentials estimated above do not reflect 'training wages' in the conventional sense of Becker. Rather, *they indicate that workers at establishments providing up-front training receive lower wages while assigned to client sites*, either before or after they have received training (or both).

To make a more formal comparison, David Autor estimated the following equation:

$$W_{ij} = a + \delta T_{ij} + \gamma_1 Ej + \gamma_2 O_i + \gamma_3 R_j + e_{ij}$$

where W_{ij} is the natural logarithm of hourly wages of individual i at establishment j. T_{ij} is a vector of establishment training variables, E_j is a vector of establishment characteristics, O_i is a vector of major occupation indicators,

[1] Occupational Compensation Survey of Temporary Help Supply Services (OCS hereafter).

Table 10.2. Comparison of log hourly wages of worker at training and non-training establishments

		Log hourly wages			Training No. workers No. estabs.	Non-training No. workers No. estabs.
		Free training	No training	Difference		
White collar						
	All	2.66	2.79	−0.13	10,497	13,034
		(0.04)	(0.05)	(0.06)	360	270
	Professional specialty	3.05	3.17	−0.13	2,918	5,016
		(0.02)	(0.03)	(0.04)	200	170
	Technical	2.41	2.45	−0.05	5,805	6,554
		(0.04)	(0.05)	(0.06)	274	213
	Accountants and auditors	2.72	2.77	−0.06	1,774	1,464
		(0.04)	(0.06)	(0.07)	187	134
Clerical/sales						
	All	2.01	2.09	−0.09	156,419	17,925
		(0.01)	(0.03)	(0.03)	693	166
	Clerical and administrative support	2.02	2.10	−0.08	145,997	16,957
		(0.01)	(0.02)	(0.03)	690	164
	Marketing and sales	1.84	1.97	−0.13	10,422	1,328
		(0.03)	(0.08)	(0.09)	435	42
Blue collar						
	All	1.76	1.78	−0.02	85,756	50,257
		(0.01)	(0.01)	(0.02)	461	294
	Precision production, craft, and repair	1.89	1.97	−0.08	8,193	6,142
		(0.04)	(0.04)	(0.06)	216	162
	Operators, assemblers, and inspectors	1.79	1.82	−0.03	19,867	12,851
		(0.02)	(0.02)	(0.03)	310	187
	Transport, material movement	1.89	1.92	−0.03	1,884	1,809
		(0.06)	(0.05)	(0.08)	186	126
	Handlers, equipment cleaners, and labourers	1.72	1.71	0.01	55,812	29,445
		(0.01)	(0.01)	(0.02)	445	252

R_j is a vector of 103 MSA indicators, and e_{ij} is a random error term assumed to be composed of a person-specific and establishment-specific component.

The parameter of interest is δ, the wage differential at training establishments. Due to the inclusion of narrow MSA and occupation indicators, δ effectively measures wage differentials among local THS establishments potentially competing for the same workers and supplying labour to the same customers.

The first three columns of Table 10.3 presents wage models for the full sample. The initial specification estimates the training wage differential with an indicator variable that is equal to one if the establishment provides computer skills training. The coefficient on this variable indicates that wages at training establishments are on average 2.0 log points lower, which is significant at the 5 per cent level. To probe alternative explanations for this wage differential, the second column introduces two additional controls. The first is the log of

Table 10.3. Estimates of the relationship between establishment training policies and worker wages

	Pooled estimates			Fixed effects estimates		
	(1)	(2)	(3)	(4)	(5)	(6)
Any training provided	−0.020 (0.010)	−0.019 (0.010)		−0.035 (0.0179)	−0.034 (0.0176)	
Up-front training provided			−0.025 (0.010)			−0.049 (0.019)
Firm selects trainees			0.005 (0.013)			−0.026 (0.040)
Client requests/pays for training			0.003 (0.012)			0.061 (0.039)
Log of establishment size		−0.026 (0.004)	−0.025 (0.004)		−0.020 (0.007)	−0.022 (0.007)
Log of THS employment in MSA-collar		0.051 (0.012)	0.050 (0.011)		0.023 (0.013)	0.024 (0.013)
Firm fixed effects	No	No	No	Yes	Yes	Yes
R^2	0.62	0.62	0.62	0.54	0.54	0.54
n	333,888	333,888	333,888	201,314	201,314	201,314

establishment size. Because large establishments typically provide more consistent THS assignments, workers at these establishments may accept lower hourly wages. And since large establishments are substantially more likely to offer training, it is plausible that the observed training–wage relationship in part reflects a size–wage differential. The second control introduced is the log of THS employment in the major occupation ('collar') in the MSA. The results do not change.

The empirical evidence provided suggests that training firms pay lower wages to workers at client firms. And these lower wages do not reflect training wages, since training is given up front. The result is thus in full contrast with the standard human capital model for general training. The next section describes a possible rationalization of this finding.

10.4.2 A POSSIBLE STORY FOR THE THS EVIDENCE

Autor has also provided a model in which not only firms sponsor general training, but also workers in THS training firms receive lower wages than workers in firms that do not provide training. The key idea of the model developed by Autor is that firms offer general skills training to induce self-selection and perform subsequent screening of worker ability.

The model has three periods. There are a large number of THS firms, some of which offer skills training, and some of which do not. These are referred to as training and non-training firms. All firms and workers are risk neutral, and there is no discounting between periods. In the first period, workers may select to work at either a training or non-training firm. Training firms provide general skills training to the workers whom they hire during the first period. Non-training firms do not. At the end of the first period, a fraction of the workers at each THS firm quits for exogenous reasons to enter the second-hand market. In addition, workers may quit their first period THS firms voluntarily to enter the second-hand market. Workers in the second-hand market are hired by other THS firms. At the beginning of the third period, all workers are hired by clients into the permanent sector.

The model can generate several equilibria. The equilibrium of empirical relevance, and consistent with the facts above, is a separating equilibrium in which workers with high-ability beliefs self-select to receive training while those with low beliefs do not. The separating equilibrium works as follows. In period 1 wages are identically zero for trainees and non-trainees and expected period 3 wages are higher for trainees. Although all workers would forgo some earnings to receive training, workers with high beliefs will forgo more because their expected period 3 gains are larger. At a separating equilibrium, the expected period 3 wage gain for high-belief workers offsets their training wage penalty in period 2, while for low-ability belief workers it does not. Consequently, at a separating equilibrium, wages at training firms are lower than at non-training firms.

The separating equilibrium depends critically upon two features of the model. The first is the complementarity between training and ability. Because training and ability are complements, high-belief workers apply to training firms, and low-belief workers apply to non-training firms. Training therefore serves as a self-selection device. If training and ability were not complements, either all workers or no workers would choose training. A separating equilibrium would be infeasible. The second critical feature of the model is that training elicits private information about worker ability. If training firms did not acquire private information about worker ability, competitive markets would ensure that each trainee received his marginal product after training. Hence, the dual roles played by training in the model, self-selection and information acquisition, are complementary. By inducing self-selection of high-ability workers, training improves the firm's worker pool. By revealing private information about worker ability, training then allows the firm to profit from this pool.

While the model is of course stylized, these private-information-based results appear consistent with the personnel policies of THS firms. After initial training and testing, THS workers are normally first placed at lower-wage, lower-skill assignments and subsequently given better placements as they demonstrate success. Workers who test and train successfully and perform well at assignments advance more rapidly while workers who perform poorly are rarely offered placements. Consequently, poor workers turn over disproportionately while good workers frequently remain.

11 Job Destruction

11.1 Introduction

Sooner or later, every firm experiences bad times. And in bad times, management often needs to reduce the size of the workforce. The choice of downsizing is obviously a key concern for personnel managers and for personnel economics. The firm needs not only to choose which workers should be targeted for lay-off, but also to realize that reducing the workforce will have an impact on the remaining workers.

Job destruction is a subtle business, even in labour markets in which employment protection legislation is not particularly stringent, and employer-initiated legislation is largely admissible. The first key concept that the chapter highlights is the difference between consensual and non-consensual separation, where the former refers to those separations that, at a given wage, are agreed by both parties, while the latter refers to those separation decisions that are not shared by both parties. Over the job destruction decision, each party (i.e. the firm and the worker) looks at his or her surplus from the job, and wants to preserve a job as long as the difference between the value of the job net of his or her outside option is positive. When the surplus of each party is negative there is obviously no point in continuing the job, and job destruction should take place without particular difficulties.

Whenever a non-consensual separation emerges, the firm has to consider whether it is possible to preserve jobs through wage cuts. Wage cuts, or an agreed reduction in future wages, are a job-preserving possibility that should always be contemplated. The chapter shows that as long as the joint surplus from the job is positive, there is always a profitable wage cut that can preserve the job. The issue is whether such *wage cuts* will be implemented in reality. There are, indeed, a number of reasons that explain why job-preserving wage cuts are barely observed in practice. A first issue to consider is whether reducing wages is allowed by the existing legislation. But there are other more subtle issues to consider, such as the effects of wage cuts on the remaining workers. In practice, firms often opt for job destruction rather than job cuts, even though there are important exceptions.

In simple and static views of labour demand, job destruction should take place each and every time the wage falls short of the value of the marginal productivity. In dynamic settings, and especially when employment protection legislation is stringent and firm-initiated separation is costly, things are more difficult. *Labour hoarding* is defined as a situation in which a firm hires a given quantity of labour even though the current marginal profit associated with such labour is negative. In an imperfect labour market, labour hoarding is a common phenomenon. An obvious reason for the occurrence of labour hoarding is the existence of employment protection legislation: when firing is costly, firms hold on to marginal losses just to delay the payment of firing costs. This is the key message of the second part of the chapter.

The final part of the chapter shows that labour hoarding emerges also when there is no employment protection legislation if two conditions hold: (i) there is surplus from a job; and (ii) there is uncertainty over the value of labour product. In a simple two-period model of job creation and destruction this type of labour hoarding naturally emerges.

The chapter proceeds as follows. Section 11.2 formally defines firm-initiated separation and distinguishes between consensual and non-consensual separation. It also discusses the conditions under which a profitable wage cut may exist. Section 11.3 defines labour hoarding and considers the optimal job destruction decision when firm-initiated separation involves a fixed cost. Section 11.4 presents the two-period model of job creation and destruction under uncertainty, and shows that labour hoarding emerges, in such a situation, even though firing is costless.

11.2 Firm-Initiated Separations and Wage Cuts in Imperfect Labour Markets

Let's focus on a single job that has been opened in the past, and let us use our standard notation for considering the value of the marginal productivity to the firm as J_t and the wage paid to the worker as W_t. The outside option to the worker is indicated with U_t.[1] The worker's surplus from the job is

$$S_w = W_t - U_t$$

A worker is clearly interested in continuing to work with a firm as long as $S_w \geq 0$, or as long as the value of the wage is larger than the outside option.

Let's define the firm's surplus from the job as

$$S_f = J_t - W_t$$

so that a firm wants to continue to hire a worker as long as $S_f \geq 0$, or as long as the marginal product is larger than the wage. For the purpose of this section we assume that the wage has already been set by collective agreements.

---

[1] In this section we use capital letter to indicate J_t, W_t, and U_t since, as we show in Appendix 11.1, such values may refer to present discounted values.

We have not formally specified what is the time horizon of the job. This was not an omission, since the concepts we are highlighting hold for both static jobs (i.e. 1 period) and multi-period jobs. In the former case, the wage W_t is simply the period wage. In the latter case, the variable W_t refers to the present discounted value of wages. Similar distinction can be made for J_t and for U_t and Appendix 11.1 reports the present discount interpretation of our discussion.

In any event, the total surplus from a single job can be written as

$$S = S_f + S_w$$
$$= (J_t - W_t) + (W_t - U_t) \qquad (11.1)$$
$$= J_t - U_t$$

We are now in a position to define consensual separation.

Consensual Separation: A separation is consensual as long as both $S_f < 0$ and $S_w < 0$. In other words, when the surplus is negative $S < 0$, or when $U_t > J_t$.

This works as follows. A worker wants to stop working for a firm as soon as $S_w < 0$ while a firm wants to fire the worker as soon as $S_f < 0$. If $W_t < U_t$ and simultaneously $J_t < W_t$, then necessarily $U_t > J_t$. In this case there is no point in continuing with this job, and it does not matter whether it is the firm that fires the worker or whether it is the worker himself that quits. In either case the job is going to be terminated.

Things are more complicated when the firm surplus is negative for the firm while positive for the worker. In this case the firm has an interest in terminating the job and proceeding to a firm-initiated separation. Nevertheless, such separation may not be consensual.

Firm-initiated separation is not consensual if $S_w > 0$ and $S_f < 0$.

When the worker surplus is positive (i.e. $S_w > 0$), there are no individual incentives to quit the job, and the worker will hold on to the job as long as the firm-initiated separation is not completed. If the firm has full authority over the continuation of the job, and there are no separation costs to be paid, the firm will initiate a separation procedure. The key question we address in the rest of this section is the following. *Is it possible for the worker to accept a sufficiently large wage cut so that the firm-initiated separation is avoided?* The remark shows that such a worker–firm transfer exists only when the total surplus is positive. A job-preserving wage cut exists when firm-initiated separation is not consensual but the surplus is positive.

To see the last conclusion, let's consider a situation in which separation is not consensual, so that

$$W_t - U_t > 0$$
$$J_t - W_t < 0$$

The worker is willing to accept a wage cut Δ (where Δ is defined in absolute terms) as long as the cut Δ leaves him or her with a positive surplus. In formula, Δ must be such that

$$(W_t - \Delta) - U_t > 0 \qquad \text{(Worker)}$$
$$\Delta < W_t - U_t \qquad (11.2)$$

The previous condition simply says that the wage cut should be lower than the initial worker surplus. Simultaneously, a firm is potentially willing to continue operation after the wage cut as long as

$$J_t - (W_t - \Delta) > 0 \qquad \text{(Firm)}$$
$$\Delta > W_t - J_t \qquad (11.3)$$

which simply says that the wage cut should be large enough to compensate the firm for the initial loss. Both conditions (Firm and Worker) hold only when the right-hand side of the (worker) condition is larger than the right-hand side of the (firm) condition so that

$$W_t - U_t > W_t - J_t$$

or when

$$U_t < J_t$$

The previous condition is the final proof, since it shows that as long as the job has a positive value, a profitable wage cut can be potentially implemented.

Another issue to consider is whether such wage cuts are possible in practice, since collective agreements specify wages and often do not allow such wage cuts to be implemented. This suggests that we may end up with inefficient separation. *A firm-initiated separation is inefficient whenever a profitable job-preserving wage cut is not implemented.* The inefficiency is linked to the fact that a job that has strictly positive surplus ends up being destroyed. Conversely, a separation that takes place when the total surplus is negative is always efficient.

So far we have only discussed firm-initiated separation, but it is clear that one can also discuss the case of worker-initiated separation. A worker-initiated separation is a situation in which the worker surplus is negative. In this case, we say that the worker would like to quit his current job. The interesting condition arises when the worker has a negative surplus while the firm enjoys a positive surplus.

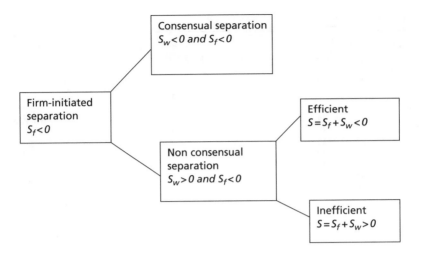

Figure 11.1. Firm-initiated separation

Worker-initiated separation is not consensual if $S_w < 0$ and $S_f > 0$.

In this scenario, rather than wage cuts, what we need to consider is whether there exists a profitable wage increase that can preserve jobs. For symmetry, it is clear that a job-preserving wage increase exists when the total surplus is positive.

A job-preserving wage increase is possible when the worker-initiated separation is not consensual but the surplus is positive.

The proof is analogous to what was described in the case of the wage cut.

11.2.1 JOB DESTRUCTION: AN EXAMPLE

Consider a firm that is hiring ten workers and needs to restructure and downsize its labour force. In other words, the firm needs to decide which workers should be kept and which workers should be offered a wage cut. The various workers act separately and the firm is able to distinguish the job of each and every worker. Table 11.1 reports the present discounted values of wages, outside option, and the production values for each of the ten workers. The firm is losing money on three workers (i.e. numbers 3, 4, and 9) and these three workers are the obvious candidates for a separation. On worker 3 the firm loses 8 while the worker enjoys a surplus of 5. Obviously, a wage cut up to 5 is profitable for this worker. But such a wage cut is not enough to compensate the firm. The total surplus is indeed negative and a separation is efficient. A similar situation exists for worker number 9, since the firm is losing 20 while the worker has

Table 11.1. Job destruction and wage cuts

Worker	Wages	Outside	Production	Firm surplus	Worker surplus	Separation	Total surplus	Action
1	70	60	70	0	10		10	
2	75	65	80	5	10		15	
3	40	35	32	−8	5	Firm initiated	−3	Separation
4	85	74	80	−5	11	Firm initiated	6	Wage cut
5	90	85	100	10	5		15	
6	25	30	25	0	−5	Quit	−5	Separation
7	65	70	71	6	−5	Quit	1	Wage raise
8	55	45	65	10	10		20	
9	90	75	70	−20	15	Firm initiated	−5	Separation
10	60	55	70	10	5		15	

a surplus of 15. On worker 4, the situation is more complicated, since the firm is losing 5 but the worker enjoys a surplus of 11. Here a job-preserving wage cut is possible, since the total surplus is positive. Indeed, a wage cut equal to 6 would make the job viable.

The situation of workers 6 and 7 is also interesting. On worker 6, the firm is indifferent while the worker has a negative surplus. This separation is not firm initiated but worker initiated, and we typically called it a *quit*. There is no surplus and the job is going to be destroyed. On worker 7, conversely, a profitable wage rise is possible.

11.2.2 JOB-PRESERVING WAGE CUTS WITH ASYMMETRIC INFORMATION

The discussion and formal analysis of the previous section suggests that in many instances, and notably when there is positive surplus, wage cuts could save jobs in an efficient manner. Yet, such wage cuts are rarely observed in reality. In this section we try to discuss why.

There are various concerns. First, there is the issue of collective agreements. Such wage cuts may not be possible by law, and in any case agreement with unions or works councils is necessary. This section focuses on another element that prevents the emergence of wage cuts, notably the presence of *asymmetric information*. The key point of this section is that when asymmetric information is pervasive, job destruction is often a preferred option to a wage cut. There are two key reasons.

1. *State of Demand.* In a large organization, the overall state of demand is known better to management than to the workers. There is asymmetric information over the state of business, and the firm is better informed than workers. In this setting, workers will not find credible the demand for a cut in wages because the state of demand is low. The problem is that the

firm could just act strategically in order to increase profits. By pretending to be in difficult business conditions, the firm may be able to increase profits. Conversely, reducing employment is a much more credible way to signal the state of demand, since firms will also incur output losses. The result is that job destruction is the only credible option.

2. *Internal labour markets.* In most organizations, the internal labour market of firms implies an implicit contract in which workers expect a rising wage profile, so that workers expect that conditional on good performance, future wage gains will be attained. Such a contract will be briefly described in Chapter 12. An overall wage cut would work as a breach of this implicit contract from the point of view of remaining workers. Conversely, employment reductions are consistent with such a contract.

This discussion suggests that downsizing ends up being a better option for the remaining workers. And since the firm acts as a forward-looking agent, it becomes the option to be pursued.

When the separation is worker initiated, in the sense that the worker is threatening to quit, the firm has to consider whether to implement a wage raise. In the case of perfect information, the situation is simple and it is the one described above. When information is asymmetric, often firms opt for a policy of not responding to wage increases obtained by employees outside the firm. The key reason to avoid matching a wage offer is the risk of inducing the rest of the workers to search more actively for a job. And if most workers behave in this way, it becomes very difficult for the firm to verify the credibility of each and every threat to quit.

11.3 Labour Hoarding and the Effect of Firing Taxes

In the previous discussion we have assumed that job termination is possible without the firm incurring any costs. Yet, in most imperfect labour markets job termination is a costly process and it involves firing costs. This section explicitly considers the situation of a firing tax to be paid by the firm in the case of a firm-initiated separation.[2] We basically assume that firm-initiated legislation is admissible, but it involves a fixed cost equal to F. The presence of the firing tax changes the outside option of the firm, which now involves the cost F. If the firm keeps the job open it will get a value that is equal to the difference between the value product and the wage, while if the firm terminates the job it will have to pay the firing tax, so that the surplus of the firm is now

$$S_f' = J - W - (-F)$$

---

[2] As we discuss in the next chapter the firing costs involve a monetary transfer to the worker as well as a tax to be paid outside the firm–worker pair.

where S' refers to the fact that we are now explicitly considering the firing cost. The surplus of the worker is unchanged and it is equal to $S_w = W - U$.

To understand the effect of firing costs let us assume that there are many jobs in the firm and that different jobs can have different values of J. In other words, we now assume that J can take any value from a minimum of zero up to a maximum of $J^{\max}$. Let's try to understand which jobs will be kept open by the firm.

Let's first analyse the case in which there are no firing costs, so that $F = 0$, and let's ask what is the minimum value of J for the firm to keep a job open. The answer is simple, since the firm will want to continue to operate any job that yields at least the wage rate. Let's call this value the *reservation productivity* J^* or a value of J that makes the firm indifferent between keeping the job open and closing it down. The reservation productivity when there are no firing costs is the value of J that makes the surplus equal to zero

$$S_f(J^*) = 0$$
$$J^* = W$$

When there are no firing costs the firm's firing decision is as follows: keep open any job that yields a marginal value that is at least as high as the wage rate. This is also the simple condition of labour demand in a static setting.

Let's now consider what happens when the firm has to pay a firing cost for implementing a job destruction. The firm will want to keep a job open as long as the continuation value is larger than the firing cost. Let's indicate with J^{**} the value of the marginal productivity to the firm when there are firing costs so that

$$S'_f(J^{**}) = 0$$
$$J^{**} - W + F = 0$$
$$J^{**} = W - F$$

where it immediately follows that $J^{**} < J^*$. The implication of this finding is obvious. When there are firing costs to be paid, the firm holds on to jobs that yield a value that is lower than the wage rate. This is called the *labour hoarding effect of firing costs*. In order to avoid the firing costs, the firm is willing to accept a loss on the marginal job and keeps open a job that yields less than the wage rate. This effect is clearly visible from Fig. 11.2.

Firing costs reduce the number of jobs that are destroyed.

This conclusion can be easily verified, since the larger the firing cost, the lower the reservation productivity. Firing costs induce firms to hold on to jobs that have lower marginal value. This is not surprising, since we have imposed a cost on the job destruction decision. Yet, in a general view of the

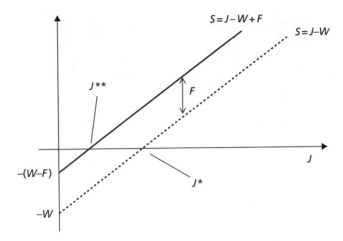

Figure 11.2. Reservation job and firing costs

firm's personnel policies, firing costs may certainly reduce job destruction, but they are also likely to have an impact on job creation. The rest of the chapter describes a two-period model of job creation and job destruction.

11.4 **Job Creation, Job Destruction, and Labour Hoarding**

We now consider the following two-period model of job creation and destruction. Assume that a firm and a worker face a potential opportunity to form a job. The salary to be paid in each period is equal to w and for simplicity we assume that it is constant in both periods. The job involves some uncertainty over the value of the labour product. We assume that in each period the value of the labour product (i.e. the value of the marginal product of labour) is akin to a random draw from a continuous distribution $G(\varepsilon)$ defined over the support $\varepsilon \in [\varepsilon_{min}, \varepsilon_{max}]$. The values of the labour product in the two periods are independent events, so that there is no link between the realization of ε in the first period and in the second period. In each period there are different stages, as is clearly indicated in Fig. 11.3.

1. In period 1 the firm first observes the realization of the productivity value ε, and then decides whether or not to create the job (this is called the *job creation decision*). If the firm creates the job, production in the first period takes place and the job moves to the second period.
2. At the beginning of the second period the firm observes the new realization of the productivity ε and it then decides whether or not the job

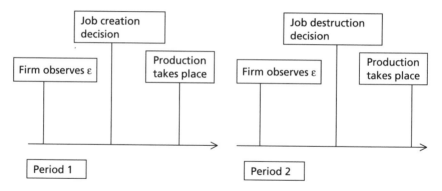

Figure 11.3. The timing of the events

should be destroyed (the *job destruction decision*). Job destruction at this point involves a firing cost equal to −F. If the firm destroys a job it has to pay F. If the job goes on production takes place and the job ends.
3. The firm has a discount rate equal to r. This means that 1 euro at time 2 yields a value at time 1 equal to $(1/1 + r)$.

There are two key decisions that the firm should make. At period 1 the firm should decide which realizations of ε should lead to a job formation. In period 2, the firm should decide which jobs should be destroyed. The problem is solved backwards. We first solve the job destruction decision at the beginning of the second problem, and then, given this decision, we move to the first problem and solve for the job creation decision.

We begin with the job destruction condition. At the beginning of the second period the firm observes a value of ε, so that if the firm operates it enjoys a marginal profit equal to $\varepsilon - w$. If the firm destroys the job it has to pay the fixed cost equal to −F. It is clear that the job destruction decision is given by the solution to the following problem

$$\text{Destroy if } \varepsilon - w < -F$$
$$\text{Continue if } \varepsilon - w > -F$$

This is the same problem as the one that we discuss in the previous paragraph, and it is clear that the firm decision will be described by a reservation productivity ε^d such that

$$\varepsilon^d = w - F$$

The value of ε^d is a reservation productivity and it is called the job destruction margin in the rest of the section. All jobs whose value of ε falls below ε^d should be destroyed. Note clearly that the job destruction decision is completely

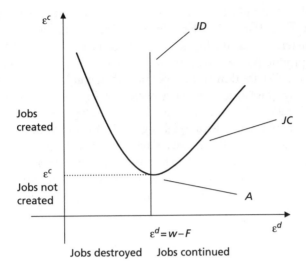

Figure 11.4. Determination of job creation and job destruction

independent from what happens in the first period. Bygones are bygones, and the firm decision is completely forward looking.

Two results are immediate:

1. Job destruction increases if the wage goes up. To see this one can notice that an increase in the wage increases the reservation productivity ε^d.
2. Job destruction is reduced if firing costs go up. To see this one can notice that an increase in the firing cost $-F$ increases the reservation productivity ε^d.

The job creation decision is more difficult to write down, but it delivers very important insights on hiring decisions in the context of firing costs. Let us indicate with $\Pi_1(\varepsilon)$ the present discounted value, evaluated at time 1 of profits at the beginning of the first period, once the firm has observed the realization of the productivity. Its expression reads

$$\Pi_1(\varepsilon) = (\varepsilon - w) + \frac{1}{1+r}\left\{\text{Expected Profits in Period 2}\right\}$$

$$\Pi_1(\varepsilon) = (\varepsilon - w) + \frac{1}{1+r}\left\{\int Max[z - w, -F]dG(z)\right\}$$

The previous expression should be read in the following manner. The left-hand side is the presented discounted profits for a job with realization in the first period equal to ε. The term in brackets $\varepsilon - w$ is simply the operational profits of the first period. The term $1/1+r$ is the discount factor, while the term inside the integral is the expected profits from the second period, taking into consideration the job destruction decision. This expression, whose formal value is given by the term inside the brackets, should be read as follows. In the second period the productivity will be equal to z, where z can take any value from the support of the distribution G. But we know that, conditional on observing z, the firm will operate as long as the expected profits are larger than the firing costs. This is reflected by the max operator. The integral symbol simply sums up all possible values of z, with weights given by the distribution $G(z)$.

At time 1 there are no firing costs to be paid, since the job has not yet been established. If the job is not going to be created, the firm does not face any cost, so that the outside option at the moment of creation is simply zero. The job creation decision is then described by the following simple condition:

$$\text{Create if } \Pi_1(\varepsilon) > 0$$

$$\text{Not Create if } \Pi_1(\varepsilon) < 0$$

This suggests that the decision to create will be regulated by a reservation productivity ε^c such that

$$\Pi_1(\varepsilon^c) = 0$$

ε^c is the creation margin, and needs to be solved with a few steps of algebra.

Solving for the Job Creation Condition

Using the definition of the job creation margin, the job creation margin is the solution to

$$\varepsilon^c - w + \frac{1}{1+r}\left\{\int Max[z-w, -F]dG(z)\right\} = 0$$

The first thing we can do is to get rid of the max operator inside the integral. The job destruction is obtained by the reservation productivity ε^d, and we know that for values of z below ε^d the job is destroyed while for values above ε^d the job continues its operation. We can then remove the max operator, by writing down two integrals for different values of z. The expression reads:

$$\varepsilon^c - w = -\frac{1}{1+r}\int_{\varepsilon^d}^{\varepsilon^{max}} (z-w)dG(z) + \frac{1}{1+r}FG(\varepsilon^d)$$

The previous expression gives the job creation as a function of the firing cost and the job destruction decision. It has important economic implications. The left-hand side is the operational profits for the marginal job, and it is equal to two terms in the right-hand side. The first term in the right-hand side is a negative term (the integral is a positive function, since z is always above w for values of z above ε^d) while the second term is positive. When $F = 0$ the right-hand side is obviously negative. This suggests that there is a tendency of the firm to take a loss in the first period, and to open up those jobs that yield a negative loss in the first period, but are offset by positive expected profits in the second period. This is a form of labour hoarding. There is labour hoarding each time the firm optimally holds on to current losses from hiring a worker.

When $F > 0$, the right-hand side tends to increase. This suggests that the larger the firing costs, the larger the operational profit of the marginal job. This makes a lot of sense, since the firm anticipates future firing costs and opens up jobs that yield larger profits. This will be confirmed in the comparative static below.

The full solution of the job creation margin can be obtained through a diagram in which on the two axes are reported the job creation and the job destruction margins $[\varepsilon^c, \varepsilon^d]$. The job destruction curve is a vertical line that crosses the axis at the point in which $\varepsilon^d = w - F$. The job creation curve is the locus that describes the combination of $\varepsilon^c, \varepsilon^d$ that yields zero expected profits. The slope of the job creation is obtained by a simple differentiation which shows that

$$\frac{d\varepsilon^c}{d\varepsilon^d} = \frac{g(\varepsilon^d)}{1 + r}[\varepsilon^d - w + F]$$

In other words, the job creation margin is akin to a quadratic function that features a minimum in correspondence to a point of the job destruction curve. To understand this property recall that along the job creation curve $\Pi(\varepsilon^c) = 0$. Consider a point on the job creation curve to the left of the job destruction curve. In such a point, an increase in the job destruction margin (which is lower than $w - F$) increases profits in the second period, and such an increase must be compensated by a decrease in ε^c for the expected profits to be zero. The opposite happens to the right of the maximum.

The Effect of Change in Firing Costs

The effect of change in firing costs is immediately obtained, and it is described by a shift to the left of the job destruction curve. The job creation shifts upward as can be immediately seen by differentiating the job creation curve with respect to F at given ε_d. The new situation is described in Fig. 11.5, and the following important result is immediately derived.

An increase in firing costs reduces job destruction in the second period but it also reduces job creation in the first period.

This conclusion is the fundamental effect of firing costs on job creation and destruction.

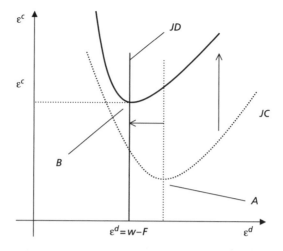

Figure 11.5. The effects of an increase in firing costs on job creation and job destruction

☐ APPENDIX 11.1 PRESENT DISCOUNTED VALUES AND MULTI-PERIOD JOBS

Employment relationships often involve a time horizon which is larger than a single period. To discuss issues linked to multi-period labour demand, we need to introduce some key concepts:

u_t: Value at time t of the alternative use of time. This is the value of the outside option at time t.

w_t: wage profile; it describes the value of the wage at each period t.

y_t: productivity profile, the value of the productivity at time t.

Let's consider a worker that potentially can be hired for T periods, and thereafter he or she retires. We call t the tenure of the worker or the years of experience with the firms. 0 is the age of youth (newly hired) workers while T is retirement age.

Let's define three key present discounted values. Note that we use capital letters for present discounted values and lower-case letters for flow payments at period t. At time $t < T$, W_t, or the presented discounted values of wages, reads:

$$W_t = w_t + \frac{w_{t+1}}{(1+r)} + \frac{w_{t+2}}{(1+r)^2} + \ldots + \frac{w_{T+t}}{(1+r)^T}$$

$$W_1 = \sum_{k=1}^{T} \frac{w_{k+t}}{(1+r)^k};$$

U_t is the present discounted value of the worker's alternative at time t so that

$$U_t = \sum_{k=1}^{T} \frac{u_{k+t}}{(1+r)^k}$$

Finally, J_t is the present discounted value of the productivity stream of the worker to the firm.

$$J_t = \sum_{k=1}^{T} \frac{y_{k+t}}{(1+r)^k}$$

When the firm problem is dynamic and multi-period, the surplus of the firm is the difference between the present discounted value of productivity and the presented discounted value of wages. If we label Π_t the present discounted value of profits (or S_{ft}) we have

$$\Pi_t = y_t - w_t + \frac{y_{t+2} - w_{t+2}}{1+r} \ldots + \frac{y_T - w_T}{(1+r)^T}$$

which can be written as

$$\Pi_t = \sum_{k=1}^{T} \frac{y_{t+k} - w_{t+k}}{(1+r)^k}$$

Further we know that the surplus is positive if

$$\Pi_t = \sum_{k=1}^{T} \frac{y_{t+k}}{(1+r)^k} - \sum_{k=1}^{T} \frac{w_{t+k}}{(1+r)^k} \geq 0$$

$$\Pi_t = J_t - W_t \geq 0.$$

12 Further Issues in Employment Protection Legislation

12.1 Introduction

The previous chapters in the book studied the role of employment protection in the context of temporary contract and in the case of job destruction. We learnt two key messages. First, employment protection biases the firm choice toward temporary contract. Second, employment protection reduces job destruction and increases labour hoarding. Yet, when job creation is also explicitly considered, employment protection also depresses job creation. While these are indeed the key messages in the literature of employment protection legislation, other important issues need to be considered.

In real life labour markets, employment protection legislation is a multi-dimensional institution. Its provisions are often very complex, and the legislation not only forces the firm to pay specific sums of money to the dismissed worker, but it also forces the firm to follow specific procedures, which inevitably involve deadweight losses to both parties. In other words, employment protection legislation involves both transfer inside the firm–worker pair as well as taxes paid outside the match. Section 12.2 documents that the largest part of the legislation refers to transfer. But the difference between taxes and transfer is economically very important when wage determination is explicitly considered. In previous chapters, the role of employment protection legislation was always analysed at a given wage. In reality, wages are likely to respond to the existence of EPL. Indeed, the model of section 12.3 shows that when wages are endogenously determined by rent sharing, the transfer component of EPL is likely to be allocative neutral. This means that employment protection legislation may have a large impact on wage profiles, but little impact on job destruction. Such a conclusion is not true in the case of the tax component of EPL, whose effects cannot be fully absorbed the wages.

Another dimension of EPL in real life labour markets is the different degree of stringency across firms of different sizes. Large firms have typically a degree of EPL that is tighter than the degree of EPL imposed on small firms. This differences is also economically important, since it may affect the scale of operation of each firm. In other words, firms may have an incentive to operate below a given EPL threshold just as a way to save on EPL provisions beyond the threshold. These issues are analysed in section 12.4, in a simple model of EPL with threshold effects.

12.2 **EPL Taxes and Transfers**

Employment Protection Legislation (EPL) is one of the most important institutions of the labour market. It refers to the set of norms and procedures to be followed in cases of dismissals of redundant workers. In almost all countries, EPL forces employers to transfer to the worker a monetary compensation in case of early termination of a permanent employment contract. Moreover, complex procedures have to be followed in case of both individual and collective lay-offs.

EPL is obviously a multidimensional institution. The most traditional dimensions of EPL are the severance payments and advance notice. Severance payments refer to a monetary transfer from the firm to the worker to be paid in case of firm-initiated separation. Advance notice refers to a specific period of time to be given to the worker before a firing can actually be implemented. Note that the severance payment and advance notice that are part of EPL refer to the minimum statutory payments and mandatory rules that apply to all employment relationships, regardless of what is established by labour contracts. Beyond mandatory payments, collective agreements may well specify larger severance payments for firm-initiated separations. Such party clauses, albeit important, are not considered in this report.

Another important dimension of EPL consists of the administrative procedures that have to be followed before the lay-off can actually take place. In most countries, the employer is often required to discuss the lay-off decisions with the workers' representatives. Further, the legislative provisions often differ depending on business characteristics such as firm (or plant) size and industry of activity. As this simple introduction shows, it is obvious that the EPL is a multidimensional phenomenon.

From the viewpoint of economic analysis, the multidimensionality of the EPL can be reduced to two components. The first component is simply a monetary transfer from the employer to the worker, similar in nature to the wage. The second, instead, is more similar to a tax, because it corresponds to a payment to a third party, external to the worker–employer relationship. Conceptually, the severance payment and the notice period correspond to the transfer, while the trial costs (the fees for the lawyers, etc.) and all the other procedural costs correspond to the tax.

12.2.1 CALCULATING TAXES AND TRANSFERS

Decomposing the total firing cost between tax and transfer components is an exercise that requires detailed knowledge of the country-specific institutions.[1] Garibaldi and Violante provide estimates of the transfer and tax components in the statutory firing cost for Italy, one of the countries with the strictest employment protection legislation (OECD 1999). The estimates show that transfers significantly exceed taxes. In this section we briefly review such calculations.

In the Italian legislation, an employer-initiated lay-off against an individual employee is legitimate only when it satisfies a 'just cause'. The Italian civil law foresees that individual dismissals are legal only under two headings: *justified objective motive*, i.e. 'justified reasons concerning the production activity, the organization of labour in the firm and its regular functioning', and *justified subjective motives*, i.e. 'a significantly inadequate fulfilment of the employee's tasks specified by the court'. The first case involves events which are outside the employee's control, while the second case requires misconduct on the part of the worker. The worker has always the right to appeal against the firm's decision, and the final judgment ultimately depends on the court's interpretation of the case. If the worker does not appeal against the firing decision, or if the separation is ruled fair, the legislation does not impose any firing cost on the firm.[2] Conversely, when the separation is ruled unfair and illegitimate, the court imposes a specific set of transfers and 'taxes' on the firm, which we analyse next.[3]

The total costs associated with this procedure can be calculated *ex post*, i.e. when the firm has already learnt that the job is no longer viable, as well as *ex ante*, i.e. when the job is still viable and production is going on.

Ex post **firing cost.** Specifically, we start by considering a situation where an employer-initiated individual separation against a blue-collar worker with average tenure (eight years) in a firm with more than fifteen employees is ruled unfair by the judge after a twelve-month trial, the average length of a labour trial in Italy. This firing cost is therefore *ex post* with respect to the court's decision. Although, this is not the exact counterpart of the cost in the firm's hiring and firing decision, it is a useful starting point.

First of all, the worker will be granted the forgone wages from the separation day up to the court ruling (i.e. twelve months under our assumptions), while

[1] This requirement goes well beyond the information published by the OECD (1999). Possibly, for this reason we are not aware of any other study trying to make this comparison.
[2] The union to which the worker is affiliated usually bears all the legal costs in this case.
[3] Concerning the definition of a legitimate separation, the Italian EPL does not make any difference in terms of firm size. Yet, the maximum compensation to which unlawfully fired workers are entitled varies with firm size in two important dimensions. For small firms (with less than fifteen employees), the choice between a full reinstatement and a severance payment rests with the firm. Further, for workers employed in firms with less than fifteen employees the maximum severance payment that can be obtained in court is limited to six months' wages.

the firm will pay the forgone social insurance contributions augmented by a penalty for delayed payment. In addition, the worker may choose between a severance payment of fifteen months or the right of being reinstated by the firm that unlawfully fired him.[4] In over 95 per cent of the cases, the worker opts for the former option. Finally, all the legal costs will be paid by the firm. Thus, if we let n be the number of months that it takes to reach a court decision, w the gross monthly wage, τ^s the social security contributions, τ^h the health insurance contribution, ϕ the penalty rate on forgone contributions, sp the mandatory severance payments for unfair dismissal, and lc the total legal cost, the total *ex post* firing cost FC is

$$FC = nw + (\tau^s + \tau^h + \phi)nw + sp + lc.$$

The pure transfer component paid by the firm to the worker is

$$S = nw + \alpha\tau^s nw + sp,$$

where α is the share of the social security contributions that is rebated to the worker in the form of increased future pensions, in which case such a payroll contribution should be counted as transfer inside the match. The tax component is

$$T = (1 - \alpha)\tau^s nw + (\tau^h + \phi)nw + lc.$$

Table 12.1 provides an estimate of the size of FC as well as of the components T and S in the total firing costs when $\alpha = 0$, the share that minimizes the transfer

Table 12.1. Tax and transfer components of firing costs in Italy

	Components of firing costs		
	Total	Tax	Transfer
Forgone wages nw	12	0	12
Health insurance $\tau^h w$	1	1	0
Social security contributions $\tau^s w$	4	4	0
Sanctions for delayed payments ϕw	3	3	0
Legal costs lc	6	6	0
Severance payments sp	15	0	15
Ex post firing costs FC	41	14	27
Share	100	34	66
Cost in out of court agreement $p_u(S + T/2)$	17	0	17
Total *ex ante* firing costs $\tilde{FC}$	18.75	3.5	15.25
Share	100	19	81

[4] See Ichino (1996) for the legal sources of this binding rule. Note that the number reported by the OECD (1999: table 2.A.2, p. 95) on the statutory severance payment in Italy is erroneous, since it refers instead to the mandatory deferred wage scheme (TFR), a very different institution.

component, i.e. the case that makes the tax component as large as possible. The estimate suggests that the total *ex post* cost is over forty months' wages, and the transfer component of the total firing costs amounts to 66 per cent.

Ex ante **firing cost.** The above computation results in an impressively high firing cost, but we should keep in mind that it is based on the worst possible scenario for the firm: once the case has been taken to court and the judge has reached a verdict favourable to the worker. Obviously, *ex ante* the firm–worker pair does not know with certainty whether the separation will be ruled unfair by the tribunal: let p_u denote the probability of such event. Many employer-initiated separations are not settled in court. Firms and workers often find a satisfactory settlement out of court and strike a deal before the full trial is over. In the case of an out of court agreement, the parties can save any court penalties that may eventually be imposed by a judge, and all the legal costs linked to the trial. In particular, if the two parties bargain in a symmetrical Nash fashion on the settlement, the joint maximization problem will solve

$$\max_{\widehat{S}} \left[\widehat{S} - p_u S\right]^{\frac{1}{2}} \left[-\widehat{S} + p_u(S + T)\right]^{\frac{1}{2}},$$

where we denote by $\widehat{S}$ the point of agreement between firm and worker. Notice that we have assumed—as common practice in Italy—that the labour union will pay the legal costs in cases where the lay-off is ruled fair. The solution gives $\widehat{S} = p_u (S + (T/2))$ which is an amount larger than the expected transfer the worker would receive, but smaller than the total cost (transfer plus tax) the firm would pay in case the firing is ruled unfair. The intuition is that half of the tax becomes part of the settlement. For the purpose of our analysis, it is important to remark that in this case the entire firing cost for the firm is a *transfer* to the dismissed worker.

Let p_a be the probability of agreement out of court. If we ignore discounting, the *ex ante* (with respect to the court's verdict) expected firing cost $\widetilde{FC}$ is

$$\widetilde{FC} = p_a p_u \left(S + \frac{T}{2}\right) + (1 - p_a) \left[p_u FC + (1 - p_u)C_L\right], \quad (12.1)$$

where C_L is the firing cost incurred by the firm when the judge rules the firing legitimate. Since, as we explained above, in the Italian legislation $C_L = 0$, the expected transfer component is

$$\widetilde{S} = p_a p_u \left(S + \frac{T}{2}\right) + (1 - p_a) p_u S \quad (12.2)$$

while the expected tax component is

$$\widetilde{T} = (1 - p_a) p_u T. \quad (12.3)$$

Galdon-Sanchez and Guell (2000), using data based on actual court sentences, compute that in Italy the probability of reaching an out of court agreement (p_a) is roughly 0.50, and the probability of the individual lay-off being ruled unfair (p_u) is also approximately 0.50. With these probabilities, using the estimates of Table 12.1, $\widetilde{FC}$ falls to eighteen months' wages. However, for the sake of our analysis, what matters is the fact that the share of the transfer rises to over 80 per cent of the total.

12.3 Outsiders, Insiders, and Tax and Transfers

Let us now consider a two-period model. A firm and a worker face a job opportunity that lasts two periods. The value product in the first period is equal to ε_h. The value of the labour product in the second period is random. It can be equal to ε_h with probability p and it is equal to ε_l with probability $1 - p$. We assume that ε_l is a large negative number so that the firm always fires the worker when the realization in the second period is ε_l. In the second period the worker is entitled to employment protection legislation. The second period is called the 'insider phase', since the worker is entitled to employment protection legislation (EPL). EPL takes two different forms. On the one hand, there is a severance payment to be paid to the worker that we indicate with the letter T. On the other hand there is firing tax that we call F. Even though both payments are technically made by the firm, there is a key difference between the two institutions. The severance payment is paid to the worker while the firing tax is paid outside the match. In the first period the worker is not entitled to employment protection legislation. We thus call such a phase the outsider phase. Note that there is no explicit firing in the first period. Yet, if the parties do not agree on a wage negotiation the worker is not entitled to any form of EPL.

We will assume for most of the section that wages are negotiated through rent sharing, and that the worker gets a fraction β of the total surplus. The surplus that each party enjoys must be properly defined in each period, since it changes between the outsider and insider phase.

- In period 1 the job is already formed and the productivity is ε_h. The firm and the worker must agree on an outsider wage which we label w_0. Production takes place and the worker, at the end of period 1, becomes an insider worker.
- At the beginning of period 2 the realization of the labour product is known to both parties. If the value product is ε_l the job ends and the firm must pays both the transfer T and the tax F. The insider workers gets the transfer T while the payment F is dissipated. If the value product is equal to ε_h,

the party must agree on a salary that we label w_i. At that point production takes place.

- We assume that there is no discount rate. This means that 1 euro at time 2 yields a value at time 1 equal to 1 euro.

12.3.1 DERIVING THE WAGES WITH SEVERANCE PAYMENTS

The problem is solved backwards. We first solve the wage in the second period, when the worker is an insider. Next we solve for the wage in the first period when the worker is an outsider, taking into account the wage of the insider.

Let's first focus on severance payments only, so that in this section we assume that $F = 0$. We begin in the second period and assume that the job continued, so that $\varepsilon = \varepsilon_h$. In the second period, the value of the profit to the firm if a wage agreement is found is $\varepsilon_h - w_i$ while if no agreement is found the firm needs to pay the severance payment T. The firm surplus at time $t = 2$ is

$$S_{f,2} = \varepsilon_h - w_i - (-T)$$

Let's now consider the worker position at time $t = 2$. The worker surplus from a wage agreement is

$$S_{w,2} = w_i - (T + u)$$

where u is the value of the outside option for 1 period and T is the severance payment. The total surplus is simply

$$S_2 = \varepsilon_h - u$$

from which follows an obvious important conclusion.

The severance payment does not enter in the total surplus.

To see this point simply notice that in the determination of the expression the severance payment does not enter. This is not surprising, since the severance payment is just a pure transfer. Nevertheless, the previous remark will have important consequences for the effect of severance payment on job destruction. Having derived the surplus, the wage of the insider is obtained in such a way that the worker gets a fraction β of the total surplus. This means that the worker surplus is

$$w_i : \qquad w_i - (T + u) = \beta S_2$$

from which it follows, after a simple substitution, that

$$w_i = (1 - \beta)u + \beta\varepsilon_h + T$$

The wage of the insider is a simple weighted average between the worker outside option and the productivity of the match. In addition, the severance payment increases the wage of the insiders. This means that insiders' wages go up with respect to a situation without severance payment.

Let's now move to the first period. The cumulative expected profits from employment at time 1 for the firm are equal to

$$\Pi_1 = \varepsilon_h - w_o + p(\varepsilon_h - w_i) - (1-p)T$$

where $\varepsilon_h - w_o$ are the operational profits in the first period. Note that the second period expected profits are random. In the second period two things can happen: with probability p the job continues and the firm gets $\varepsilon_h - w_i$ (w_i is the insider wage), while with probability $(1-p)$ the job is destroyed and the firm pays the severance payment to the worker.

Let's now turn to the workers' value of employment at time 1, which can be written as

$$W_1 = w_o + pw_i + (1-p)(u+T).$$

The total value of the outside option, which we indicate with U, is simply equal to the total sum of the per period outside option u, so that $U = 2u$.

As we mentioned above, at time $t = 1$ the worker is an outsider and he or she is not entitled to severance payment. This means that the total surplus to the worker is

$$S_{w,1} = W_1 - U_1.$$

As for the firm, if agreement is not reached, there is no severance payment involved so that $S_{f,1} = \Pi_1$. This means that the total surplus at time $t = 1$ is

$$S_1 = W_1 - U_1 + \Pi_1$$

which, after a simple substitution of the functions, leads to

$$S_1 = \varepsilon_h - u + p(\varepsilon_h - u)$$

The previous expression simply says that the total surplus from the match is the difference between the value of the labour product and the worker's outside option in period 1, plus the same difference in period 2 multiplied by the probability that the job continues (which is equal to p). Note that the severance payment does not enter in the determination of the surplus also in the first period. To obtain the insider wage consider that

$$W - U = \beta S_i$$

which is an expression that says that the worker gets a fraction β of the total surplus. The total outsider wage is then

$$w_o + pw_i + (1-p)T - u - u = \beta\varepsilon_h - \beta u + \beta p(\varepsilon_h - u)$$
$$w_o = u(1-\beta) + \beta\varepsilon_h - T$$

The wage of the outsider worker is reduced by the full amount of the severance payment. While it is true that the insider workers get an increase in their wage equal to T, the analysis has also shown that such a wage increase is fully prepaid by the outsider worker. This has also a further important consequence.

> *When wages are flexible, the severance payment has no impact on firm profits. In other words, the severance payment with wage flexibility is neutral.*

This can be seen by showing that the severance payment has no impact on the firm's expected profits. One simply substitutes the outsider wage and the insider wage into the firm's profits to obtain

$$\Pi_1 = \varepsilon_h - w_o + p(\varepsilon_h - w_i) - (1 - p)T$$
$$= \varepsilon_h - u(1 - \beta) - \beta\varepsilon_h + T + p\varepsilon_h - p(1 - \beta)u - p\beta\varepsilon_h - pT - (1 - p)T$$
$$= (\varepsilon_h - u)(1 - \beta) + p(1 - \beta)(\varepsilon_h - u)$$

From the previous conclusion it follows immediately that the firm's hiring decision is not affected by the presence of severance payments. If the cumulative profits are unchanged, the firm clearly does not change its hiring policy, even though the hiring decision is not explicitly modelled in this section.

12.3.2 DERIVING THE WAGES WITH THE FIRING TAX

In this section we carry out a similar exercise without severance payments with a firing tax. In other words we can now assume that $F > 0$ while $T = 0$. In the second period, the value of the profit to the firm if a wage agreement is found is $\varepsilon_h - w_i$ while if no agreement is found the firm needs to pay the firing tax F. This implies that the firm surplus at time $t = 2$ is

$$S_{f,2} = \varepsilon_h - w_i - (-F)$$

Let's now consider the worker position at time $t = 2$. The worker surplus at time $t = 2$, following a wage agreement, is

$$S_{w,2} = w_i - u$$

where u is the value of one period of unemployment. The total surplus is simply

$$S_2 = \varepsilon_h - u + F$$

from which follows an obvious important conclusion. **The firing tax enters in the total surplus.** This is not surprising, since the firing tax enters into the threat point of the firm and does not enter into that of the worker. Nevertheless, it will have important consequences for the effect it will have in the labour market.

Having derived the surplus, the wage of the insider is obtained so that the worker gets a fraction β of the total surplus. This means that

$$w_i: \qquad w_i - u = \beta S_2$$

from which it follows, after a simple substitution, that

$$w_i = (1 - \beta)u + \beta \varepsilon_h + \beta F$$

The wage of the insider is then a simple weighted average between the worker's outside option and the productivity of the match. In addition, the firing tax increases the wage of the insiders by a factor that is proportional to the workers' bargaining power. This means that insiders' wages go up with respect to a situation without firing tax.

Let's now move to the first period. The expected profits from employment at time 1 for the firm are equal to

$$\Pi_1 = \varepsilon_h - w_o + p(\varepsilon_h - w_i) - (1 - p)F$$

where $\varepsilon_h - w_o$ are the operational profits in the first period. The second period expected profits are random. In the second period two things can happen: with probability p the job continues and the firm gets $\varepsilon_h - w_i$ (w_i is the insider wage), while with probability $(1 - p)$ the job is destroyed and the firm pays the firing tax. Let's now turn on the workers' value of employment at time 1, which can be written as

$$W_1 = w_o + p w_i + (1 - p)u.$$

The total value of the outside option, which we indicate with U, is simply equal to the total sum of the per period outside option u, so that $U = 2u$.

As we mentioned above, at time $t = 1$ the worker is an outsider and he or she is not entitled to the firing tax. This means that the total surplus to the worker is

$$S_{w,1} = W_1 - U_1.$$

As for the firm, if agreement is not reached, there is no severance payment involved so that $S_{f,1} = \Pi_1$. This means that the total surplus at time $t = 1$ is simply

$$S_1 = W_1 - U_1 + \Pi_1$$

which, after a simple substitution of the functions, leads to

$$S_1 = \varepsilon_h - u + p(\varepsilon_h - u) - (1 - p)F$$

The previous expression simply says that the total surplus from the match is the difference between the value of the labour product and the outside option in period 1, plus the same difference in period 2 multiplied by the probability that the job continues (which is equal to p). In addition, the presence of the firing tax reduced the surplus at time $t = 1$. To obtain the insider wage consider that

$$W - U = \beta S_i$$

so that

$$w_o + pw_i + (1 - p)u - u - u = \beta\varepsilon_h - \beta u + \beta p(\varepsilon_h - u) - \beta(1 - p)F$$
$$w_o = u(1 - \beta) + \beta\varepsilon_h - \beta F$$

The wage of the outsider worker is reduced by a fraction β of the firing tax. While the insider worker gets an increase in his wage equal to βF, the analysis has also shown that such a wage increase is fully prepaid by the outsider worker. This has also a further important consequence.

Even when wages are flexible, the firing tax has impact on firm profits, and it is not neutral.

This can be seen by showing that the firing tax reduces expected profits. One simply substitutes the outsider wage and the insider wage into the firm's profits to obtain

$$\Pi_1 = \varepsilon_h - w_o + p(\varepsilon_h - w_i) - (1 - p)F$$
$$= (\varepsilon_h - u)(1 - \beta) + p(1 - \beta)(\varepsilon_h - u) - F(1 - \beta)(1 - p)$$

The previous expression clearly shows that the firing tax F negatively affects the present discounted profits.

12.4 Threshold Effects

EPL is traditionally modelled as a firing tax on labour shedding, and the original theoretical framework is the dynamic labour demand under uncertainty. Bentolila and Bertola (1990) characterize the optimal employment strategy of a monopolistic firm subject to idiosyncratic shocks and firing costs, holding wages fixed. Most of this literature takes EPL as given, and looks at the employment effect of different degrees of job security provisions. A very simple exposition of the Bertola–Bentolila model is that of Schivardi (2000). The present section studies employment dynamics when EPL is binding only for firms larger than a given size. We introduce threshold effects in a toy model of labour demand. This section proceeds as follows. First, we solve for the efficient allocation, next we show the properties of the model with an extreme form of EPL. Finally, we introduce threshold effects, and derive the main empirical predictions on firm level dynamics.

12.4.1 THE SET-UP OF THE MODEL

We assume that there is a continuum of firms of mass 1, and that wages are exogenously fixed and equal to w. Each firm hires only labour and produces and sells a homogeneous output with a convex production function $y = f(\alpha, \varepsilon, l)$, where α is a stochastic shifter of labour demand, l is the quantity of labour employed, and ε is a fixed firm-specific parameter heterogeneous across firms. The shifter parameter α is an index of business conditions at each firm. It can take two different values, $\alpha = a_b$ in bad business conditions and $\alpha = \varepsilon$ (with $\varepsilon > a_b$) in good business conditions. Firms are subject to an i.i.d. (identical and independently distributed) idiosyncratic shock and in each period there is a probability p that business conditions are bad and a probability $(1 - p)$ that business conditions are good. The parameter ε differs across firms, and is distributed according to the distribution function $F(x) = Prob(\varepsilon <= x)$, where F is continuous with no point mass and defined over the support $\Omega \in [a_b, \varepsilon^{max}]$. This implies that firms are identical when business conditions are idiosyncratically bad, but differ in their profit schedule when business conditions are good. Since firms differ only for their idiosyncratic parameter ε, in what follows we index firms simply by ε. Firms are dislocated in islands, there is no entry or exit, and profits exist in good and bad times as long as $a_b > w$. In this respect, the analysis is left at the partial equilibrium level. The model is stationary and we do not need to explicitly keep track of the time index t, even when we introduce EPL. If the production function is quadratic in labour, firm's profit for a type-ε firm can be written as

$$\Pi(\alpha, \varepsilon, l) = \alpha l - \frac{1}{2} l^2 - wl$$

where

$$\alpha = \begin{cases} a_b & \text{with probability } p \\ \varepsilon & \text{with probability } 1 - p \end{cases}$$

12.4.2 THE EFFICIENT ALLOCATION

Assume now that each type-ε firm can choose the optimal employment level after observing the realization of the shock α, and assume that hiring and firing can take place at no cost. Firm optimal employment behaviour is obtained simply by maximizing profits in each period, so that the firm continuously sets the marginal product equal to the wage, or

$$l^*(\varepsilon) = \begin{cases} l_b = a_b - w & \text{if } \alpha = a_b \\ l_g(\varepsilon) = \varepsilon - w & \text{if } \alpha = \varepsilon \end{cases}$$

This implies that a type-ε firm, in steady state, spends a fraction p of its time in bad business conditions with $l^* = l_b$ and a fraction $(1-p)$ in good business conditions with $l^* = l_g(\varepsilon)$, where the asterisk refers to the efficient allocation. In this situation firms shed all labour in excess of l_b when business conditions turn bad and hire up to $l_g(\varepsilon) = \varepsilon - w$ when business conditions turn good. Expected profits for a type-ε firm are

$$E\Pi^*(\varepsilon) = \frac{p}{2}[a_b - w]^2 + \frac{(1-p)}{2}[\varepsilon - w]^2$$

Profits are obviously increasing in ε.

12.4.3 THE RIGID SYSTEM

Assume now that EPL is so strict that firing is impossible. A type-ε firm will then choose a level of employment that maximizes average profits, and will keep its employment constant at all time. In other words, a type-ε firm will choose a level of employment to maximize average expected profits:

$$\Pi^R(\varepsilon, l) = p\left(a_b l - \frac{1}{2}l^2 - wl\right) + (1-p)\left(\varepsilon l - \frac{1}{2}l^2 - wl\right)$$

where $\Pi^R(\varepsilon, l)$ are the profits for a type-ε firm in the rigid system. If we indicate with $l^R(\varepsilon)$ the result of the maximization, its expression reads

$$l^R(\varepsilon) = pa_b + (1-p)\varepsilon - w$$

Confronting the rigid and the efficient allocation, an important implication immediately follows.

Average employment for a type-ε firm in the efficient and in the rigid allocation is identical. The result is obtained by simple inspection of $l^R(\varepsilon)$, which can be written as $l^R(\varepsilon) = p(ab - w) + (1-p)(\varepsilon - w)$. But then $l^R(\varepsilon)$ is the average level of employment of a type-ε firm in the efficient allocation. Further, profits are larger in the efficient allocation, as long as p is different from 0 and 1.

To obtain the latter result simply observe that profits in the rigid system are

$$\Pi^R(\varepsilon) = \frac{1}{2}[pa_b + (1-p)\varepsilon - w]^2$$

which is an expression that is always lower than $E\Pi^*(\varepsilon)$ as long as p is strictly positive and less than one. In addition, one can also observe that firm employment in the rigid system is less volatile than in the efficient allocation, since firms never hire and fire. These results are the standard implications of the EPL literature with fixed wages, and are just reported for introducing threshold effects, to which we turn next.

12.4.4 THE ROLE OF THRESHOLD EFFECTS

Assume now that the rigid regime is enforced only for an employment level larger than l^{thr}, where l^{thr} is an exogenous threshold specified by the legislation. The only restriction we impose is that $l^{thr} > a_b - w$, otherwise the problem is not even interesting. In this setting, once a firm grows beyond the employment level l^{thr} firing becomes impossible, while it can take place at no cost for employment levels less than or equal to l^{thr}. With threshold effects, some type-ε firms have the option to permanently fluctuate in the flexible fringe of the firm size distribution, or in the interval $l \in [l_b, l^{thr}]$, where l_b is the efficient level of employment when business conditions are bad. We label these type of firms 'constrained firms', and their formal definition follows.

> Constrained Firm: A type-ε firm with efficient employment allocation in good business conditions larger than the threshold ($l_g(\varepsilon) > l^{thr}$) is constrained when it employs $l = l_b$ in bad business conditions and $l = l^{thr}$ in good business conditions.

Thus, a constrained firm never passes the threshold, sheds labour up to l_b when business conditions turn bad, and hires up to l^{thr} when business conditions are good, and features an average employment level $l^{SC} = pl_b + (1-p)l^{thr}$. A constrained firm follows a stay-small policy, since in good times it is reluctant to grow beyond the threshold. Expected profits of a constrained firm are

$$\Pi^{SC}(\varepsilon, l) = p\left(a_b l - \frac{1}{2}l^2 - wl\right) + (1-p)\left(\varepsilon l^{thr} - \frac{1}{2}l^{thr2} - wl^{thr}\right)$$

while its employment behaviour is

$$l^*(\varepsilon) = \begin{cases} l_b = a_b - w & \text{if } \alpha = a_b \\ l_g(\varepsilon) = l^{thr} & \text{if } \alpha = \varepsilon \end{cases}$$

so that the average level of profits is increasing in the idiosyncratic level ε.

With threshold effects, some firms have to choose between a rigid allocation and a stay-small policy. In the former case they have an employment base larger than the threshold, they permanently employ $l^R(\varepsilon)$, and never fire. In the latter case, they permanently fluctuate inside the flexible fringe of the size distribution.

To complete our description, we need to characterize the conditions that ensure that constrained firms exist in equilibrium. In general, a type-ε firm will be constrained and will follow a stay-small policy as long as its average profits are higher than the average profits from the rigid system, or when $E\Pi^{SC}(\varepsilon) > E\Pi^{R}(\varepsilon)$. Among other things, this condition clearly depends on the specific value of the idiosyncratic parameter ε, as we show in our next result.

> Firms in the interval $\varepsilon \in [\varepsilon^*, \varepsilon^{**}]$ are constrained, where $\varepsilon^* = l^{thr} + w$ and ε^{**} is a positive number larger than ε^*. In light of this result, the firm size distribution is partitioned in three intervals. Firms with idiosyncratic component ε lower than ε^* are totally efficient and do not interact in any way with the threshold (their employment level in good times is lower than the threshold). Firms with idiosyncratic component in the interval $[\varepsilon^*, \varepsilon^{**}]$ are constrained, and in good times bunch with employment $l^{thr} = \varepsilon^* - w$. Finally for idiosyncratic values of ε larger than ε^{**}, firms are rigid and hire $l^R(\varepsilon)$.

To prove this result one needs simply to introduce the function

$$z(\varepsilon) = E^{SC}(\varepsilon) - E^{R}(\varepsilon)$$

whose expression reads

$$z(\varepsilon) = \frac{p}{2}(a_b - w)^2 + (1 - p)\left(\varepsilon l^{thr} - \frac{1}{2}l^{thr^2} - wl\right)$$

$$- \frac{1}{2}[pa_b + (1 - p)\varepsilon - w]^2$$

First note that the threshold is irrelevant for those firms for which $lg(\varepsilon) < l^{thr}$, which is a condition that is satisfied as long as $\varepsilon < \varepsilon^*$, with $\varepsilon^* = l^{thr} + w$. Type-$\varepsilon$ firms with idiosyncratic component below ε^* are totally efficient and do not interact in any way with the threshold.

Second, note that $z(\varepsilon*) = p(1-p)[a_b - w - l^{thr}]^2 > 0$ and that $z\prime(\varepsilon^*) > 0$ so that firms with $\varepsilon > \varepsilon^*$ are certainly constrained. To find the upper support of the interval $[\varepsilon^*, \varepsilon^{**}]$ one needs to solve the quadratic equation $z(\varepsilon) = 0$ whose largest root reads

$$\varepsilon^{**} = \frac{\varepsilon^* - (pa_b)^{1/2}}{1 - p^{1/2}}$$

It is immediately clear that $\varepsilon^{**} > \varepsilon^*$ strictly, so that all firms in the interval $[\varepsilon^*, \varepsilon^{**}]$ are constrained. Conversely, for $\varepsilon > \varepsilon^{**}$ $z(\varepsilon) < 0$ and firms choose the rigid system.

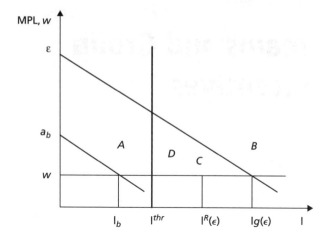

Figure 12.1. Labor demand in good and bad times and threshold effects

An important result easily follows.

A type-ε firm that is constrained has an average employment level that is lower than the average employment level in the efficient allocation and in the fully rigid system.

From the definition of constrained firms it follows immediately that $lg(\varepsilon) > l^{thr}$ for all $\varepsilon \in (\varepsilon^*, \varepsilon^{**}]$ where $lg(\varepsilon) = \varepsilon - w$. Since $l^R(\varepsilon) - l^{SC}(\varepsilon) = (1 - p)[\varepsilon - \varepsilon^*]$, it is obvious that all constrained firms with $\varepsilon \in (\varepsilon^*, \varepsilon^{**}]$ feature average employment that is lower than the average employment in the rigid system.

This result is important, since it shows that one of the standard predictions of traditional EPL models, summarized in the first result above, no longer holds when constrained firms exist. The last result is further summarized by looking at Fig. 12.1, where we report the optimal employment level for a type-ε firm under three regimes: the efficient allocation, the rigid system, and a stay-small policy. Points A and B in the figure refer to the employment level under the efficient allocation, when the firm switches its employment level between l_b and $l_g(\varepsilon)$. Point C refers to the employment level under the rigid system, and $l^R(\varepsilon)$ is the amount of labour that the firm permanently employs, independently of business conditions. When a firm is constrained, its employment level shifts between point A in bad times and point D in good times. Clearly, the average between A and D is lower than the employment level associated with point C.

13 Teams and Group Incentives

13.1 **Introduction**

Team-organized production is a key feature of many organizations. Most job advertisements explicitly look for workers that possess team-specific skills, and are motivated to work in teams. Indeed, team production and group-based incentives pose a great challenge to personnel economics. As it turns out, a simple approach to the problem would argue that organized team production is likely to lead to a reduction in productivity. This is the so-called $1/N^{th}$ problem, whereby effort put forward by workers under team production is likely to be less than what would be exerted under individual-based incentives. If this is indeed the case, all we can do under team production is to find ways to preserve the right incentives, even though it appears that overall productivity will hardly be larger than what it would have been if individual-based incentives were in place.

Yet, to fully understand team production, and all the emphasis that real life organizations do place on teams, we have to move forward and explicitly recognize that there exist benefits and costs linked to team production. After all, if so many firms are interested in workers able to work in teams, it has to be the case that team-specific skills (such as communication skills) and the possibility of mutual learning among team members may increase the total surplus generated by the workforce. The personnel economics literature is still growing in this dimension. Many good questions exist, but answers are often limited. In this context, we prefer to offer a case study approach.

Does the adoption of a team increase or decrease productivity? How does team composition affect productivity? Are teams more productive if members are homogeneous or heterogeneous? As we argued above, personnel economics has no full answer to this problem. What we can do is to bring empirical research to the topic, and analyse in close detail a case study on the adoption of team production in the garment industry. Surprisingly, and contrary to what the $1/N^{th}$ problem would predict, we will see that in the specific study analysed, individual productivity under group incentives has increased, rather than decreased. This suggests that there is still a lot to be learnt in the area of team production.

13.2 **The Team Production Problem**

We begin by presenting the simple team production problem, or the $1/N^{th}$ problem, as it is often defined in the literature. Consider a group of individuals of size N that work together on a specific project. The price of the output is normalized to 1 and the production is such that the total revenue produced by the entire team depends on the effort of every team member via the simple, additive production function:

$$Q = e_1 + e_2 + e_3 + \cdots + e_N$$

where e_i is the effort of individual i.

We can think of a team of software developers engaged on a project with a time deadline. There is an agreed payment and a target delivery date for the final product, but each day of delay reduces the fee received by the entire team by $\$X$. Total output is the simple sum of the effort of all individuals.

Note that, according to the above example, (i) all team members are equally productive, and that by assumption (ii) the production function is linear, so that there are no complementarities between the team members' efforts. While complementarities make team production more advantageous, neither of these assumptions affects the main results we will come up with below.

Finally, assume that each agent's disutility of effort is given by:

$$C(e) = \frac{e_i^2}{2} \qquad \forall i$$

We now ask two questions in turn. First, what is the efficient effort level for each member of this team? Second, given a simple revenue-sharing compensation scheme, how hard will each team member actually work (the 'worker's problem')?

Efficient effort level. To calculate the efficient effort of each and every team member we have to consider the benefits and the costs associated with increasing effort of each agent. Total output is given by $\sum_i e_i$ while the total cost of this effort is $\sum_i C(e_i)$. This suggests that the efficient effort level is the solution to

$$Max_{e_1,e_2,\dots,e_n} = \sum_i e_i - \sum_i C(e_i) = e_1 + \cdots + e_N - \frac{e_1^2}{2} - \cdots - \frac{e_n^2}{2}$$

where the maximization is to be taken for each and every member

$$1 - e_i = 0 \qquad \forall i$$

Therefore the efficient outcome is for each worker to supply at the point in which the marginal benefit of effort to aggregate team production (which is 1) is equal to the marginal cost of effort, which in this case is equal to e_i.

Worker's problem. Beside the efficient level, we know that each individual solves their own maximization problem by maximizing their utility. The utility of the individual depends, as always, on the compensation scheme and on the cost of effort, so that

$$U_i = compensation_i - \frac{e_i^2}{2}$$

The most obvious compensation scheme is one in which the total output from the team is shared proportionally among its team members. In other words, each worker maximizes his or her individual utility, given a compensation schedule, or 'output sharing rule'. Further suppose this sharing rule implies the following compensation, $compensation_i = \frac{\sum e_i}{N} \forall i$. In other words the team members agree to share the total revenues of the team equally. In this situation, how hard will people actually work?

Individual i's pay-off: $Y_i = \frac{e_1 + e_i + ... e_N}{N}$; Individual i's disutility of effort: $C(e_i) = \frac{e_i^2}{2}$. So the individual's problem is:

$$\max_{e_1} \frac{e_1 + e_i + ... e_N}{N} - \frac{e_i^2}{2}$$

with the following first-order condition:

$$\frac{1}{N} - e_i = 0$$

An Individual's (privately) optimal effort is therefore given by $e_1^* = 1/N$.

How can the previous conclusion be explained, and why is the individual optimal effort so different from the efficient level? The intuition is as follows. While the worker is still bearing the full cost of his or her additional effort, the compensation scheme implies that the marginal benefit of one additional unit of effort is only $1/N$. This is called the 'free rider problem' or the '1/N problem'. The total effort of all agents is $N \times \frac{1}{N} = 1$ instead of N, which is the efficient level.

Note that this result has nothing to do with the assumption that the group's output is shared equally among its members. It is true for any fixed sharing rule, where worker i receives a share γ_i of the total, as long as $\sum \gamma_i = 1$ (all the workers' shares must add up to 100 per cent).

Under the above rule in our example each worker's effort will equal γ_i, and the sum of all the workers' efforts will equal $\sum \gamma_i = 1$, rather than N which is needed for efficiency. Summarizing our result:

Any group compensation rule that shares group output according to a fixed rate induces sub-optimal effort due to free riding. The problem increases in severity as the group size, N, increases.

The free rider problem associated with team production is quite common in reality, even outside strict personnel economics examples. Among students, when group projects are associated with a common grade, it is very difficult to induce efforts by all members, and there is always a tendency to rely on other people's effort and ability. A somewhat similar problem takes place when a group of friends decide to share restaurant bills. Each individual has a tendency to consume expensive meals, so as to rely on other friends' contributions.

13.3 **Team Norms as Remedies to the Team Production Problem**

In the above example the individual reward was assumed to be $1/N\, Q$ or γQ where γ can be any share as long as $\sum \gamma_i = 1$. Such a revenue-splitting game can be thought of as a special case of our linear compensation scheme, which is based on a fixed amount α plus a bonus component β. Think of these as special cases of a linear compensation schedule based on the group's output which can be written as

$$compensation_i = \alpha + \beta Q$$

We can ask what should be the value of β that induces the efficient level of effort, which we know should be $e^* = 1$. In other words the problem becomes one of finding β to induce an efficient effort $E^* = 1$ by every team member. The individual problem is

$$Max\ \alpha + \beta[e_1 + \cdots + e_n] - \frac{e_1^2}{2}$$

Hence individual i's problem yields

$$e_i = \beta$$

Therefore to get the worker to choose $e^* = 1$, we need to set $\beta = 1$. This is not surprising, since we know very well that effort is maximum when the individual is the full residual claimant, as the following conclusion highlights.

To induce efficient effort by every member of a team, each team member's individual compensation must increase by 1 for every 1 increase in the group's output. Each individual must be the full residual claimant.

This makes clear how difficult it is to find such a scheme. The difficulty with the previous comment is that the output of all individuals must increase by $1 for every $1 increase in the group's output. It sounds quite hard.

One way to obtain this scheme is that the 'firm' or some agreed-on team member sets a target output M, which we can call **team norm** M.

- Everyone is paid zero if the output M is not reached, and the firm keeps the difference.

- The output is split evenly among team members if the output norm is reached, while the pay is zero otherwise.

- If the team norm M is the output when all individuals produce at the efficient level $e^* = 1$, then each worker gets paid \$1 and the firm breaks even.

As you can see, establishing a team norm is the way to keep the incentive right for workers, since that marginal increase of producing at the efficient level is exactly \$1. But the very difficult task is to establish the proper norm, and to enforce it.

13.4 **Teams in Reality**

Many firms use teams. Using teams involves both costs and benefits. The existing literature argues that teams are desirable for three main reasons: (i) to make possible gains in complementarities in production among workers; (ii) to facilitate gains from specialization by allowing workers to accumulate task-specific human capital; (iii) to encourage gains from knowledge transfer. Yet teams also have costs. The most important cost is the free rider problem, which was analysed above. So it is difficult to say *ex ante* what is the impact of teams on output. Let's see some key questions. Does the adoption of a team increase or decrease productivity? How does team composition affect productivity? Are teams more productive if members are homogeneous or heterogeneous? In a case study of the garment industry at Koret it is possible to answer some of these questions.

Worker heterogeneity Theoretically, worker heterogeneity in teams has two advantages. It facilitates mutual learning and can influence the group production norm. (i) *Mutual learning* suggests that more able workers are able to teach less able workers to be more productive. If the mutual learning effect is significant, then teams that are initially more heterogeneous in ability will perform better. (ii) *Team norm*. A relationship between worker heterogeneity and team performance could also be the result of forming a team norm, a concept that we formally defined above.

Worker decision to join a team Let us imagine a context in which workers are given the possibility of joining a team, and let us also imagine a setting in which non-team jobs are available in the workplace. Then each worker will solve a cost–benefit analysis over the decision to enter team production. Obviously, the highest-ability worker will join a team only if he or she obtains an additional source of surplus from team production. In terms of output performance, high-ability workers are bound to suffer, since they are going to share production with less productive co-workers. This suggests that for a high-ability worker to join the team, there must be additional reasons, which can be conceptualized in two ways: (i) productivity gains may derive from multi-skill abilities; (ii) socialization within the team may compensate high-ability workers in terms of income. As we see in the case study below, these phenomena do exist in reality.

13.5 **A Case Study: Production at Koret**

The case study is based on weekly productivity reports from a Koret garment manufacturing facility in Napa, California. The establishment produces 'women's lowers' including pants, skirts, shorts, etc. Prior to 1995, production was organized with individual piece rate. Over 1995–7, production organization shifted to team production. The organization change was introduced in response to demand by retailers that companies make just-in-time deliveries. Such demands required a more flexible production system, and many firms in the industry responded to such demands with team-based production.

Garment production is done in three stages. First, cloth is cut into pieces that conform to garment patterns. Second, garments are assembled by sewing pieces together. Third, garments are finished by pressing. The case study we are considering focuses on the sewing operation.

The change that we analyse is a passage from progressive bundling system production (PBS) to module production (MP). In PBS sewing operations are broken down into distinct operations. PBS is a piece rate scheme while MP is a team-based remuneration. Sewers are paid on the basis of *individual piece rates* according to a standard set for the operation they undertake. The standards are usually set by the management in accordance with the unions. Quality is evaluated by randomly selecting six out of forty garments and the sewer's name is recorded. In this setting piece rate is appropriate and possible.

In 1994 the plant manager began experimenting with flexible teams, which in the garment industry are called module production (MP). The manager asked for volunteers. After joining a team sewers could return to PBS if they preferred. The data are described in Table 13.1. In module production, each team includes six or seven team members who work in a U-shaped work space of 4×8m. The close proximity of workers and machines reportedly facilitated

Table 13.1. Summary statistics for individual and team incentives at Koret

Variable	Overall (1)	Not in team (2)	Team member (3)
Productivity			
25%	80.12	71.55	87.58
50%	99.33	86.8	105.45
75%	118.3	108.5	120.38
Weekly earnings			
25%	$197.52	$159.64	$226.66
50%	$274.02	221.77	$301.03
75%	$350.26	291.51	$369.06
Hours/week			
25%	28.52	24	30.01
50%	34.4	32	35.72
75%	38.8	38.33	38.86
Age			
25%	30	30.9	30.1
50%	37	39.7	35.9
75%	45.4	48	44.3
Observations	20,626	6,688	13,938

team members' ability to identify bottlenecks and changes in productivity. Teams (or modules) are compensated with a *group piece rate* for each operation. The team's net receipts are shared and divided equally. Worker productivity in PBS and MP is measured in the same standards and it is comparable.

The case study is based on personnel data of employees at Koret from 1 January 1995 until 31 December 1997. The data consist of weekly information on worker productivity, pay, hours worked, and team membership for all individuals employed at Koret. There are no data on individual education. It is possible to use individual data observed under both regimes to assess the impact of teams on productivity. The productivity variable is measured as efficiency relative to the standard described, with numbers above 100 indicating performance above the standard level. Figure 13.1 plots median weekly productivity at the plant from the first week of 1995 (week 0) to the last week of 1997 (week 156). In addition, the fraction of plant workers engaged in team production is also presented. The figure shows that *median productivity at Koret increases after most Koret workers are working in teams.* This is clearly visible in the Figure after *week 70.* The picture shows also that there is substantial cyclical variation in productivity.[1]

Table 13.1 presents summary statistics for the person-week data, overall and by membership status. Consistent with Fig. 13.1, columns 2 and 3 indicate that productivity was higher under team production rather than lower, as

[1] In technical terms the presence of cyclical variation implies that a proper multivariate analysis should include also time dummies.

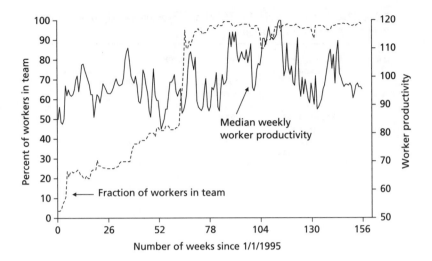

Figure 13.1. Average Productivity and percentage of workers employed in teams

would be predicted if free riding were dominant. Table 13.2 reports average weekly worker productivity for individuals prior to joining the team and team productivity after joining the team. Productivity increased in fourteen of the twenty-three teams for which data are available. Teams formed in 1995 are the most likely to show an increase in productivity, suggesting that workers with greater collaborative skills joined the early teams.

The case study analysed three questions in detail:

1. Did the use of teams lead to higher productivity, contrary to what might be predicted by simple models of free riding?
2. Which type of workers (in terms of ability) joined the teams? Is there an adverse selection into teams (with less able workers joining teams) as the free riding problem would suggest? Or maybe there are collaborative skills that were not used in PBS?
3. How does team composition affect team productivity?

13.5.1 THE IMPACT OF TEAMS ON PRODUCTIVITY AT KORET

Let y_{it} be the natural log of productivity of worker i in week t at Koret. A worker's productivity is modelled as

$$y_{it} = X_{it}\beta + \alpha \, TEAM_{it} + \epsilon_{it} \tag{13.1}$$

where the indicator variable $TEAM_{it}$ equals one if worker i is a member of a team in week t and zero otherwise. The variables included in the vector X

Table 13.2. Dates of team formation and average weekly productivity before and after team formation

Team	Date of team formation (1)	Average weekly productivity	
		Individuals prior to joining team[a] (2)	Team (for weeks 21+)[b] (3)
1	12 March 1994	97.8	114.3
2	7 January 1995	82.9	122.6
3	28 January 1995	79.4	97.6
4	28 January 1995	94.0	106.0
5	28 January 1995	117.8	118.9
6	28 January 1995	89.4	88.3
7	29 April 1995	89.6	107.8
8	7 October 1995	122.6	115.6
9	28 October 1995	127.4	131.3
10	13 April 1996	85.6	83.6
11	30 March 1996	100.4	111.8
12	13 April 1996	87.3	109.3
13	13 April 1996	94.6	106.1
14	13 April 1996	85.6	91.2
15	18 May 1996	78.3	76.8
16	22 June 1996	81.1	82.6
17	20 July 1996	81.7	122.9
18	13 April 1996	92.6	95.5
19	13 April 1996	86.1	79.7
20	10 August 1996	127.5	114.4
21	7 December 1996	...[c]	139.1
22	18 January 1997	94.0	80.0
23	1 February 1997	89.2	70.9
24	15 March 1997	92.1	61.2
25	6 September 1997	76.9	...[c]

[a] Entries in col. (2) are calculated by averaging the individual person week productivity values of workers who subsequently join the particular team (individuals are weighted by the length of time they spent on the team).
[b] Team averages in col. (3) are calculated after excluding the first 20 weeks.
[c] Team 21 consisted of almost all new hires, and so the pre-team productivity data are not available.

include individual age (and squared), monthly data on US women's retail apparel sales (as well as future sales up to six months), and monthly dummies. The key parameter is α and the results are reported in the table.

Contrary to the predictions of moral hazard models that emphasize free riding, the estimate of the productivity parameter α was positive. After the adoption of teams, productivity increase was 18 per cent.[2] There are potentially two factors that can explain this finding. First, for any particular individual, joining a team may lead to an increase in productivity. Second, high-ability workers may systematically choose to join teams. The first effect would be a pure team productivity effect while the second one would be an adverse selection effect. To distinguish between these two potential explanations, consider

---

[2] Using quantile regression, the productivity increased to roughly 21%.

the following specification of the above equation

$$y_{it} = \theta_i + X_{it}\beta + \alpha\, TEAM_{it} + \eta_{it} \qquad (13.2)$$

where θ_i represents a set of unobserved characteristics that influence productivity of worker i under both PBS and MP. In this new specification the term α offers the productivity impact of team production once we control for individual specific characteristics. The results of the new regressions suggest that, on average, a particular productivity increases by roughly 14 per cent after joining a team. Basically, the estimate of α in model (13.1) falls to 14 per cent in model (13.2). Of the 18 per cent early increase in productivity associated with teams at Koret, one-fifth reflects the systematic selection of high-ability workers under the PBS system. Overall, the finding is consistent with the utilization of collaborative skills but also with bargaining and mutual learning, which appear (in this particular case) to more than offset any possible free riding.

Were early teams more productive?

One possible drawback of the model above is that it considers the productivity of all teams to be the same, independent of the data of team formation. Since team formation was voluntary, one may expect that early teams were more productive since workers with higher collaborative skills might be the first to participate in teams. The estimate of this effect is done by adding the following three variables to the model above:

$$y_{it} = \theta_i + X_{it}\beta + \alpha\, TEAM_{it} + \delta_1\, TEAM95 + \delta_2\, TEAM96 + \delta_3\, TEAM97 + \eta_{it}$$

There is substantial heterogeneity across teams in their impact on output. Workers on teams formed in 1995 had double the impact on productivity. Since these effects could be due to team tenure effects, with early teams characterized by more experience with team membership, the estimates in Table 13.3 distinguish among the impact on productivity of different teams at different weeks. The results are confirmed, and do reflect a team effect. Overall, the estimates suggest that the introduction of teams led to higher productivity for teams formed in the first year and that the productivity declined as more workers in the firm engaged in modular production. They suggest that workers with higher levels of collaborative skills that were productive in a team setting tended to participate in teams first.

13.5.2 WHO JOINS A TEAM?

The results of the previous section suggest that there are important self-selection mechanisms that operate under team formation at Koret. This is not particularly surprising. The surprising result, however, is that it seems that

Table 13.3. Relationship between teams and productivity

| | Dependent variable: Ln(productivity) | | | |
| | No individual dummies | | Individual dummies fixed effects | |
	OLS	Median	OLS	Median
A. All teams grouped together				
TEAM	0.178	0.211	0.136	0.116
	(0.053)	(0.044)	(0.035)	(0.032)
B. Teams grouped by year of formation				
TEAM95	0.221	0.234	0.177	0.169
	(0.052)	(0.048)	(0.034)	(0.038)
TEAM96	0.06	0.092	0.088	0.072
	(0.07)	(0.061)	(0.044)	(0.038)
TEAM97	−0.09	−0.094	−0.072	−0.082
	(0.12)	(0.186)	(0.065)	(0.068)
C. Team effects by year of formation and team tenure				
TEAM95				
Weeks 1–10	0.394	0.221	0.31	0.11
	(0.183)	(0.175)	(0.161)	(0.095)
Weeks 11–20	0.331	0.286	0.241	0.167
	(0.071)	(0.055)	(0.074)	(0.055)
Weeks 21+	0.201	0.237	0.183	0.204
	(0.05)	(0.043)	(0.046)	(0.039)
TEAM96				
Weeks 1–10	−0.087	−0.073	−0.046	−0.081
	(0.118)	(0.118)	(0.081)	(0.06)
Weeks 11–20	−0.019	0.057	−0.023	0.039
	(0.084)	(0.074)	(0.065)	(0.04)
Weeks 21+	0.079	0.118	0.15	0.131
	(0.063)	(0.059)	(0.048)	(0.047)
TEAM97				
Weeks 1–10	−0.365	−0.235	−0.277	−0.18
	(0.092)	(0.169)	(0.102)	(0.144)
Weeks 11–20	0.064	0.128	0.101	0.161
	(0.086)	(0.357)	(0.121)	(0.19)
Weeks 21+	−0.034	−0.165	0.002	−0.043
	(0.166)	(0.279)	(0.075)	(0.102)

Notes: Number of observations is 20,627 person weeks. Standard errors are in parentheses. Each regression also includes a constant, age of the worker and, its square, dummies for each month, and cyclical variable measuring women's retail garment sales.

more productive workers, rather than less productive, were the first to join teams. The $1/N$ problem would suggest that most able workers have the most to lose from team membership. One can examine the issue in more detail. To investigate the self-selection into teams, one can estimate a 'pre-team' regression for the 151 non-team workers employed in week 0, when teams were not yet formed. This simple regression takes the form

$$y_{i0} = X_{i0}\beta + \gamma \, FTEAM_{i0} + \varepsilon_{i0}$$

Table 13.4. The impact of future team participation

Dependent variable: Ln (productivity) Variable	OLS (1)	Median (2)
A. All future teams pooled		
FTEAM (joins team in the future)	0.156	0.145
	−0.07	−0.129
B. Future teams formed in 1995 and 1996		
FTEAM95 (joins team in 1995)	0.206	0.154
	−0.078	−0.131
FTEAM96 (joins team in 1996)	0.061	−0.015
	−0.093	−0.186

Notes: Number of observations is 151. Standard errors are in parentheses (robust standard errors for OLS). Standard errors for the median regressions are bootstrapped using 500 replications. All regressions include a constant and age and its squares.

where y_{i0} is the ln(productivity) of worker i in the first week of January 1995 (week 0) and the indicator variable $FTEAM_{io}$ equals one if worker i joins a team by mid-1996 and zero if she does not. Basically the coefficient γ captures the productivity under PBS of the individuals that later decided to enter team production. Because future team membership cannot affect current productivity, γ measures the selection into teams. Panel A of Table 13.4 indicates that workers who joined teams in future are approximately 15 per cent more productive in non-team work in January 1995. This result goes against the free rider problem. It is not that low-productivity workers are sorted into teams because of the adverse selection problem. Just the opposite occurs. Either technical ability is somewhat positively correlated with collaborative skills or teams offer non-pecuniary benefits that are larger for high-ability workers. In addition, it may be that the disutility imposed by a team norm on low-productivity workers was so large as to discourage many of them from joining teams at the beginning.

The big puzzle is what happens to earnings. Regressions of the log of hourly pay on team membership (controlling for demographics and cyclical factors) in Table 13.5 show that while average pay increased after the introduction of teams, workers at the top end of the pay distribution experienced an 8 per cent reduction in hourly pay under teams. The overall increase in average pay is not surprising, especially since we saw that overall productivity increased. The surprise is the fall in wage at the top of the distribution. This suggests that non-pecuniary benefits of team membership, such as more control over the work environment and less repetition, are important factors for many workers.

Further analysis shows also that the pay results are not caused by the fact that high-ability workers participated in teams only for a few periods and then quit the firm when they learned that their pay was unlikely to rise.

Table 13.5. The impact of teams on hourly and weekly pay

	OLS	0.05	0.25	0.5	0.75	0.95
Variable	−1	−2	−3	−4	−5	−6
A. Dependent variable: ln (hourly pay)						
TEAM	0.158	0.101	0.233	0.222	0.148	−0.083
	−0.035	−0.044	−0.38	−0.045	−0.046	−0.039
B. Dependent variable: ln (weekly pay)						
TEAM	0.26	0.285	0.348	0.312	0.24	0.026
	−0.039	−0.076	−0.042	−0.041	−0.039	−0.063

*Note:*The number of observations is 20,193. Standard errors are in parentheses (robust standard errors for OLS regressions). Each regression also includes a constant, age of the worker and its square, dummies for each month.

13.5.3 HOW DOES A TEAM COMPOSITION AFFECT TEAM PRODUCTIVITY?

While it is obvious that teams with high-ability members should be on average more productive, an interesting question concerns the links between heterogeneity and productivity. The question here is whether worker heterogeneity increases or decreases team productivity. Theoretically, it may be the case that better workers may be able to impose a higher team norm output level, especially when there are non-team jobs at the plant. Similarly, if mutual learning is more important, heterogeneity may lead to an increase in productivity. Thus, the ability composition of teams must be carefully defined.

The estimates show that more heterogeneous teams are more productive, with average ability held constant, since the coefficient on the ratio of the maximum to the minimum individual productivity of team members is positive and significant. When one is forming a team, *it appears better to have a mix of high-ability and low-ability* workers rather than a set of workers with identical technical abilities. It may be that high-ability workers are able to enforce a higher team norm by exerting their bargaining leverage. On the other hand, the results may reflect mutual learning, in which more able workers are able to teach their less able teammates to be more productive.

13.5.4 DISCUSSION AND CONCLUSION

The case study at Koret can be summarized by four key findings. First, the adoption of teams at Koret improved worker productivity by 14 per cent on average, even after we accounted for the self-selection of high-productivity workers under the PBS production system onto teams. Second, this productivity improvement was greatest for the teams that formed earliest and diminished as more workers in the firm engaged in modular production. Third, high-ability workers not only tended to join the teams first, but were no more likely to subsequently leave the firm after joining a team. Finally, more heterogeneous teams are more productive, when average ability is held constant.

These results obviously suggest that *group piece rate incentives achieved higher productivity than individual piece rate incentives.* Free riding does not appear to be the dominant behaviour response at Koret. The lack of free riding may be simply due to the ease of peer monitoring within teams at Koret. However, the possibility of straightforward mutual monitoring cannot explain why productivity increased significantly.

These results are certainly consistent with the view that workers have both technical and collaborative skills (such as communication and leadership skills and flexibility), the latter of which were not utilized under *PBS* production. In this respect, team production may have expanded production possibilities by utilizing collaborative skills.

It is also difficult to escape the conclusions that workers received some non-pecuniary benefit by participation in teams: some high-ability workers joined teams despite an absolute decrease in pay. Teams offered more varied and less repetitive work and also reduced variation in weekly pay. The results are also consistent with the predictions of bargaining and mutual learning models. More heterogeneous workers are more productive, and 'stars' are influential in raising team productivity.

Overall, these arguments suggest that it may be feasible for a firm to reduce turnover and increase production by introducing team production, even if some workers earn lower pay after joining the team. Overall, this chapter suggests that team production is a complex behavioural phenomenon that presents a challenge because it involves multiple mechanisms.

☐ APPENDIX A LABOUR DEMAND AT THE FIRM LEVEL

PRODUCTION FUNCTION

The production function is the technology that the firm uses in the production process. For simplicity, in Appendix A we assume that there are only two factors of production (two inputs): the number of employee-hours hired by the firm (L) and capital (K). We write the production function as

$$q = f(L, K)$$

where q is the firm output, and f is the technological relationship that transforms inputs into output. The production function specifies how much output is produced by any combination of labour and capital. With respect to the labour input, there are two key assumptions to be discussed in detail. First, the number of employee-hours L is given by the product of the number of workers hired times the average number of hours worked per person. Chapter 3 considers the distinction between the number of workers hired and the number of hours worked. In this appendix we simply refer to labour input L as the number of workers hired. Second, the production function assumes that different types of workers can be aggregated into a single input that we call labour. In fact workers are heterogeneous, and Chapter 2 discusses issues of workers' heterogeneity.

MARGINAL PRODUCT

The marginal product of labour, which we denote as MP_L, is defined as the change in output resulting from hiring an additional worker, holding constant the quantities of all other inputs. The MP_L is formally given by

$$MP_L = \left. \frac{\Delta q}{\Delta L} \right|_K$$

where the notation $|_K$ should be read as holding capital constant.[1]

---

[1] The marginal product of capital is similarly defined as

$$MP_k = \left. \frac{\Delta q}{\Delta K} \right|_L$$

The marginal product of labour is the slope of the total curve, which can be thought as the relationship between output and labour holding capital constant. There are two important properties of the marginal product

1. *The marginal product is non-negative.* This property is a minimum basic requirement that we assume to be satisfied throughout the book. Adding more of one input, holding constant the other input, never leads to a reduction in output, and in general it increases. This condition simply means that adding one extra employee inside the firm, at given capital stock, increases output. While such an assumption is most of the time reasonable, one can envisage conditions in which it does not hold, mainly because extra workers lead to increased congestion inside the firm.

2. *Output increases at a decreasing rate.* The assumption that the marginal product of labour declines follows from the **law of diminishing returns**: as more and more workers are added to a fixed capital stock, the gains from specialization decline and the marginal product of workers declines. While we will often *assume that the law of diminishing returns operates over some range of employment,* various chapters in the book assume that the marginal product is constant.

It is easy to understand how to calculate the marginal product of labour by using a numerical example. The baseline data are reported in Table A.1, where we summarize the firm's production when it hires different numbers of workers, holding capital constant. If the firm hires one worker, it produces 11 units of output. The marginal product of the first worker hired, therefore, is 11 units. If the firm hires two workers, production rises to 21 units of output, and the marginal product of the second worker is 10 units. Figure A.1 illustrates the total product curve. This curve describes what happens to output as the firm hires more workers. The total product curve is obviously upward sloping. The marginal product of labour is the shape of the total product curve, and it is plotted in Fig. A.2. In our example, output first rises at an increasing rate as more workers are hired. This implies that the marginal product of labour is rising. Eventually, output increases at a decreasing rate. In our example, the marginal product of the fourth worker declines further at 8 units.

Table A.1. Labour demand at the firm level

Employment	Output	Marginal prod	$Wage_1$	$Wage_2$
0.00	0.00	—	5.00	8.00
1.00	11.00	11.00	5.00	8.00
2.00	21.00	10.00	5.00	8.00
3.00	30.00	9.00	5.00	8.00
4.00	38.00	8.00	5.00	8.00
5.00	45.00	7.00	5.00	8.00
6.00	51.00	6.00	5.00	8.00
7.00	56.00	5.00	5.00	8.00
8.00	60.00	4.00	5.00	8.00
9.00	63.00	3.00	5.00	8.00
10.00	65.00	2.00	5.00	8.00

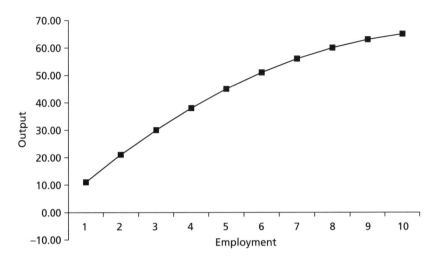

Figure A.1. Production function with constant capital

PROFIT MAXIMIZATION

We assume that the firm's employment decision maximizes profits. The firm's profits are given by:

$$\pi = pq - wL - rK$$

where p is the price at which the firm can sell its output; w is the wage rate (that is, the cost of hiring an additional worker) and r is the price of capital. In this appendix we assume that the firm is perfectly competitive, both in the output market and in the input market. This simply means that the firm takes as given the price p, the wage w, and the cost of capital r. Further, such quantities are independent of how much the firm produces and hires. If we substitute the production function into the profit equation we obtain

$$\pi = pf(L, K) - wL - rK$$

Since p, w, and r are constant, the previous equation makes clear that the only actions the firm can take to influence profits involve the decisions of how much labour and capital to hire. The firm maximizes profits by hiring the right amounts of these inputs.

EMPLOYMENT DECISION IN THE SHORT RUN

The short run is a time span in which the stock of capital is constant at K_o. The firm profit in the short run is then given by

$$\pi = pf(L, K_o) - wL - rK_o$$

this implies that in the short run the only variable that the firm can 'play around with' is the number of workers it hires. In this dimension, the key variable to the firm is the *dollar value of what an additional worker produces.* Its expression in formula is

$$VMP_L = pMP_L$$

Since we apply the law of diminishing returns and the price is constant, it is clear that the VMP_L will eventually decline.

In our example, to obtain the dollar value of what an additional worker produces, we multiply the marginal product of labour times the price of the output. If the price is equal to $1, then the value of the marginal product is identical to the marginal product.

The competitive firm can hire all the labour it wants at a constant wage of w dollars. Since each additional worker yields to the firm an amount equal to VMP_L it is obvious that the optimal employment decision in the short run is to hire up to a point in which the wage rate is equal to the VMP_L and the law of diminishing returns applies. In formula, the employment decision is

$$VMP_L = w \qquad \text{and} \qquad VMP_L \text{ is decreasing}$$

While the first condition is fairly intuitive (as long as an additional worker yields to the firm more than his cost he should be hired) the second condition is less obvious. Indeed, if an additional worker yields as much as he costs, but adding another worker increases profits more than it costs (i.e. if the VMP_L is increasing), then it cannot be optimal to stop hiring. In Fig. A.2 the second condition is satisfied.

Note that it is possible to obtain the optimal hiring condition also with the help of a little algebra. If we assume that the production function is differentiable, we can say that the problem of the firm is to maximize profits with respect to labour. In formula, this is equivalent to

$$\text{Max}_L \qquad \pi = pf(L, K_o) - wL - rK_o$$

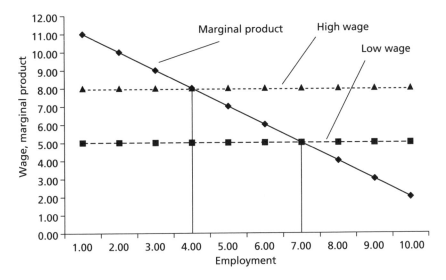

Figure A.2. The marginal product and labor demand

The first-order condition requires putting the marginal profits to zero

$$\frac{\Delta \pi}{\Delta L} = 0$$

$$p \left. \frac{\Delta q}{\Delta L} \right|_K - w \frac{\Delta L}{\Delta L} = 0$$

which implies that

$$VMP_L = w$$

This is just a first-order condition for profit maximization. To be sure that the quantity chosen is optimal, it is also necessary that less the second-order condition be negative, which is like saying that VMP_L is decreasing. Let's now turn to our numerical example: it is clear that for our competitive firm it is not optimal to hire more than seven workers when the wage is 5.

LABOUR DEMAND

The demand for labour tells us what happens to the firms' employment as the wage changes, holding capital constant. From Fig. A.1, it is clear that the optimal quantity of labour hired depends on the wage rate. If the wage rate increases to 8, the amount of labour hired falls, while if the wage rate falls, the amount of labour hired increases. All this happens as long as the marginal product of labour is downward sloping. It follows that the *firm's demand for labour in the short run is equivalent to the downward-sloping segment of its value marginal product of labour schedule.*

THE DEMAND FOR LABOUR IN THE LONG RUN

In the long run both labour and capital can be set optimally. This implies that not only labour but also capital should be set optimally. In formula this yields that the conditions are

$$VMP_L = w$$

$$VMP_K = r$$

which can be expressed as

$$pMP_L = w$$

$$pMP_K = r$$

which can be written (using the fraction of the to conditions to eliminate the price) as

$$\frac{MP_L}{w} = \frac{MP_K}{r}$$

$$pMP_L = w$$

The first condition is the new key condition for long-run profit maximization. The left-hand side yields the output of the last dollar spent on labour. Indeed an additional worker yields MP_L and costs w so that the ratio gives the output of the last dollar spent on labour. Similarly, the right-hand side gives the output yield of the last dollar spent on capital. The condition can be used to obtain the capital–labour ratio. Once the capital–labour ratio is obtained we can obtain the actual level of labour from the second condition, which is identical to the short-run maximization.

☐ **APPENDIX B** CONSTRAINED OPTIMIZATION

Constrained optimization lies at the heart of many problems in personnel economics. The central mathematical problem is that of maximizing or minimizing (as in the case of the optimal skill ratio of Chapter 2 and of the hours–employment trade-off of Chapter 3) a function of several variables, where these variables are bound by some constraining equations. The typical problem is

$$\text{maximize } f(x_1, x_2)$$

where x_1 and x_2 must satisfy the constraint

$$h(x_1, x_2) = C$$

The function f is called the objective function while h is the constrained function.

The geometric solution to the problem is easy and should be familiar from intermediate microeconomics. First, draw the constraint in the $x_1 x_2$ place, the thick line in Fig. B.1. Then, draw a representative sample of the level curves of the objective function f (we typically call the level curves indifference curves). Geometrically, our goal is to find the highest-valued level curve f which meets the constraint set. The highest level curve of f (consistent with the constraint) cannot cross the constraint curve C; if it did, nearby higher-level sets would cross too, as occurs in point b in Fig. B.1. This highest-level set of f must touch C (so that the constraint is satisfied) but must otherwise lie on one side of C (since it cannot cross over C). Another way of saying this is that the highest-level curve of f to touch the constraint set C must be tangent to C at the constrained max. This situation occurs at point (x_1^*, x_2^*) in Fig. B.1.

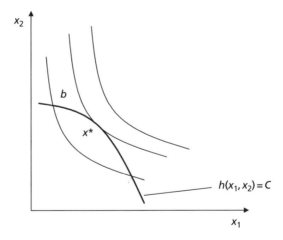

Figure B.1. The Lagrange method

The fact that the level curve f is tangential to the constraint set C at the constrained maximizer (x_1^*, x_2^*) means that the slope of the level set of f equals the slope of the constraint curve C at (x_1^*, x_2^*). The slope of the level set f at (x_1^*, x_2^*) is

$$-\frac{\frac{\partial f}{\partial x_1}}{\frac{\partial f}{\partial x_2}}(x_1^*, x_2^*)$$

and the slope of the constraint set at (x_1^*, x_2^*)

$$-\frac{\frac{\partial h}{\partial x_1}}{\frac{\partial h}{\partial x_2}}(x_1^*, x_2^*)$$

The fact that these two slopes are equal at (x_1^*, x_2^*) means

$$\frac{\frac{\partial f}{\partial x_1}}{\frac{\partial f}{\partial x_2}}(x_1^*, x_2^*) = \frac{\frac{\partial h}{\partial x_1}}{\frac{\partial h}{\partial x_2}}(x_1^*, x_2^*)$$

which can be written as

$$\frac{\frac{\partial f}{\partial x_1}}{\frac{\partial h}{\partial x_1}}(x_1^*, x_2^*) = \frac{\frac{\partial f}{\partial x_2}}{\frac{\partial h}{\partial x_2}}(x_1^*, x_2^*)$$

To avoid working with (possibly) zero denominators in the previous expression, let us indicate with μ the common value of the two quotients in the previous expression so that

$$\frac{\frac{\partial f}{\partial x_1}}{\frac{\partial h}{\partial x_1}}(x_1^*, x_2^*) = \frac{\frac{\partial f}{\partial x_2}}{\frac{\partial h}{\partial x_2}}(x_1^*, x_2^*) = \mu$$

and the previous condition can be written as

$$\frac{\partial f}{\partial x_1}(x_1^*, x_2^*) - \mu \frac{\partial h}{\partial x_1}(x_1^*, x_2^*) = 0 \tag{B.1}$$

$$\frac{\partial f}{\partial x_2}(x_1^*, x_2^*) - \mu \frac{\partial h}{\partial x_2}(x_1^*, x_2^*) = 0 \tag{B.2}$$

We basically have now three unknowns (x_1, x_2, μ), so that we now need three equations, one more than what is listed above. But we have the third equation and it is simply the constraint $h(x_1, x_2) = C$. Including the constraint equation with the two equations in (B.1) and (B.2) yields a system of three equations in three unknowns that read

$$\frac{\partial f}{\partial x_1}(x_1^*, x_2^*) - \mu \frac{\partial h}{\partial x_1}(x_1^*, x_2^*) = 0$$

$$\frac{\partial f}{\partial x_2}(x_1^*, x_2^*) - \mu \frac{\partial h}{\partial x_2}(x_1^*, x_2^*) = 0 \tag{B.3}$$

$$h(x_1, x_2) = C.$$

There is a convenient way of writing the system. Form the Lagrangian function as

$$L(x_1, x_2, \mu) + \mu[C - h(x_1, x_2)]$$

and find the critical values of the Lagrangian L by computing

$$\frac{\partial L}{\partial x_1} = 0$$

$$\frac{\partial L}{\partial x_2} = 0$$

$$\frac{\partial L}{\partial \mu} = 0$$

One can easily see that the result of this process is precisely the system of equation (B.3). Note also that since μ just multiplies the constraint in the definition of L, the equation $\partial L / \partial \mu$ is just the constraint $h(x_1, x_2) = C$. This new variable μ which multiplies the constraint is called a Lagrange multiplier.

This process is somewhat magical. When we want to maximize a function in an unconstrained problem, we simply solve for its critical points by setting its first-order partial derivatives equal to zero. However, by the introduction of the Lagrange multiplier μ into the constrained problem, we have transformed a two-variable constrained problem to the problem of finding the critical points of a function $L(x_1, x_2, \mu)$ of one more variable. In other words, we have reduced a constrained optimization problem in two variables to an unconstrained problem in three variables.[1] The cost of this operation is the inclusion of a new and artificial variable μ. Yet, in economic application μ has a clear economic meaning. In most economic applications the multiplier measures the sensitivity of the optimal value of the objective function to changes in the right-hand sides of the constraints and, as a result, it provides a natural measure of the value of scarce resources in a maximization problem.

The problem:

$$\text{maximize } f(x_1, x_2)$$

$$\text{subject to } h(x_1, x_2) = c$$

whose solution is x_1^*, x_2^* is solved (as long as x_1^*, x_2^* is not a critical point of h) by setting up a Lagrange function

$$L(x_1, x_2, \mu) = f(x_1, x_2) + \mu[C - h(x_1, x_2)]$$

and the solution x_1^*, x_2^* is obtained by finding a critical point x_1^*, x_2^*, μ^* of the Lagrangian so that

$$\frac{\partial L}{\partial x_1} = 0, \qquad \frac{\partial L}{\partial x_2} = 0, \qquad \frac{\partial L}{\partial \mu} = 0$$

---

[1] The process would not have worked if both $\partial h / \partial x_1$ and $\partial h / \partial x_2$ were zero at the point $x_1^* x_2^*$. This implies that we need to make the assumption that these partial derivatives are not zero at the constrained maximizer. In a case where the constraint is linear this additional condition is automatically satisfied.

If we were minimizing f instead of maximizing f on the constraint set C we would have used the same arguments that we used above, so that the previous remark holds whether we are maximizing or minimizing f on C. The difference in the second-order condition we describe below.

The second-order condition is obtained by studying the determinant of a matrix that is called the bordered Hessian.

Second-order condition for a maximization. Suppose that x_1^*, x_2^*, μ^* are a critical point of the Lagrangian so that

$$\frac{\partial L}{\partial x_1} = 0, \qquad \frac{\partial L}{\partial x_2} = 0, \qquad \frac{\partial L}{\partial \mu} = 0$$

To check whether x_1^*, x_2^* is a local max of $f(x_1, x_2)$ on $h(x_1, x_2)$ one needs to check that

$$\det \left\{ \begin{matrix} 0 & \frac{\partial h}{\partial x_1} & \frac{\partial h}{\partial x_2} \\ \frac{\partial h}{\partial x_1} & \frac{\partial^2 L}{\partial x_1^2} & \frac{\partial^2 L}{\partial x_1 \partial x_2} \\ \frac{\partial h}{\partial x_2} & \frac{\partial^2 L}{\partial x_1 \partial x_2} & \frac{\partial^2 L}{\partial x_2^2} \end{matrix} \right\} > 0$$

at x_1^*, x_2^*, μ^*

If the problem is one of minimizing a function, the second-order condition involves finding a determinant that is negative, so that in the previous condition the determinant of the 3 by 3 matrix should be negative.

Second-order condition for a minimization. Suppose that x_1^*, x_2^*, μ^* are a critical point of the Lagrangian so that

$$\frac{\partial L}{\partial x_1} = 0, \qquad \frac{\partial L}{\partial x_2} = 0, \qquad \frac{\partial L}{\partial \mu} = 0$$

To check whether x_1^*, x_2^* is a local min of $f(x_1, x_2)$ on $h(x_1, x_2)$ one needs to check that

$$\det \left\{ \begin{matrix} 0 & \frac{\partial h}{\partial x_1} & \frac{\partial h}{\partial x_2} \\ \frac{\partial h}{\partial x_1} & \frac{\partial^2 L}{\partial x_1^2} & \frac{\partial^2 L}{\partial x_1 \partial x_2} \\ \frac{\partial h}{\partial x_2} & \frac{\partial^2 L}{\partial x_1 \partial x_2} & \frac{\partial^2 L}{\partial x_2^2} \end{matrix} \right\} < 0$$

at x_1^*, x_2^*, μ^*

☐ REFERENCES

Abowd, J. M., Kramarz, F., Margolis, D. N., and Philippon, T. (2000), *The Tale of Two Countries: Minimum Wage and Employment in France and the United States*, IZA working paper.

Acemoglu, D. (1997), 'Training and Innovation in an Imperfect Labour Market', *Review of Economic Studies*, 64: 445–64.

Acemoglu, Daron, and Pischke, Jorn-Steffen (1998), 'Why Do Firms Train: Theory and Evidence', *Quarterly Journal of Economics*, 113: 79–199.

—— (1999), 'The Structure of Wages and Investment in General Training', *Journal of Political Economy*, 107: 539–72.

Adam, Paula, and Canziani, Patrizia (1998), *Partial De-regulation: Fixed Term Contracts in Italy and Spain*, Centre for Economic Performance Discussion Paper 306.

Akerlof, G. A., and Katz, L. (1989), 'Workers' Trust Funds and the Logic of Wage Profiles', *Quarterly Journal of Economics*, 104/3: 525–36.

Alvarez, F., and Veracierto, M. (2001), 'Severance Payments in an Economy with Frictions', *Journal of Monetary Economics*, 47: 477–98.

Autor, David (2001), 'Why Do Temporary Help Firms Provide Free General Skills Training?', *Quarterly Journal of Economics*, 116/4 (Nov.): 1409–48.

Autor, D., Katz, L., and Krueger, A. (1988), 'Computing Inequalities: Have Computers Changed the Labor Market', *Quarterly Journal of Economics*, 113: 1169–213.

Baker, George (1992), 'Incentives Contracts and Performance Measurement', *Journal of Political Economy*, 100: 598–614.

—— (1994), 'The Internal Economics of a Firm: Evidence from Personnel Data', *Quarterly Journal of Economics*, 109/4: 891–919.

—— and Holmstrom, Bengt (1995), 'Internal Labor Markets: Too Many Theories, Too Few Facts', *AER*, 85/2: 255–9.

—— Gibbons, Robert, and Murphy, Kevin (1984), 'Subjective Performance Measures in Optimal Incentive Contracts', *Quarterly Journal of Economics*, 109/4: 921–55.

—— Jensen, Michael, and Murphy, Kevin (1988), 'Compensation and Incentive: Practice vs. Theory', *Journal of Finance*, 43: 593–616.

Barron, J. M., Black, D. A., and Loewenstein, M. A. (1987), 'Employer Size: The Implications for Search, Training, Capital Investment, Starting Wages, and Wage Growth', *Journal of Labor Economics*, 5/1: 76–89.

—— (1993), 'Gender Differences in Training, Capital, and Wages', *Journal of Human Resources*, 28/2: 343–64.

Barron, J. M., Berger, M. C., and Black, D. A. (1997), 'How Well do we Measure Training?' *Journal of Labor Economics*, 15/3: 507–28.

Barron, J., Berger, M., and Black, D. (1999), 'Do Workers Pay for On-the-Job Training?' *Journal of Human Resources*, 34/2: 235–52.

Bartel, A. (1995), 'Training, Wage Growth, and Job Performance: Evidence from a Company Database', *Journal of Labor Economics*, 13: 401.

Barton, H. Hamilton, Nickerson, Jack A., and Owan, Hideo (2003), 'Team Incentives and Worker Heterogeneity: An Empirical Analysis of the Impact of Teams on Productivity and Participation', *Journal of Political Economy*, 111/3: 465–97.

Becker, G. S. (1962), 'Investment in Human Capital: A Theoretical Analysis', *Journal of Political Economy*, 70: 9–49.

Becker, Gary (1964), *Human Capital*, Chicago: University of Chicago Press.

Becker, G. (1993), *Human Capital: A Theoretical and Empirical Analysis with Special Reference to Education*, 3rd edn. Chicago: University of Chicago Press.

Bentolila, Samuel, and Bertola, Giuseppe (1990), 'Firing Costs and Labor Demand: How Bad is Eurosclerosis?', *Review of Economic Studies*, 57: 381–402.

Bertola, Giuseppe (1990), 'Job Security Employment and Wages', *European Economic Review*, 851–66.

—— (2004), 'A Pure Theory of Job Security Provisions', *Review of Economic Studies*.

—— and Rogerson, R. (1997), 'Institutions and Labor Reallocation', *European Economic Review*, 1147–71.

Blanchard, O. (1998), *Employment Protection and Unemployment*, mimeo, MIT, **http://econ.www. mit.edu/faculty/blanchar/index.htm**.

Blanchard, Olivier, and Landier, Augustin (2000), 'The Perverse Effects of Partial Labor Market Reform: Fixed Duration Contracts in France', *Economic Journal*, 112: F214–F244.

Boeri, T. (1999), 'Enforcement of Employment Security Regulations, on the Job Search and Unemployment Duration', *European Economic Review*, 43: 65–89.

Boeri, Tito (1999), 'Enforcement of Employment Security Regulations, On-the-Job Search and Unemployment Duration', *European Economic Review*, 43: 65–89.

Booth, A. (1993), 'Private Sector Training and Graduate Earnings', *Review of Economics and Statistics*, 75/1: 164–70.

Booth, Alison, Francesconi, Marco, and Frank, Jeff (2002), 'Temporary Jobs: Stepping Stones or Dead Ends?', *Economic Journal*, 112: F189–F213.

Borjas, G. (2004), *Labor Economics*, 3rd edn. New York: McGraw-Hill.

Brown, J. N. (1989), 'Why do Wages Increase with Tenure? On-the-Job Training and Life-Cycle Wage Growth Observed within Firms', *American Economic Review*, 79: 971–91.

Brown, C. (1990), 'Firms' Choice of Method of Pay', *Industrial and Labor Relations Review*, 43/3: 165–82.

Burda, M. (1992), 'A Note on Firing Costs and Severance Payments in Equilibrium Unemployment', *Scandinavian Journal of Economics*, 94/3: 479–89.

Calmfors, L., and Hoel, M. (1988), 'Work Sharing and Overtime', *Scandinavian Journal of Economics*, 90: 45–62.

Cobb, C., and Douglas, P. (1928), 'A Theory of Production', *American Economic Review, Papers and Proceedings*, 18: 139–65.

Crépon, Bruno, and Kramarz, Francis (2002), 'Employed 40 Hours or Not-Employed 39: Lessons from the 1982 Mandatory Reduction of the Workweek', *Journal of Political Economy*, 110/6: 1355–89.

Davis, Steven, Haltiwanger, John, and Schuh, Scott (1996), *Job Creation and Destruction*, Cambridge, Mass.: MIT Press.

Ehrenberg, R. G. (1971), 'Heterogeneous Labor, the Internal Labor Market, and the Dynamics of the Employment–Hours Decision', *Journal of Economic Theory*, 3: 85–104.

Ehrenberg, Ron, and Bonanno, Michaeal (1990), 'The Incentive Effects of Tournaments Revisited: Evidence from PGA Tour', *Industrial Labor Relation Review*, 43: 74–89.

Ehrenberg, R., and Smith, R. (2003), *Modern Labor Economics: Theory and Public Policy*, 8th edn. New York: Addison Wesley Longman Inc.

Elliot, R. F. (1999), *Labor Economics: A Comparative Text*, New York: McGraw-Hill.

Galdon-Sanchez, J., and Guell, M. (2000), 'Let's Go to Court! Firing Costs and Dismissal Conflicts', Industrial Relations Sections, Princeton University, working paper no. 444.

Garibaldi, Pietro (1998), 'Job Flow Dynamics and Firing Restrictions', *European Economic Review*, 42: 245–75.

—— (2004), 'Search Unemployment with On the Job Search', *Macroeconomic Dynamics*.

—— and Pacelli, Lia (2004), 'Employment Protection and the Size of Firms', *Giornale degli economisti*.

Garibaldi, P., and Violante, G. (2005), 'The Employment Effects of Severance Payments with Wage Rigidities', *Economic Journal*, November.

Gibbons, Robert (1987), 'Piece Rate Incentives Scheme', *Journal of Labor Economics*, 5: 413–29.

—— (1996), 'Incentives and Careers in Organization', in David Kreps and Ken Wallis (eds.), *Advances in Economics and Econometrics: Theory and Applications*. Cambridge: Cambridge University Press, vol. ii, ch. 1.

Gibbons, R. A. (1998), 'Incentives in Organizations', *Journal of Economic Perspectives*, 12: 115–32.

Gibbons, R., and Murphy, K. J. (1992), 'Optimal Incentive Contracts in the Presence of Career Concerns', *Journal of Political Economics*, 100: 468–506.

Goux, D., Maurin, E., and Pauchet, M. (2001), 'Fixed Term Contract and the Dynamics of Labor Demand', *European Economic Review*, 45: 533–52.

Grubb, D., and Wells, W. (1993), 'Employment and Regulations and Patterns of Work in OECD Countries', *OECD Economic Studies*, 7–58.

Guell, M. (2000), *Fixed-Term Contracts and Unemployment: An Efficiency Wage Analysis*, Industrial Relations Sections, Princeton University, Working Paper 433.

Hamermesh, D. (1993), *Labor Demand*, Princeton: Princeton University Press.

Hart, R. (1987), *Working Time and Employment*, Boston: Allen and Unwin.

Holmstrom, Bengt (1979), 'Moral Hazard and Observability', *Bell Journal of Economics*, 10: 75–91.

—— (1982), 'Moral Hazard in Teams', *Bell Journal of Economics*, 13: 324–40.

Hunt, J. (1999), 'Has Work-Sharing Worked in Germany?', *Quarterly Journal of Economics*, Feb.: 117–48.

Hunt, Jennifer (2000), 'Firing Costs, Employment Fluctuations and Average Employment: An Examination of Germany', *Economica*, 67: 177–202.

Ichino, P. (1996), *Il lavoro e il mercato*, Milan: Mondadori.

Ichino, Pietro (1996), *Lo stato e il mercato*. Milan: Mondadori.

Kandel, Eugene, and Lazear, Edward P. (1982), 'Peer Pressure and Partnerships', *Journal of Political Economy*, 100: 801–17.

Knoeber, Charles, and Thruman, Walter (1994), 'Testing the Theory of Tournaments: An Empirical Analysis of Broiler Production', *Journal of Labour Economics*, 12/2: 155–79.

Kuhn, P. (1986), 'Wages, Effort, and Incentive Compatability in Life-Cycle Employment Contracts', *Journal of Labor Economics*, 4/1: 28–49.

Lazear, E. P. (1979), 'Why is there Mandatory Retirement?', *Journal of Political Economy*, 1261–84.

—— (1981), 'Agency, Earnings Profiles, Productivity, and Hours Restrictions', *American Economic Review*, 71/4: 606–20.

—— (1988), 'Employment at Will, Job Security, and Work Incentives', in Robert Hart (ed.), *Employment, Unemployment and Labor Utilization*, Boston: Unwin Hyman.

—— (1990), 'Job Security Provisions and Employment', *Quarterly Journal of Economics*, 699–726.

Lazear, Edward (1989), 'Salaries and Piece Rates', *Journal of Business*, 59/3: 405–31.

Lazear, Edward P. (1995), *Personnel Economics*, Cambridge: MIT Press.

—— (1998), *Personnel Economics for Managers*, New York: Wiley.

—— (2000), 'Performance Pay and Productivity', *American Economic Review*, 90: 1346–61.

Leuven, Edwin (2004), *The Economics of Training: A Survey of the Literature*, Amsterdam: Department of Economics, University of Amsterdam.

Ljungqvist, L. (2002), 'How Do Layoff Costs Affect Employment?', *Economic Journal*, 112: 829–53.

Lynch, L. (1992), 'Private Sector Training and the Earnings of Young Workers', *American Economic Review*, 82: 299–312.

MacLeod, B., and Malcolmson, J. (1993), 'Investments, Holdup and the Form of Market Contracts', *American Economic Review*, 83: 811–37.

McLaughlin, K. (1991), 'A Theory of Quits and Layoffs with Efficient Turnover', *Journal of Political Economy*, 99: 1–29.

McConnell, Campbell R., Brue, Stanley L., and Macpherson, David A. (1999), *Contemporary Labor Economics*, New York: McGraw-Hill.

Mortensen, D. T., and Pissarides, C. A. (1994), 'Job Creation and Job Destruction in the Theory of Unemployment', *Review of Economic Studies*, 61: 397–415.

—— (1998), 'New Developments in Models of Search in the Labor Market', in O. Ashenfelter and D. Card (eds.), *Handbook of Labor Economics*, Amsterdam: North Holland.

OECD (1996), *Employment Outlook*, Paris: Organization for Economic Development.

—— (1997), *Employment Outlook*, Paris: Organization for Economic Development.

—— (1998), *Employment Outlook*, Paris: Organization for Economic Development.

—— (1999), *Employment Outlook*, Paris: Organization for Economic Development.

—— (2002), *Education at a Glance*, Paris: Organization for Economic Cooperation and Development.

—— (2002), *Education at a Glance*. Paris: Organization for Economic Development.

—— (2003), *Employment Outlook*, Paris: Organization for Economic Development.

O'Flaherty, B., and Siow, A. (1995), 'Up-or-Out Rules in the Market for Lawyers', *Journal of Labour Economics*, 13: 709–35.

Oi, W. (1962), 'Labor as a Quasi-Fixed Factor', *Journal of Political Economy*, 70/6: 538–55.

Parsons, D. (1972), 'Specific Human Capital: An Application to Quit Rates and Layoff Rates', *Journal of Political Economy*, 80/6: 1120–43.

Pissarides, C. A. (2000), *Equilibrium Unemployment Theory*, Cambridge, Mass.: MIT Press.

Prendergast, C. A. (1999), 'The Provision of Incentives in Firms', *Journal of Economic Literature*, 37: 7–63.

Rosen, S. (1969), 'Short-Run Employment Variation on Class-I Railroads in the U.S., 1947–1963', *Econometrica*, 36: 511–29.

Schivardi, Fabiano (2000), 'Labor Market Rigidities, Unemployment and Growth', *Giornale degli economisti e annali di economia*, 115–41.

Shapiro, Carl, and Stiglitz, Joseph (1984), 'Equilibrium Unemployment as a Discipline Device', *American Economic Review*, 74: 434–44.

Spence, Michael (1973), 'Job Market Signaling', *Quarterly Journal of Economics*, 87: 355–74.

Spence, A. M. (1974), *Market Signaling: Informational Transfer in Hiring and Related Screening Processes*, Cambridge, Mass.: Harvard University Press.

Trejo, S. J. (1991), 'The Effects of Overtime Pay Regulation on Worker Compensation', *American Economic Review*, 81/4: 719–40.

Wassmer, Etienne (1999), 'Competition for Jobs in a Growing Economy and the Emergence of Dualism in Employment', *Economic Journal*, 109/457: 349–71.

Yashiv, Eran (2000), 'The Determinants of Equilibrium Unemployment', *American Economic Review*, 90/5: 1297–322.

☐ INDEX